FRENCH AND FRA[NCOPHONE]

Wine Drinking

Series Editors

Hanna Diamond (University of Bath)
Claire Gorrara (Cardiff University)

Editorial Board

Ronan le Coadic (Université Rennes 2)
Nicola Cooper (Swansea University)
Maxim Silverman (Leeds University)
Didier Francfort (Université Nancy 2)
Sharif Gemie (University of Glamorgan)
H. R. Kedward (Sussex University)
Margaret Majumdar (Goldsmiths College, University of London)
Nicholas Parsons (Cardiff University)

Wine Drinking Culture in France

A National Myth or a Modern Passion?

Marion Demossier

UNIVERSITY OF WALES PRESS
CARDIFF

© Marion Demossier, 2010

All rights reserved. No part of this book may be reproduced in any material form (including photocopying or storing it in any medium by electronic means and whether or not transiently or incidentally to some other use of this publication) without the written permission of the copyright owner except in accordance with the provisions of the Copyright, Designs and Patents Act 1988. Applications for the copyright owner's written permission to reproduce any part of this publication should be addressed to the University of Wales Press, 10 Columbus Walk, Brigantine Place, Cardiff, CF10 4UP.
www.uwp.co.uk

British Library Cataloguing-in-Publication Data
A catalogue record for this book is available from the British Library.

ISBN   978-0-7083-2208-6 (hardback)
        978-0-7083-2321-2 (paperback)
e-ISBN 978-0-7083-2285-7

The right of Marion Demossier to be identified as author of this work has been asserted by her in accordance with sections 77 and 78 of the Copyright, Designs and Patents Act 1988.

Typeset by Mark Heslington Ltd, Scarborough, North Yorkshire
Printed in Great Britain by CPI Antony Rowe, Wiltshire

Contents

Series Editors' Preface	vi
Acknowledgements	vii
Map of French vineyards	x
Introduction: Wine Drinking Culture: A Myth or a Reality in Decline?	1
Chapter One: Drink, Consumption and Identity	18
Chapter Two: Changes to a National Wine Drinking Culture	41
Chapter Three: A New Wine Drinking Culture?	70
Chapter Four: Contemporary Discourses and Representations	101
Chapter Five: Ethnographies and Contexts	132
Chapter Six: Passion for Wine and Life-Stories	155
Chapter Seven: Between Self-Reflexivity, 'Distinction' and Social Connectedness	175
Chapter Eight: Globalization, Nation and the Region: The New Wine Drinking Culture	196
Conclusion	216
Glossary	222
Bibliography	223
Index	231

Series Editors' Preface

This series showcases the work of new and established scholars working within the fields of French and francophone studies. It publishes introductory texts aimed at a student readership, as well as research-orientated monographs at the cutting edge of their discipline area. The series aims to highlight shifting patterns of research in French and francophone studies, to re-evaluate traditional representations of French and francophone identities and to encourage the exchange of ideas and perspectives across a wide range of discipline areas. The emphasis throughout the series will be on the ways in which French and francophone communities across the world are evolving into the twenty-first century.

Hanna Diamond and Claire Gorrara

Acknowledgements

This book is the result of fifteen years of intense fieldwork and of constant interaction with the wine profession in France. I started my Ph.D. on the Burgundian wine industry in the 1990s and completed my analysis of the anthropology of wine with this book in the summer of 2008. Without my conversations with wine growers, professionals, experts, oenologists, consumers, wine lovers and others in the field, this work would not have seen the light of day and many of my questions would have remained unanswered. It is an impossible task to thank everybody who has assisted my research, but I should like to assure them all that the world of wine is filled with passion and interest, and this work is dedicated to all the enthusiasts with whom I have shared a fascination with wine. The picture I propose here of French wine culture and consumption is unlikely to be that expected by my compatriots, but it arises, in part, as a result of my displacement and 'exile' in Great Britain and as a reflection of the ambiguities of my position as a 'social anthropologist at home'. Because of the multi-sited nature of my own investigation, I have tried to propose an original perspective, that of the relationship between culture and consumption in an era of globalization. Therefore it will not be an exhaustive and self-indulging construction of the world of wine, but more a nuanced and constructive analysis of a changing world adapting to globalization.

I began my fieldwork nearly twenty years ago researching the winemaking techniques of Burgundian producers, and I completed it with an ANR-INRA research project on wine with lower alcohol content involving Pernod Ricard and the Fédération des Vins de Pays (Bernard Augé). This latter research project has proved to be extremely helpful, enabling me to discover the region of Languedoc-Roussillon and its political landscape. I should like to thank my colleagues who have shared their extensive knowledge of French wine production, especially Patrick Aigrain, Clementina Sebillotte, Hervé Hannin, Étienne Montaigne and François d'Hauteville, and also the two organizers Jean-Louis Escudier and Guy Albagnac and the whole ANR team.

I should like to thank all the institutions and organizations which have provided generous financial help that has enabled me to complete my research: the British Academy for supporting me financially during my year in France by granting me a Large Research Grant (LRG35396); the Department of European Studies and Modern Languages at the University of Bath for giving me research leave in 1999 and in 2003–4 which enabled me to finalize my research and to complete the writing of this manuscript. My colleague Professor Bill Brooks for his continuous support, and all my colleagues in the French section, in particular Hanna Diamond, Nina Parish and Steve Wharton, who had to endure my constant obsession with talking about wine drinking; Claire Gorrara and Hanna Diamond, the series editors, who have provided me with constant support, and the anonymous reader for his/her constructive comments; and Sarah Lewis from the University of Wales Press who has been a very dedicated and efficient commissioner.

Finally, this work has benefited from invaluable discussions with French and British colleagues working in the field of sociology and anthropology of food and drink. Among them, I would like to acknowledge the help of Thomas M. Wilson (Binghamton University, New York), Jean-Pierre Corbeau (University of Tours), Gilbert Garrier (University of Lyon), and the AoFood team headed by Virginie Amilien, Isabelle Techoueyres and Florence Bergeaud-Blackler. A special thanks to all the professionals I have met throughout the fieldwork and for the wine tastings shared with them, especially Mauricette Pion, David Cobbold and the team of the École du Vin in Paris. I should also like to thank all the wine lovers, and especially Thierry Meyer, for sharing his sociological knowledge of this world of passions.

I should like to thank the following individuals, organizations and institutions who helped me with the publication of this book and granted me permission to reproduce materials previously published elsewhere. Berg Publishers for allowing me to reproduce parts of the chapter 'Consuming Wine in France: The 'Wandering' Drinker and the Vin-Anomie', published by Berg in the volume edited by Thomas Wilson and entitled *Drinking Culture*. In France, I am grateful to the INA (Institut National de l'Audiovisuel) for its help in assisting me with the constitution of a database on wine from

1945 until 2004. Special thanks in particular to Sylvie Fegar and Didier Nottin, the technical team who were consistently helpful and patient during my work on this project, and who have made this part of the research a real pleasure. The INA is a unique place of research located in the heart of the Bibliothèque Nationale de France, and it provides a rich and original source of materials. The Bibliothèque Forney kindly granted me permission to use the image on the front cover.

Special thanks also to my husband, Julian Swann, who has constantly supported me during the process of writing and editing, and to our daughters, Margot and Louisa, who have always kept my feet on the ground. Finally I wish to dedicate this book to my father and my brother, who were both invaluable sources of inspiration and support, and whose critical comments were always constructive during the intense periods in the 'field of action'.

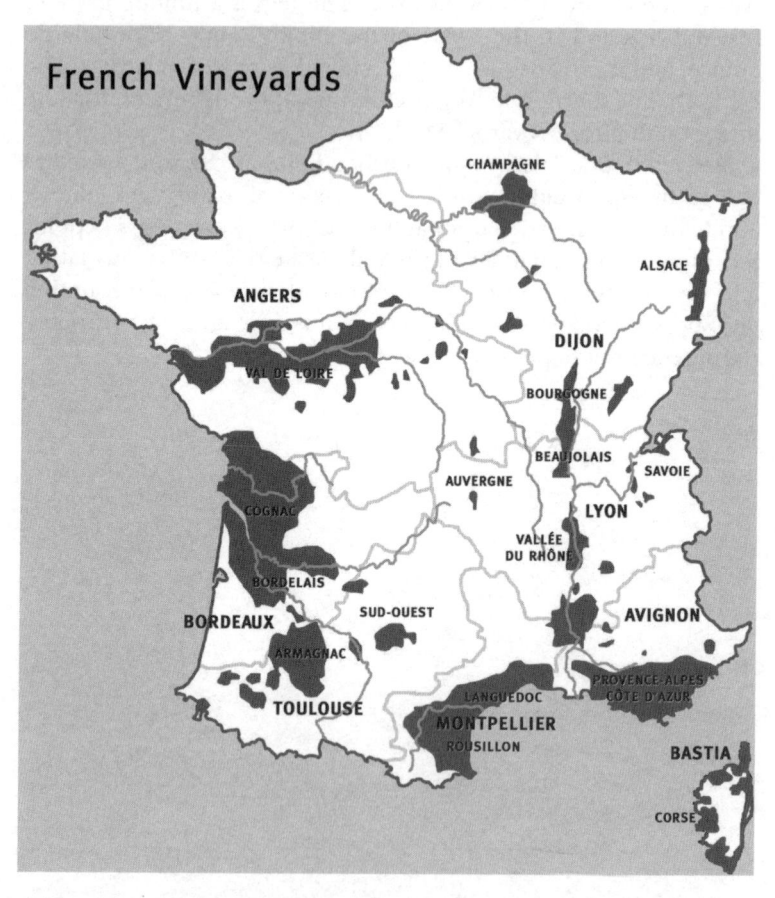

The wine regions and, in bold type, the major cities of the French vineyards (adapted from ONIVINS, 2002; *www.onivins.fr*)

Introduction
Wine Drinking Culture: A Myth or a Reality in Decline?

> *Whenever a great wine crisis erupts, no one has the courage to say that the real problem is the need to rip up a third of French vineyards ... not at all, the problem always appears to come down to the fact that the French are bad citizens who shirk their national duty, which is to drink up the production of their vines.*
>
> François de Closets, *La France et ses mensonges* (Paris: Denoël, 1977)

My 'exile' in England, as it has often been described by my French compatriots, has for me always been defined by two specific cultural elements: my accent and my passion for wine. On countless occasions, the banal conversation of the dinner table has turned to the supposed knowledge that French people have about wine, something which, for many Britons, contributes to their neighbours' superiority as a nation. The fieldwork conducted in France during 2003–4[1] made me realize that the British perception of the French was not only confined to this side of the Channel, but was shared by most French people, who believe that they 'are actually the best wine drinkers in the world because they are surrounded by quality wine production'. However, if it is true that wine production is one of the most economically important branches of French agriculture[2] and that the quality of wine has dramatically improved since the beginning of the twentieth century, it is also true that the majority of French people have little or no knowledge of wine.[3] Yet, paradoxically, wine drinking and the culture associated with it are seen by many as an essential part of what it means to be French. For French people, wine, or more precisely the love of good wines, characterizes Frenchness in much the same way as being born in France, fighting for liberty or speaking French.[4] This image of a strong national wine drinking culture still prevails in the national imagination despite the changes affecting wine production and consumption.

Since the beginning of the twentieth century, France has been one of the countries at the top of the European table in terms of annual per capita alcohol consumption, despite a steady decrease in alcohol drinking since the Second World War.[5] Even though this decline primarily concerns wine drinking, wine has remained the principal alcoholic beverage consumed in France.[6] These changes in consumption have taken place against the background of rapid economic modernization, political integration and globalization.[7] On the eve of World War II, annual wine consumption in France was around 170 litres per capita.[8] Just over sixty years later, wine consumption has drastically declined to 54.8 litres in 2007. However, this sharp reduction has to be balanced against the fact that there is a clear distinction between the consumption of *vin ordinaire* (everyday wines), which has continuously declined, and the consumption of quality wines or those with an AOC (*Appellation d'origine contrôlée*) label or denomination of origin, which has increased from 15,535 hectolitres in 1994–5 to 17,536 in 2005–6.[9] This trend has been accompanied by the rise of *vins de pays* (country or regional wines).

Consumption of the traditional *vin ordinaire* has followed the downward demographic trend of the rural and urban working classes, its principal consumers,[10] and the rise of the AOC wines is a sign of growing affluence and the numerical importance of the middle class in France. A major revolution has taken place in the wake of these socio-demographic changes and economic modernization, and most French people are not even aware of it. Since 1980, the percentage of regular drinkers of wine has continuously decreased, while the proportion of occasional drinkers continues to rise as a new social phenomenon. In 1980, 50.7 per cent of the French population aged fourteen years or over consumed wine nearly every day, while in 2005, only 20.7 per cent did. This trend has affected both genders, with a decline from 69.2 per cent to 30.1 per cent for men and 36.8 per cent to 12 per cent for women. Both Garrier and Nourrisson have demonstrated that historically a new drinker has emerged characterised by new patterns of consumption, orientated towards festive and occasional drinking.[11] Yet a growing number of French people do not drink wine at all, and that is seen as a 'dreadful prospect' by some commentators.[12] The percentage of non wine consumers had increased to 38 per cent in 2005, with nearly 50 per cent for women and 30 per cent for men. The statistics demonstrate that, from the early 1990s onwards, the number of litres of mineral water sold started to overtake the number of litres of wine.[13] Meanwhile wine tasting, according to various national surveys and reports, has become an obsolete national technique and French people can no longer differentiate 'good' from 'bad' wines.[14] Yet this negative view of French wine drinking culture has more to do with the greater social differentiation and the heterogeneous nature of the field of wine consumption than a long-term historical trend.

From the 1970s onwards, France has experienced the emergence of a wine drinking culture which symbolizes at the same time the decline of this commodity as part of the staple diet of much of the nation, and its rise as a cultural and aesthetic object. There have never been so many wine clubs, wine bars and wine activities on offer in France as there are today, and wine culture has diversified, democratized and proliferated to such an extent that it could be argued that there have never been so many wine lovers with such a prolific knowledge of wine. In some cases, wine has acquired the status of an art object. However, it is the white middle-class male that stands out as the predominant figure in this new cultural field. The expansion of the media and the literary production devoted to wine under its various guises reflects the new relationship between French people and wine. The development of internet forums has also radically transformed wine culture, which was traditionally confined to the private sphere, to family circles and to professional and social networks, and it has now become a subject of global debate. Wine drinking culture is therefore in the process of transformation, offering an ideal opportunity for an analysis of the relationship between consumption and culture from an anthropological perspective.

When I began my detailed research for this project in 2003–4,[15] my investigations coincided with a major crisis for French wines both at home and abroad, resulting, amongst other things, from the increasing foreign competition of New World wines, the decline of exports, the controversial Évin law,[16] a questioning of the old fashioned AOC system and the draconian drink-drive laws introduced by Nicolas Sarkozy, then the French minister of the interior. French politicians, winemakers and the wider public were confronted by the realization that major changes had to take place in order to preserve France's pre-eminent position in the international market and to protect its cherished national industry. Many wine growers had taken to the streets to protest, even in some of the wealthiest and most prestigious regions such as Burgundy or Bordeaux. On 25 February 2004, the French prime minister, Jean-Pierre Raffarin, met the main delegates and representatives of the fragmented and regionalized French wine industry. The delegation of professionals from France's major wine-producing areas told the prime minister that the combination of declining wine exports and the fall in domestic sales had caused a crisis that had driven some of their colleagues close to despair. Following this meeting, Alain Suguenot, president of the Groupe d'Études Viticoles (viticulture study group) in the National Assembly and mayor of Beaune (capital of wine in Burgundy) was asked to submit a white paper on the future of wine in French society. Amongst the issues highlighted by Suguenot was the increasingly intense debate about the need to revise the old AOC system[17] created after the First World War and founded on the concept of *terroir*,[18] the Évin law and the drink-driving debate. Suguenot succeeded in his fight against the Évin law in January 2005 when the government agreed to the adoption of an amendment to the law on alcohol advertisement which was a compromise between wine supporters and public health specialists.[19] He had less success in reforming the AOC system, which, as we shall see, is central to the debate about the past and the future of the industry.

The previous year saw the wine boards in Bordeaux (CIVB, Comité Interprofessionnel des Vins de Bordeaux) and in Burgundy (BIVB, Bureau Interprofessionnel des Vins de Bourgogne) being taken to court by the ANPAA (Association Nationale pour la Prévention de l'Alcoolisme) which is 90 per cent funded by public authorities, among them the Ministry of Health, for advertising campaigns whose content did not conform to the Évin law. The government's determination to enforce the previously neglected laws on drink-driving also threatened wine consumption, especially in restaurants, as most consumers were suddenly forced to limit themselves to a glass of wine or half a bottle, or even to drink only water. The wine growers complained that this strict governmental attitude sounded the death knell for wine drinking culture in France.

Yet the French government's enthusiasm for public health and safety manifest in these campaigns against excessive alcohol consumption was more than just a challenge to a symbolic and cherished aspect of Gallic culture. In 2002, the wine industry was represented by 124,000 wine producers, 850 co-operatives, 240,300 permanent workers, 52,000 employees and 1,400 wine merchants, and had a turnover of 11 billion euros, of which 5.8 billion came from exports. For the state, the wine industry represented no less than 2.94 billion euros in indirect taxes in 2000 alone.[20] The combination of these fiscal and economic factors makes wine production a vital sector in the French economy and one which has considerable political influence with a cross-party lobby of more than 120 members of Parliament in 2005.

From the perspective of an anthropologist, the crisis of these early years of the new century provided the ideal platform for an investigation of French wine production and the wider significance of contemporary wine drinking culture. This crisis revealed much deeper long-term tensions between the various socio-cultural processes affecting French society as a whole. If statistics on consumption reveal profound changes in French society since the 1950s, they also suggest that drinking wine has become more than ever a strong social and cultural marker, and therefore, a growing sign of social differentiation. Changes in the structure of France's population have undoubtedly exerted a major influence on long-term patterns of consumption, but this is only one part of the story. Technical progress, growing affluence and a burgeoning media interest in almost every aspect of French viticulture have all been contributory factors behind these changes, and they have been accompanied by a growing concern about the effects of alcohol on health and well-being. Desperate attempts have been made by the professionals and the various ministries (Agriculture and Trade for example) to fight the crisis. The creation in 2000 of AFIVIN[21] (Agence Française d'Information sur le Vin), an association devoted to the diffusion of wine, is a good illustration of the attempt to re-establish the position of wine in contemporary French society. Education is seen as the cornerstone of the vast campaign conducted to rehabilitate the position of wine as a unique product with a strong emphasis on its cultural significance at national and European level. Yet, simultaneously, government legislation and the discourse of both the Ministry of Health and the medical profession have tried to control wine drinking and to present wine as just another type of alcohol.

These tensions have always coexisted in the various discourses on wine, but they have acquired a new resonance in the context of the economic crisis in the wine industry. As the journalist Matthieu de Bord noted in a provocative article: 'France has gone from being almost synonymous with wine in the minds of international consumers to being a nation whose wines are now viewed as inaccessible, old-fashioned and out of step with the contemporary wine market.' [22] It is not the first time that French wine producers have experienced periods of rapid change, but international competition now poses a serious challenge to the very existence of many vineyards, which no longer enjoy the prerogatives and pre-eminence they have possessed for centuries. It is true that the current data of worldwide production still confirms the predominant position of France, Italy and Spain, which together account for nearly half of the total, compared with the USA and Argentina with 8.4 per cent and 5.6 per cent respectively, but this European hegemony is being undermined as the New World expands its production. The USA, for example, increased its production from 16 million hectolitres in 1990 to 23,800,000 in 2001, while French production decreased from 65,530,000 hectolitres to 58,243.000 during the same period. European vineyards are now subject to major restrictions, partly imposed by the European Union, [23] which claims to be concerned about the imbalance between supply and demand, and the complexity of the rules governing the definitions, processing and marketing of wines. The new global market situation is presented as a challenge for European wine producers, and the European Commission called in 2006 for a root-and-branch reform of the wine market. Different scenarios were proposed, but the new Council regulation introduced a wide-ranging reform of the Common Market Organization for wine, which was formally adopted by the Council of Ministers in April 2008. The changes are intended to restore balance to the wine market by phasing out wasteful and expensive market intervention measures and by allowing the budget to be used for more positive, proactive measures which will boost the competitiveness of European wines.[24]

The crisis in French wine drinking culture can therefore be said to have complex roots that stretch back at least to the end of the Second World War. From the perspective of the anthropologist, it is potentially fruitful to use this example to question some of the cultural and social processes at work in the formation of individual, collective and national identities. Such a study also poses real methodological challenges for the anthropologist seeking to apply the experience of qualitative fieldwork and micro analysis to a broader national canvas, which is in turn transformed by the forces of globalization.

1. Anthropology of drinking

In a recent report published online by the SIRC (Social Issues Research Centre, Oxford), the authors concluded that 'there is a clear and urgent need for large-scale systematic research on social and cultural aspects of drinking in Europe, and for continuous monitoring of shifts and changes in mainstream European drinking cultures, particularly in terms of the effects of cultural convergence'.[25] The publication of Mary Douglas's pioneering study *Constructive Drinking* (1987) and of Dwight B. Heath's remarkable and eclectic work *Drinking Occasions: Comparative Perspectives on Alcohol and Culture* (2000) have been followed more recently by two important works, *Drinking: Anthropological Approaches* by de Garine and de Garine (2001) and *Drinking Cultures* by Thomas Wilson (2005).[26] Together they have established drinking as a distinct academic field of anthropological inquiry and have argued that it should be studied in a comparative context. For Mary Douglas, the specificity of the anthropological perspective is to examine drinking as a 'constructive' activity, a way of life, one element of a given culture;[27] while, for de Garine and de Garine, drinking endorses a negative as well as a positive activity.[28] According to both authorities, anthropologists have traditionally turned their attention to the issue of drinking as a 'social act performed in a recognised social context'.[29] However, until recently, very little research had been focused on social and cultural aspects of drinking in modern western societies, and perhaps surprisingly, this was also true of wine drinking in France. Yet both eating and drinking offer unique insights into the nature of any society, and they present manifold channels for cultural analysis.[30] This book therefore aims to provide a new interpretation of the relationship between wine drinking and identity in an age of economic globalization and political change.

If few studies have focused on drinking as a marker of national and regional identity and as a complex arena for asserting and negotiating questions of competition, power, identity and social ordering, that is to say as a 'field for action',[31] it is also true that most of the studies on drinking cultures have employed traditional ethnographic methods which focus on a specific fieldwork project or locale. The complexity of the national or regional character of drinking, or even the issue of changes affecting it, have been largely ignored by anthropologists. The recent volume edited by Peter Scholliers (2001) addressed some of these issues from a historical perspective, but the groundwork remains to be done. As Dwight B. Heath has pointed out, 'Just as drinking and its effects are embedded in other aspects of culture, so are many other aspects of culture embedded in the act of drinking.'[32] Wine drinking culture in France has been transformed radically and it offers a window on to the expression of identity at national, regional and community level. As Thomas Wilson has argued in his book *Drinking Cultures*, 'Drinking is itself cultural; it is not so much an example of national and other cultural practices, in the sense that it is a performance of something that runs deeper in the national or ethnic makeup, as much as it is itself a bedrock of national and ethnic culture.'[33]

2. Studying wine drinking culture

The case study of France gives us the opportunity of conducting a wider anthropology of alcohol drinking by focusing on a highly 'national', regional and collective social activity that is undergoing a major transformation. By questioning the position of wine in an increasingly heterogeneous French society, I examine the various discourses and practices shaping its consumption. Looking at the decline of wine consumption as a facet of everyday life, I argue that wine drinking provides a window on to the changing nature of what it means to be French. Can wine be seen as the last bastion of national identity? Is it a vehicle for the revival of regional identity in a new Europe where questions of territoriality and essentialism have come to the fore? Or, perhaps more controversially, is wine drinking increasingly a passion at an individual level, but less an element of national identity?

In answering these questions, this study aims to challenge some of the traditional ethnographic methods employed in the study of wine by exploring, through a multi-sited ethnography, the complex position of wine in France. By employing the technique of a multi-sited ethnography,[34] it is possible to analyse different cultural perspectives on drinking as a place for the production, performance, expression and reception of drinking cultures. The practice of wine drinking and the culture attached to it provide a space for exploring the renegotiation of specific values and defining the changing relationship between national and regional identities in France. In this context, ethnography offers a fruitful way to explore the dynamic, globalized and fragmented character of this complex social act embodying attributes of social organization and general culture.

The main objective is to use the multiplicity of meanings that actors use and ascribe to wine consumption in different contexts of social action in order to examine what Wilson has described as the wider cultural formations and expressions of power and identity related to wine drinking culture and their dynamics. The intention is to explore the diversity of meanings, discourses and actions encountered in relation to the concept of 'wine drinking culture' as a cultural object. This is understood as a 'cultural production' (in the sense underlined by Ulin[35]), as 'a medium in which other levels of categorisation become manifest'[36] as a national and regional emblem that is expressed both through the media of literature and scholarship and through patterns of consumption. Using a series of detailed ethnographies of wine culture, presented in chapters five, six and seven, and a multi-sited ethnography of drinking places, it will address the complex and dynamic nature of wine drinking in France by discussing the ambiguities raised by a changing wine drinking culture set against the background of the constant work of 'cultural production' led by specific national and regional social actors to construct drinking wine as 'an ideal world'.[37] Here I argue that the study of a single good, such as wine in France, in its various contexts can offer a methodological entry-point for analysing both the complexity and the diversity of social relations and social action. It begins with what Arjun Appadurai calls 'the social life of things', exploring the social relationship between socially constructed knowledge, practice and social differentiation.[38]

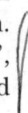

For a female anthropologist trained in French ethnology, comparative sociology and social anthropology, and brought up as a wine and food lover, I know that studying my own national drinking culture requires an awareness and sensibility to my own position as an observer. On more occasions than I care to remember, I was taken for an 'oenologist' by my informers, and I was asked to comment on the wines being drunk. My position as a woman studying an intoxicating culture defined and controlled mostly by men was in itself highly problematic. Participant observation in drinking contexts led to situations where both the anthropologist and her informers found themselves in awkward situations resulting from the relaxation of gender relations and social norms, threatening to make the study less scientific and objective. Throughout my many years of fieldwork, I have learned how to master this kind of social challenge, and I must confess that being brought up as the granddaughter of a Burgundian wine merchant has given me some insights into wine drinking culture. I have deliberately adopted a culture of moderation and controlled drinking during the fieldwork.

Anthropology at home, as it is very often described by British colleagues, is a recent development in the Anglophone world, while in France it has been established since at least the 1950s as one of the disciplines of the social sciences. As an almost inevitable consequence of the modernization of our societies and the erosion of the distance separating the researcher from the researched group, western scholars have increasingly turned their attention to their own societies. In France, the closure of some of the more popular sites for fieldwork following decolonization was undoubtedly linked to the growth of French ethnology, giving legitimacy to the new branch of the profession. Yet there is a consensus of scholarly opinion that 'anthropology at home' opens a wide range of methodological, epistemological and practical questions which I hope I have tried to address throughout the book. By adapting available fieldwork techniques to the topic under scrutiny and locating myself as a French researcher living in the UK and therefore at the crossroads of two cultures, I have tried to maintain a critical distance in line with Marilyn Strathern's statement on conducting 'anthropology at home'.[39] She argues that because of the continuity between 'culture' and 'society' in the western tradition, between the ideas of the people and the concepts that comprise the anthropological method, anthropology at home is highly relevant to the study of contemporary society. It is because of my involvement in wine drinking culture, and having published a book on Burgundian wines which is perceived as 'technical and serious', that I have been able to be integrated and seen as a native. It is also because I know what I am talking about when I ask questions about *grands crus* or *fermentation malolactique* that I go beyond the superficiality of everyday conversation. It is also one of the main challenges of social anthropology to demonstrate that the discipline has something to say about the social world it contributes to.

The evidence presented in this study is based on ten years of participant observation of wine production in France compiled in fieldwork notebooks, and combines a multi-sited ethnography of wine festivals, wine fairs and wine clubs as well as extensive interviews with professionals in the wine trade all over France. My research has taken me from Paris to Bordeaux, from Beaune to Agen and Albi, from Reims to Corsica and several other locations where observations and interviews have taken place following the vicissitudes of the fieldwork. I have been able to become an observer of wine drinking situations organized around wine schools (Paris, Bordeaux and Beaune) or clubs. This material forms the bulk of chapter five with a selection of snapshots providing me with a substantial amount of ethnographic information. More than fifty semi-directed interviews were conducted with the main actors of the wine industry, and all the professions have been represented, from oenologists to *sommeliers* and chefs. The interviews with politicians and representatives of the professional world of wine have permitted me to contextualise some of the key local issues by examining them from a wider perspective. I have met and interviewed a number of wine lovers using life history as a key element to explore their relationship to wine. This has provided me with an original insight into the wide range of tastes and the field of representations surrounding their expression. A number of writers, cultural actors and experts on wine have been selected and interviewed in relation to their contribution to local and regional identity, with Burgundy and Bordeaux providing the basis of my case studies.

In addition to the fieldwork, I have consulted various archives from professional bodies in Paris, Burgundy and Bordeaux. I have also compiled a vast corpus of literary writings about wine (and its synonyms) since 1945. I have examined the archives of wine magazines such as *La Revue des Vins de France* (*RVF*) and *Cuisines et Vins de France*, and consulted articles from such diverse publications as *Elle* and *Le Monde* to follow the progressive emergence of wine as part of public discourse since 1945. This work is examined in parallel with gastronomic writings and the revival of a regional culture through tourism, cultural artefacts and the marketing of regions. I have created an original and unique database of all documentaries, news and television programmes broadcast on wine (and its thematic associations) between 1945 and 2004 with the help of the INA (Paris). This corpus, which forms part of chapter four, compares the construction of wine in literature and the visual media. Finally, I identified three main internet forums devoted to wine culture and conducted a systematic analysis of the exchanges taking place between wine lovers during a specific period of time. Some of the wine lovers were subsequently contacted by email and interviewed as part of my research. This material represents a major part of chapter seven, illustrating how wine has, for some consumers, become a pretext for engaging in a quest for individual identity because, when talking about wine and tastes, people talk about themselves. Drinking is central to our sense of individual identity, beliefs and collective representations, and for many individuals the choice of which wine to buy, when, how and with whom to drink it, is part of an active process of identity building.

3. Synopsis of the chapters

The book is presented around the themes of wine and French national identity, consumption and wine drinking culture. Chapter one discusses the theoretical background to the concept of a national wine drinking culture and examines, amongst other things, the relevant literature on identity, consumption, regionalism and taste, locating them within the context of the concept of wine drinking culture in France. The chapter argues that the national dimension of wine culture no longer relies on mass consumption of 'plonk' but has more to do with specific emblematic values such as taste and 'distinction'. Today consumption in France could be seen as a way of reshaping old ideologies, and it is certain that contradictory values are embedded in wine drinking culture. For French people, despite the modernization of their society, wine remains a part of the French 'cultural exception'.

Chapter two looks at the historical development of a national drinking culture by focusing on three essential elements: the construction of a regulated economic space from the late nineteenth century onwards, organizing national wine production on the ideological foundations of the concept of *terroir* and AOC at a time of growing international demand for wine, agricultural modernization and urbanization. Secondly, it focuses on the consolidation of regional wine cultures in wine-producing regions, and the parallel development, of French gastronomic and oenological cultures in Paris and elsewhere. Finally, it considers the construction of the myth of French wine as an element of national heritage and patrimony.

Chapter three will examine how major social changes, such as increased leisure time, the expansion of social and associative life, the revival of the hygienist movement, the economic crisis affecting French wines, the rise of *ruralisme* and the internet to name just a few, have inspired a new wine drinking culture. It will argue that wine drinking has become socially fragmented and differentiated, and its study sheds light on social and intellectual debates such as the definition of modernity, the French response to economic liberalization and the quest for identity through consumption. For many individuals, drinking wine has become an identity-building process by which they become part of a new form of civil community constructed around a nostalgic view of a rural and authentic France. By defining the relationship between wine culture and consumption, the book will argue that a new wine culture is now emerging which reveals many of the contradictions contained within contemporary French society.

Chapter four looks at wine consumption in the media and at the discourses and representations that have emerged since 1945, in the literary field, in films and on television, and demonstrates the increasing politicization of the debate on wine drinking culture. It follows the development of a specialized oenological discourse in the media embracing the various themes underlined in the historical construction of the nation and argues that a series of contradictions is at the core of wine drinking culture. These contradictions, which include technical progress versus artisanship, *vignerons* versus wine merchants, *terroir* versus brands, nation versus region, health versus alcohol consumption, are all amongst the ingredients of a heterogeneous culture that creates tensions between various socio-economic interests in French society. International competition and its effects are analysed, demonstrating how groups such as *vignerons*, wine consumers and local political institutions have responded to economic change.

Chapter five focuses on five ethnographic case studies. Each ethnographic episode will be followed by a brief presentation underlining some of the major points to be developed in the next chapters: the construction of taste and regional identities, the contradictions surrounding wine consumption (national versus regional interests), the social lives of wine drinkers (by exploring the world of wine lovers and its rules), the fragmentation of wine drinking as a social activity. The aim is to enable the reader to follow the progression of the representations and actions in ethnographic context and to discover the complexity of wine culture and consumption.

Chapter six explores the way in which identities are contextualized through wine consumption and how they are articulated relative to the broader concepts of tradition and modernity. Examining individual life stories through wine consumption, it argues that occasional, fragmented and festive consumption enables individuals and specific groups to create a sense of solidarity and sociability that intensifies the nature of their relationships through alcohol consumption. In their quest for landmarks, wine and food, tourism and the discovery of regional heritage and direct contact with the producer, they seek a sense of stability or timelessness in reaction to the fluidity of modern life, the salience of contemporary identities and the ephemeral nature of our societies. This combination of values underlining wine consumption challenges traditional understandings of consumption and demonstrates the positive responses of both producers and consumers to economic change by examining how they contribute to the redefinition of individual and collective identities.

Chapter seven examines wine lovers as an example of wine consumption arguing that, through both a self-reflexive and an interactive process, individuals are engaged in an identity-building process. By competing with others around the definition of taste and the importance of regions, they seek to establish territories and networks of relationships provoking positive but also some negative responses and reactions. An essentialist vision of France emphasizing the traditional work of the wine grower as the paragon of quality dominates the content of their debates, but it is increasingly confronted by a more liberal perspective. Amongst the core values that define their consumption are: work, artisanship, quality, sociability and commensality, all of which can be seen as providing reassurance and a sense of stability in this period of rapid transition.

Finally chapter eight discusses the ways France has responded to the forces of globalization. The construction of the concept of *terroir*, which has provided the foundation of the French wine industry since the early twentieth century, and the recent controversial debate about the AOC system call into question the policies

Introduction 15

attached to the notion of quality. Recent developments in the GATT (General Agreements Tariffs and Trade) discussions and the WTO (World Trade Organization) show how the ideal of a 'French exception' has struck a chord, and that the French response to modernization has proved to be profitable. Discussing the various elements which have shaped the debate about French national drinking culture, the chapter looks at some of the effects it has had on rural communities, regions and their identities, but it also addresses the global implications. It concludes that national identity, far from declining, has repositioned itself in the international arena at least in relation to wine and regionalism.

Notes

1 I should like to thank the British Academy, which awarded me Large Research Grant 35396 in 2003–4 to complete this study, and the Department of European Studies and Modern Languages of the University of Bath (Great Britain) which granted me study leave in 1999 and 2003–4.
2 Wine has always contributed significantly to the French economy. According to the General Directorate of Foreign Trade, in 2000, the wine sector paid more than 2,94 billion euros of VAT and 117 million euros of indirect taxes. The activity is seen as a determining factor in the economy of several regions and contributes to the development of tourism and gastronomy. France is amongst the first two exporting countries of wines in Europe in volume. For recent statistics on French wine economy, consult *http://www.onivins.fr* (consulted 30 September 2008).
3 See for example recent surveys conducted by Sofres and *Figaro* magazine in 1999.
4 See the survey conducted by the historian Jean-Pierre Rioux, 'Être Français?', *L'Histoire*, 100, 43 (1987), 11–17.
5 According to the WHO (World Health Organization), in 2002, France was ranked in the ninth position in terms of litres of pure alcohol consumed per person per year after the following countries (in descending order): Luxembourg, Czech Republic, Hungary, Germany, Ireland, Austria, Republic of Moldova and Spain.
6 For a statistical overview of the evolution of alcohol consumption in France, consult ONIVINS (*http://www.onivins.fr*) or INSEE (*http://www.insee.fr*) (consulted 30 September 2008).
7 See Special issue of the journal *Aofood* on globalization, 3 (2004) (*http://edition.cens.cnrs.fr/revue/aofood/2004/v/n3/*).
8 Gilbert Garrier, *Histoire sociale et culturelle du vin* (Paris: Bordas, 1995), p. 391.

9   For more information on wine consumption, see statistics produced by Viniflhor and the INSEE in chapter 3.
10 L.-A. Loubère, *The Wine Revolution in France: The Twentieth Century* (Princeton: Princeton University Press, 1990), p. 263.
11 Garrier, *Histoire sociale*, pp. 292–344 ; and Didier Nourrison, *Le Buveur du dix-neuvième siècle* (Paris: Albin Michel, 1990), pp. 63–72.
12 Garrier, *Histoire sociale*, p. 292.
13 Danielle Besson, *Boissons alcoolisées. 40 ans de baisse de consommation*, INSEE, 966 (May 2004).
14 See for example Ipsos-Insight, Marketing 1999 and 'Perception des pratiques oenologiques par les Français', document communicated by Christian Mélani, ONIVINS, 1990. There are several other documents which could be consulted on the website of AFIVIN to support this argument (*http://www.afivin.fr*).
15 This book is based on an intensive period of fieldwork conducted between 1999 and 2004. Some of the ethnographic materials were collected during my previous ethnographic research on Burgundian wine growers. I should like to thank the British Academy for giving me the opportunity to study wine drinking culture for a year in France and the University of Bath for granting me study leave in 1999 and 2003.
16 For the full Évin law, see *http://www.sante.gouv.fr/htm/pointsur/tabac/loi-evin.htm*.
17 A wider debate has followed at European level concerning a possible reform of the AOC labelling system, which is facing increasing competition at international level and is part of the negotiations between the European Union and the United States in the context of GATT. For more details, see E. Barham, 'Translating Terroir: the global challenge of French AOC labeling', *Journal of Rural Studies*, 19, 1 (January 2003), 127–38.
18 For a working definition of *terroir*, see Barham, 'Translating Terroir' and chapter 8.
19 In France, alcohol still kills 45,000 people and costs the health service 17.6 billion euros each year.
20 These figures come from the Recensement Général de l'Agriculture (French Agricultural Census 2000).
21 AFIVIN is composed of the main professional actors of the chain of production and commercialization. It has been financially supported by the European Commission.
22 See *http://msnbc.msn.com/id/3225796/* M. de Bord, 'The latest crisis in France', *Newsweek*, 17 October 2003 (consulted 30 September 2008).
23 For more information about the reform of the wine sector in Europe, see the European Union website on agriculture, *http://ec.europa.eu/agriculture/markets/wine/index_en.htm*.
24 See *http://ec.europa.eu/agriculture/capreform/wine/index_en.htm*.
25 See *http://www.sirc.org/publik/drinking6.html*.

26 Mary Douglas, *Constructive Drinking: Perspectives on Drink from Anthropology* (Cambridge: Cambridge University Press, 1987) and Igor de Garine and Valérie de Garine (eds.), *Drinking: Anthropological Approaches* (Oxford: Berghahn, 2001).
27 Douglas, *Constructive Drinking*, p. 3.
28 De Garine and de Garine, *Drinking: Anthropological Approaches*, p. 2.
29 Douglas, *Constructive Drinking*, p. 4.
30 For more development of this argument, see the remarkable volume edited by Carole Counihan and Penny Van Esterik, *Food and Culture: A Reader* (London: Routledge, 1997).
31 Mary Douglas, *Food in the Social Order: Studies of Food and Festivities in Three American Communities* (New York: Russell Sage Foundation, 1984).
32 Dwight B. Heath, *Drinking Occasions: Comparative Perspectives on Alcohol and Culture* (Philadelphia: Brunner-Mazel, 2000).
33 Thomas M. Wilson (ed.), *Drinking Cultures: Alcohol and Identity* (Oxford and New York: Berg, 2005), p. 4.
34 Douglas R. Holmes, *Integral Europe: Fast-Capitalism, Multiculturalism, Neofascism* (Princeton: Princeton University Press, 2000).
35 Robert C. Ulin, *Vintages and Traditions: An Ethnohistory of Southwest French Wine Cooperatives* (Washington: Smithsonian Institution Press, 1996).
36 Douglas, *Constructive Drinking*, p. 30.
37 This notion of 'ideal world' is essential to the analysis of representations surrounding wine drinking culture in France. For more discussion, see Douglas, *Constructive Drinking*, p. 11.
38 Arjun Appadurai, *The Social Life of Things* (Cambridge: Cambridge University Press, 1986).
39 Marylin Strathern, 'Grande-Bretagne: anthropology at home', *Ethnologie Française*, 37, 2 (2007), 197–212.

Chapter One
Drink, Consumption and Identity

Wine consumption in France provides a window on to the changing nature of what it means to be French. What follows is a case study exploring the construction of a national drinking culture – the myths, symbols and practices surrounding it – and then through a multi-sited ethnography of wine consumption a demonstration of how that culture is in the process of being transformed. The aim is to provide an original account of the various causes of the long-term decline in alcohol consumption and of the emergence of a new wine drinking culture since the 1970s, and to analyse its relationship to national and regional identity. To do this it is necessary to examine a number of key developments, including the broader shifts in attitudes towards the drinking of alcohol, and to consider how individuals engage with the past and build their future through the consumption of wine as a cultural artefact and as a commodity. It is also important to analyse the impact of economic globalization on wine culture as well as its wider cultural resonances. In addressing these and other questions an anthropological approach is particularly valuable because wine as a product and a cultural object is a repository of memories enabling French people to position themselves in relation to the past through the process of consumption. However it is also helpful to draw upon other theoretical models, and by consciously seeking to combine the insights of other disciplines it is possible to analyse wine culture and consumption in a French national context by using a multilevelled analysis that embraces producers, the wine profession and the consumer.

This chapter sets out the theoretical background to the study of a national drinking culture by presenting the dominant theories dealing with national identity, regionalism, consumption, taste and memory. These are, in turn, examined in relation to the concept of wine drinking culture, arguing that the national dimension of

French wine culture no longer relies on consumption, but has more to do with specific emblematic values which are today used as markers of identification through *culturalization*, which I define here as a process of creating cultural meanings. Wine consumption in France can be seen as a way of reshaping old ideologies, and it is certain that paradoxes such as tradition versus modernity, or wine as an alcohol opposed to wine as a cultural product, are embedded in French wine drinking culture. For wine producers and wine lovers, despite the modernization of their society, wine remains very much a part of the wider phenomenon of the French 'cultural exception'. Yet this belief is not shared equally by the whole of French society.

1. Drinking and national identity

In the debate about the nature of national identity, political and social scientists have generally been divided into two dominant camps, placing more or less emphasis upon culture and identity in the formation of the nation. The essentialist approach to identity formation argues that political identities flow more or less directly from the underlying cultural raw material, while the constructivists/ modernists contend that the connection is more tenuous. Both interpretations share the assumption that the nation is inherently a cultural entity, as cultural as it is political.[1] While the essentialist approach to identity formation is driven primarily by cultural background variables, which are constituted of roots, heritage, language and religion, the constructivists place greater emphasis upon politics seen as an active process of identity formation entailing the manipulation of cultural symbols. Their points of divergence are connected to the wider debate about whether or not there is a biological or other deep 'essence', a fixed character to any particular identity or whether identities are socially constructed.

Anthony D. Smith,[2] who has produced an influential definition of the nation that combines the insight of both models, provides us with a multidimensional definition of the nation, listing five main attributes: historic territory or homeland, common myths and historical memories, a collective mass public culture,[3] shared legal rights and duties for all members, and a single economy with territorial mobility for members. National identity is therefore a cultural phenomenon through which a community sharing a particular set of characteristics is led to the belief that its members are ancestrally related. One of the means to foster this cultural dimension is to transmit values, beliefs, customs, conventions, habits, languages and practices to the new members who receive the culture of a particular nation. The process of identification with a specific culture implies a strong emotional investment, one that is able to create bonds of solidarity amongst the members of a given community.[4] Thus they imagine and feel their community to be separate and distinct from others.[5] But how does it apply to wine production and consumption as an element of national identity?

The link between French national identity and wine is complex. Wine refers to both a political process – with the progressive emergence throughout French history of an increasingly unified, regulated economic space divided between production and consumption, and the establishment of a regional wine hierarchy symbolized by the AOC and constructed around the idea of *terroir* – and a cultural construction establishing and promoting wine as an essentialist element at the core of French identity.[6] Indeed wine's powerful imagery in France has become especially important because of the way it is presented as the essence of the French nation, illustrated by the old expression *boire un pot* (have a drink together), which is still used and associated with red wine and shared sociability. Another patriotic example is *le pinard* (red plonk), which was associated with French soldiers during the Great War. At the mobilization in August 1914, the soldiers of the Midi were said to have shouted: 'We'll be back home for the wine harvest.'[7] Later, in 1939, wine came to be the *vin triste* of the conscripts, as poignantly described by Jean-Paul Sartre in his *Carnets de Guerre* (Wartime Diaries). Another example of this strong involvement of the nation with wine is exemplified by the Creation of the Comité de Propagande du Vin, which was established in 1931 by the government and embodied official views of wine in inter-war France and its role at the heart of various debates surrounding issues such as national and rural identity, health and patriotism.[8] Wine has, therefore, deep historical resonances for French national culture, inspiring patriotic sentiments with its representations rooted in the essentialist concept of the nation, and it remains a powerful symbol of cultural continuity in the face of the changing relationship between global, national and regional identities in France.

According to Thomas Wilson, culture should not been seen simply as a good tool with which to understand the real or true nation, and culture and identity are not windows on to the nation, they are the nation itself.[9] Wilson further contends:

> *Drinking [...] is a historical and contemporary process of identity formation, contributing to its maintenance, reproduction and transformation [...] Rather, drinking is the stuff of everyday life, quotidian culture which at the end of the day may be as important to the lifeblood of the nation as are its origin myths, heroes and grand narratives.*

In the case of France, drinking wine is not only an element of a shared culture, but it is embedded in other characteristics of the nation encompassing its five dimensions: psychological, cultural, territorial, historical and political.

The psychological dimension of this traditional French drinking culture is marked by the role of moderate consumption through the ritualization of drinking, its association with the process of eating and a collective and public demonstration of self-control. Historically, local landowners and professional elites played a crucial role in transmitting this cultural model, with their clubs, confraternities and gastronomic associations, as well as the public festivities that punctuated the republican calendar.[10] It provided the basis for the consciousness of forming a group based on the sharing of conviviality in an atmosphere of pleasure and enjoyment.[11] Proverbs and songs collected during the nineteenth century in Burgundy, Bordeaux and elsewhere attest the formation of a drinking culture emphasizing the relationship between moderate consumption and the quality of wine production at a time of major tensions for both elements. A convincing illustration of this new literature is exemplified by Alexandre Grimod de la Reynière and his *Almanach des Gourmands* which in 1803 published an 'Eloge du vin de table' encouraging wine consumption and moderation. At a regional level, the image of elitism and wine consumption was strongly promoted, as is illustrated by the example of the engraving of the figures of *L'Amateur de Bordeaux* or *L'Amateur de Bourgogne*, which were in circulation promoting the wine drinker to the rank of the bourgeois.

It was through eating and drinking that the French nation essentialized the link between wine and the public republican sphere, enabling a strong identification between the daily collective consumption of wine and the imaginary consumption of the nation. In other words, drinking wine provided until recently a means of belonging to the nation by consuming one of its main ingredients in a way that was impossible for other alcoholic products. This is exemplified by the figure of Nectar created by the wine retail chain Nicolas in 1922, which incarnates the Parisian delivery man, a handlebar moustache, big eyes full of charm and his arms full of bottles of wine. Another example is provided by the state campaign to encourage wine drinking conducted in 1930 and entitled 'Drink wine and be happy', illustrated by a young couple represented on the background of a France made of grapes. Yet the situation was more complex than simply seeing wine as an expression of being French because it also emphasized regionalism (Burgundy, Bordelais, etc.), and the situation was also different for non-wine-producing regions such as Brittany and Normandy. In fact, the national model which emerged coexisted with touristic and regional literature promoting local products and regional identities. It could be argued that each region had its unique formulae to promote its drinking culture.

Through the creation of the notion of *terroir* and its corollary, the label of denomination of origin, the French landscape attached to wine production has become historicized and politicized, and is presented as a major component of a certain image of the French nation, an element of the national heritage and history that is worth fighting for. French wine production is an economic space delineated by boundaries and markers, differentiating one area from another on the same basis as French national identity is constituted by the diversity of regional identities. For the historian Loubère the 'wine revolution' of the late nineteenth and early twentieth century corresponded to a major transformation of wine consumption in France which can be better understood by five dimensions: progress of science with the birth of oenology, major technological changes, an economically considerable increase of wealth accruing chiefly to the makers and sellers of fine wines, rise of an affluent bourgeoisie and decline of the industrial and rural proletariat, and finally reversal of governmental policy that was a great stride away from the traditional 'hands-off' attitude and towards control and regulation.[12] These changes have been accompanied by an intense democratization of the wine market by the social fragmentation of drinking patterns and the increasing competition from alcohol beverages offered to the consumer.[13] If patterns of wine consumption have drastically changed, it could nevertheless be argued that the French population was always less homogeneous in its alcohol consumption than we have been made to believe.[14]

Wine drinking culture was thus presented as a homogeneous mythical element of the French nation and became a feature of a shared culture defined by its associated sociability, self-control and culture of moderation inscribed in its rituals and its practices, while it was, in reality, marked by class representations, excessive consumption in specific contexts and urban/rural cleavages. Thierry Fillaut has shown how the traditional peasant society of Brittany suffered a reputation for serious alcoholism when in fact its per capita consumption was quite low.[15] Peasants drank little overall but heavily on special occasions, when their drunkenness would be particularly public, and binge or public displays of drunkenness, no matter how infrequent, caused more outrage on the part of polite society than did the much larger but more discreet drinking of the better-off levels of society. According to Bologne the variety of alcoholic beverages created and distributed in the national economy has always played a major role in the shaping of regional and national identity.[16] Cider and Calvados were associated with Normandy while wine and marc de Bourgogne were associated with Burgundy. Didier Nourrison noted that in the nineteenth century cider imposed itself as the regional drink, and as an element of Norman regional identity.[17] The establishment of regional drinking cultures lies in the historical and economic development of a specific local drink, the creation of a clientele at local, national and international levels, the fostering of a regional imagery through folkloric iconography and texts, and finally the promotion as a marketing tool of the elements forming its visual representations. Regional drinking cultures were progressively and paradoxically fitted together into a national model of drinking culture constructed around a promotion of alcohol consumption and a shared sociability. Representations and cultural imaginary are thus at the core of the constitution of a drinking culture which could be described as heterogeneous and fragmented in historical terms.

2. Regional identity and regionalism in a new Europe

Paradoxically regional identity can be seen as both an obstacle to, and a vital component of French national identity. Anne-Marie Thiesse has argued convincingly that more than a century ago, there was a dual French identity formed by the regional/national cleavage.[18] The Third Republic asserted that France was 'one and indivisible', but also that the country was diverse. This exaltation of diversity repressed by the state permitted the reaffirmation of a French superiority over other nations. Regional identities were constructed on the basis of a dual relationship between the local and the national, and a checklist was established during this period by each nation encapsulating symbolic and material items: a history establishing its continuity through the ages, a set of heroes embodying its national values, a language, cultural monuments, folklore, historic sites, distinctive geographical features, a specific mentality and a number of picturesque labels such as costume, national dishes and an animal emblem or a drink.

Wine was, like cheese, one of the elements that helped to form the French nation on the foundations of its regional diversity. The regional character of wine drinking culture was linked to the area of production and, as Loubère noted, 'all the regional wine economies were strongly influenced by geographic, economic and cultural ties to the nation'.[19] Wine offers a mode of differentiation, and each region has a unique and differentiated drinking culture firmly tied to the nation and its 'imagined community'. The INAO (Institut National des Appellations d'Origine Contrôlées) and the various national bodies intended to direct wine production were all created during the nineteenth century and were organized around the regions, with more power given to emblematic and prestigious vineyards such as Bordeaux and Burgundy. Diversity was the key element in this process and it continues today to provide the main obstacle to the promotion of wine at a national level as the regions compete vigorously. In her innovative study, Kolleen M. Guy has demonstrated how the development of the champagne industry between 1820 and 1920 combined private interests and the nation-building process.[20] She argues convincingly that

> Champagne and wine brand names offered consumers a sense of continuity. In the face of the complexities of the new social world of the late nineteenth century that made the individual consumer feel incompetent or insecure, the timeless tradition of champagne offered reassurance that one was upholding the highest standards of social intercourse, thus reinforcing the individual's sense of membership in a civilized community.[21]

By creating a rhetoric of French identity around the consumption of champagne, the producers promoted their own marketing success as national. Yet this process of being a regional product promoted as a national good in advertising and marketing spectacles was not unique. Other wine-growing regions were following a similar path and in inter-war Burgundy, for example, wine merchants and wine growers developed and successfully promoted a regionalist and commercial folklore representing their wines as the authentic product of a timeless peasantry.[22] The elite used folklore as a tool to promote their wines during the economic depression that was affecting wine production. It was also a difficult time for the producers, notably when the battle around the *terroir* and its legal recognition developed from the 1930s. By co-operating with political elites, academics and industrialists in the construction of a cultural and economic regionalism, they sought to take over the control of the wine market by imposing their vision of wine production as based upon *terroir*.

The museum of wine, established in Beaune in 1938 by Georges Henri Rivière, curator of the national museum of the Arts et Traditions Populaires, is an excellent example of this process. The aim behind its creation was to promote a timeless image of Burgundian viticulture based upon the traditions of its unique *terroir* and the unchanging techniques of the *vignerons* (wine growers) who tended the precious vines. In its original displays, the museum presented already extinct techniques dating back to before the great phylloxera crisis of 1880 which had destroyed the province's vines. This fantasy regional world of wine and the contents of the display were based on the fieldwork and the collection of objects conducted by the folklorist and ethnographer André Lagrange, who was later the author of the novel *Moi je suis vigneron*, published in the 1950s. Neither the *propriétaires-viticulteurs* (wine growers who own the land) nor the *négociants* (wine merchants) were represented in this modern Burgundian rustic idyll. The rhetoric was indeed part of a regionalist construction orchestrated from Paris, but its purpose was above all to dissolve social tensions at a time of economic crisis and to give a more prominent voice to the world of *vignerons*. The heritagization of a disappearing world was seen as a way to maintain social unity in a climate of social tensions and economic difficulty. This was also a period of major negotiations about the recognition of specific plots of lands under the AOC system and by the same token, a major redefinition at an economic level of the concept of *terroir* as a hierarchical device.

As Élise Marie Moentmann has shown, at the Paris exhibition of 1937 some regions, notably Burgundy, presented themselves in a backward-looking fashion emphasizing the folklore of artisans, whereas others were already emphasizing the role of modernity.[23] She argues that rather than an all-encompassing idea, the very diversity of the regions characterized the essence of France, an evolving synthesis of traditional and modern industries, as well as the cultural traditions that would continue to define the country in the post-war period. In this promotion of French identity through the regions, the organizers of the regional centre saw artisans and their high-quality, human-based production methods as long-standing economic and cultural strengths of the country that still embodied France in the 1930s. Yet as Moentmann demonstrates, differing visions of the individual regions suggest that there was no consensus about how to define France aesthetically, economically or culturally, given the frictions between rural and rapidly industrializing parts of France. Lebovics and Peer have shown that by the 1930s, the diverse regional cultures had come to represent a heterogeneous but deep-rooted national identity, as opposed to the seemingly monotonous, industrialized and distant modern culture.[24] During the post-war period, the so-called *Trentes Glorieuses* were associated with the urbanization and industrialization of French society and a wider access to consumption. This was a period marked by the Cold War, reconstruction, decolonization and various internal political problems, most notably governmental instability.

Many of these debates about both French regional and national identity have surfaced again as a result of the crisis in the wine industry. Further European integration and the recent revival of hygienist preoccupations under the World Health Organization's directives have put the emphasis upon a new control of wine production and consumption at a time of increasing international economic competition and major societal changes. The region has to renegotiate its position in the global arena, and wine drinking in this context provides a space for renegotiating identities, reinforcing cohesiveness and creating an 'ideal world'. This attempt to consolidate national identity takes place through the work of the region as a place of strong identification, and wine drinking culture is one example of such a process. The emphasis upon regional identities and *terroir* offers a response to the growing preoccupations attached to globalization and fast food. The diversity of French wine production guarantees the existence of good-quality wines, but it is also the main obstacle to its survival at a time of global political processes.

3. Consumption and Identification

In his book *Food, Drink and Identity*, Peter Scholliers,[25] responding to the criticism of the sociologist Alan Warde, who sees 'limits to the capacity of food to express personal identity', argues that it is important not to underestimate the bond between use value and identity value, that is to say between food as fulfilling a biological function and food as a means of constructing identity.[26] If it is sensible to question the place and importance of food as an identity builder, it is equally important to stress its functional aspect. In the case of wine, the functional aspect is difficult to separate from the social, and this is, in part, determined by the national context in which the consumption takes place.

As Claude Fischler has argued, 'food is central to our sense of identity' as it is defined by the principle of incorporation which touches the very nature of a person.[27] In the case of wine and alcohol, this same process of incorporation is accompanied by the possibility of intoxication, alcohol playing the role of a social fluid. Wine consumption in France is very often presented as an obligation, and a refusal to conform risks immediately classifying the individual. It could be argued that such attitudes are stronger in rural areas than in cities because social constraints are stronger in small and close-knit communities than they are in large and anonymous urban settings. In all societies, alcoholic beverages are used as powerful and versatile symbolic tools, to construct and manipulate the social world. What, where and when we drink allows others to make judgements about us and for us to make judgements about them. As Thomas Wilson has noted, 'Who we are and the actions which substantiate identity, also give substance to the spatial and temporal dimensions to society, polity and economy.'[28]

Wine drinking in France was traditionally one element of social demarcation and identification, which was part of the ordinary life cycle of most of the population. If recent generations have not been initiated into wine consumption to quite the same degree as previous ones, they have nevertheless been obliged to conform to the ritual of drinking together, as it is the foundation of most social occasions. The failure to do so signifies your exclusion from the group. For the older generation, education included not only the transmission of beliefs, values and specific practices, but also the transmission of particular tasks or duties to perform. Women received instruction in the art of cooking from their mothers, while men were educated in the *savoir boire* (the know-how of drinking) by their fathers. However, this clear gender division was called into question by the late 1960s as part of a complete transformation in social attitudes as more women joined the workforce.

In terms of the contemporary generational divide, wine drinking is clearly an arena where groups now define themselves in relation to drinking or not drinking and in relation to the knowledge they have about wine. There have never been so many wine-tasting schools organized by the *grandes écoles* and by companies aiming at training people in wine tasting. Traditionally French secondary schools used to serve wine at lunchtime with the meals, and it was often cut with water, and this practice was commonplace in the 1950s and 1960s. Today such practices would be inconceivable, and young people are showing less interest in wine drinking, and many of them recognize that they know little about it. New beverages such as beer or alcopops have flooded the market and have taken over from wine as the alcoholic beverage of choice in many social situations. As a result, most of the leaders fighting the modernization of wine production in France and representing the *terroir* belong to the now middle-aged 1968 generation. They are the heirs of the conservative, bourgeois tradition of *bon vin, bonne chère*, and they have played a major role in revitalizing French culinary heritage at the regional level. Despite having been largely educated in cities and having experience of travel and other cultures to a degree unknown before, they define themselves against the changes brought about by modernity. In this context, consumption plays a major role as it indicates to what extent, issues of identity and culture are at stake.

In the classical sociological tradition, consumption was 'an expression of a central social hierarchy, inequalities of resources being turned into tools of class and status group struggle'.[29] Differential consumption practices were thus explained in terms of the location of social class in the system of production. The concept of *habitus* and *distinction* theorized by Pierre Bourdieu are very often used to explain these mechanisms when looking at wine culture and its recent developments. Yet his key text, *La Distinction*, published in 1979, examining the consumption practices generated by the *habitus* of various social classes as a learned set of dispositions that underpin and generate social and judgements, had nothing to say about wine and social distinction.[30] According to Jean-Pierre Albert, this absence can be explained by the fact that wine was not yet the object of such differential consumption.[31] Wine consumption was traditionally either confined to the social activity of the upper classes in the case of *grands vins* or more generally was the object of everyday consumption without any particular meaning or function attached to it. The 1980s and the emergence of a new wine culture transformed wine drinking into a highly distinctive sign of status and thus a new means of identification.

However, this type of interpretation leaves only a minimal role for 'choice', freedom and the rise of identity which are the new ingredients of lifestyle theory.[32] Consumption in contemporary societies is considered crucial, for commodities are some of the principal channels for the communication of self-identity.[33] According to social theorists such as Bauman and Giddens, people define themselves through the messages they transmit to others by the goods and practices they possess and display. Such an explanation is certainly relevant for some types of consumption or particular contexts, nonetheless it does not enable us to analyse the complexity of the social mechanisms hidden behind wine consumption and the multiple meanings individuals attach to it in specific contexts. Moreover, the collective nature of identity remains largely overlooked by social commentators when displayed and performed in the social arena. Yet changes affecting wine consumption help to illustrate growing social fragmentation and the emergence of a new drinker that I have termed 'the wandering drinker',[34] defined as the newly affluent and educated man or woman who is free to choose what to drink and in which context to drink it. Through wine consumption, individuals compete and construct their identity and relate to concepts of what it means to be French, exploring the relationship between regions and the nation. The source of identity is the lifestyle image that individuals purposively appropriate or construct and the shared normative orientations underlying their consumption.

If it is true that drink like food marks social differences, boundaries, bonds and contradictions,[35] it is equally true that the negotiation of these differences is an ongoing process by which individuals and societies renegotiate their identities in relation to a particular context. Both eating and drinking are linked to overall social hierarchies and power relations.[36] According to Pekka Sulkunen, who questions the modernity of wine drinking in France, the middle class, defined by a strong cultural capital, provides a new model of drinking which is based on moderate consumption.[37] Growing affluence and an expanding middle class have meant that new strategies of social distinction were needed to cultivate differentiation. Social constraints have loosened, and individuals are now free to choose what they want to drink, and in this regard, complex processes of differentiation take place. Thorstein Veblen has argued that ostentatious consumption was long associated with alcohol beverages,[38] notably elite French wines, and Douglas has confirmed that connoisseurship in the matter of wine is in itself a field for competition and has the power to identify the person as well as the wine.[39]

However the evidence from my research suggests that social differentiation between individuals has been greater than assumed even within the confines of the middle classes. What is particularly striking is the heterogeneity of wine culture, and wine consumption cannot be analysed simply as a matter of 'distinction'; other issues are at stake, such as sociability, friendship, globalization and regionalism. Yet what is specific to the French national context is the active role of the state, groups and individuals in shaping wine consumption. Individuals engage in different ways with alcohol and wine consumption, and an analysis that is based uniquely on class distinction does not do justice to the richness of the act of drinking. Moreover, wine drinking has become a transnational activity, and a cosmopolitan perspective enables us to grasp the modernity of wine consumption in France with greater accuracy. Drinking is above all a socially constructive act, and wine consumption cannot be reduced to a single interpretative framework. Wine consumption has multiple meanings and has produced sometimes contradictory values and views. As Brewer and Trentmann have suggested, 'The processes of consumption and their different meanings can only be properly recovered if we analyse the links that connect the different places in which goods are produced, distributed, purchased or consumed and given meaning'.[40] This book will therefore link wine production with its consumption, integrating the various meanings offered by producers, actors and consumers, and social fragmentation will be the framework of interpretation for making sense of the socially constructive act that is drinking.

By focusing on wine lovers and *amateurs*, who could be defined as a group of cultural mediators occupying a key position in wine culture and consumption, and by examining their behaviour, I argue that they occupy a central position in terms of both social transmission and the reproduction of specific values and ideas about wine drinking culture, and therefore they are vectors of identification through the sharing of a common experience. Yet this identification is far from being a homogeneous process, as self-reflexivity and appropriation define their engagement with wine as a social product. Those studies that have chosen to analyse the world of wine lovers and *amateurs* in France or elsewhere have concentrated on know-how, perceptions, norms, distinction, aesthetics and judgements of quality, but have neglected to place the debate in wider contexts such as those of globalization, national identity and modernity.[41] They remain also very close to their subjects. What could be constructively concluded from such studies is that the concept of wine lovers is far more complex than a simple typology might lead us to expect, because individuals engage and define themselves through the act of drinking wine in a personal and self-reflexive fashion. Another crucial characteristic is that wine lovers and *amateurs* could not be defined along a specific and objective continuum enabling them to shift from one position to another through the acquisition of knowledge or competence. In France, there is no single definition of how to assess the quality of wine, but several coexist. Therefore the amateur is defined by his/her individual characteristics and his/her passion for wine, and the act of drinking becomes a highly constructive act of identification.

4. Memory between embodiment and textuality

In the process of identification through incorporation, individuals define themselves in society by positioning their performed identity in relation to wine drinking culture defined as constituted, amongst other things, by words, discourses, images, representations and bodily or sensorial practices. In this context, wine culture can be seen as a culturally constructed site, including not only embodied practices, synaesthesia and gestures, but also a material and visual culture related to wine drinking which has become a cultural realm in itself.[42] By acquiring a wine culture, wine consumers distinguish themselves from others and locate themselves by the same token in French society as a whole. Drinking wine or not drinking wine, but also becoming a wine connoisseur or not, have implications for group identity and thus for the individual's decision to engage with the performative nature of the act of wine drinking. As noted by David E. Sutton, 'Food does not simply symbolise social bonds and divisions; it participates in their creation and recreation.'[43] The evidence from this study confirms that wine drinking culture and its acquisition have facilitated the internal definition of the male middle class in France, in particular at a time when broader processes of modernization were affecting wine production and consumption, gender roles and social fragmentation. The changes affecting wine drinking culture go beyond a simple socio-economic explanation, and it can be seen as encapsulating some of the salient features of contemporary French culture and society.

In the various processes by which wine has come to play a new role, memory as a locus of culture occupies a central position. Anthropologists and historians have argued that dietary changes can be seen as crucial to social transformations in a wide range of contexts, serving as a means both of characterizing the past and of reading the present through the past.[44] Wine drinking here serves as a medium for understanding perspectives on modernity that are often invisible in public debate. Wine has, for example, been treated historically as a mythic symbol of the Republic, and French national identity and the memory of groups and individuals conveyed through wine consumption could be interpreted as both the articulation and the representation of a politics of memory fostered by specific groups of actors – wine professionals, the wine lobby, wine lovers, wine experts, politicians and the state as represented by the Ministry of Agriculture. Wine consumption has thus become an issue of debate within the state between the Ministry of Agriculture and the Ministry of Health, and between consumers. One of the most fruitful strategies for the wine profession has been to encourage the constitution of a cultural realm by constituting a wine culture based on specific values attached to French national identity such as *régionalisme, ruralité, terroir*, authenticity, artisanship – values which have been at the core of the cultural construction of the nation for over two centuries.

Through the commensality of the exchange and the sharing of a bottle of wine, a sense of belonging is created and social attachments are encouraged. People bereft of social attachments create imagined communities, seeking to compensate for the lack of a sense of belonging associated with the supposed excessive individualism of the modern condition.[45] Drinking wine is a compelling medium for memory, and in this context it offers an occasion for remembering other social situations during which wine was shared and the membership of the group was constituted. Through this process, the male middle classes in particular localize and recall their memories, which form part of a whole ensemble of thoughts common to a group. When interviewed about how they define a good wine, most French people always evoke the necessity of recalling it through the social situation and its characteristics. The best wines are the ones shared with special people, when an exchange has taken place and a sense of occasion has been involved. Experiences of sharing a good wine refer back to the earlier examples of the company and the performativity of the social experience, and remind us that its sensual and euphoric effects transmit powerful mnemonic cues. Wine clubs in general offer the right context for experiencing the sense of being part of the same community around the product, and recollections of these particular episodes are probably epitomized through the sensual and emotional dimension of such experiences. Most of the wine tastings observed for this study demonstrate that groups are both formed and maintained through the sharing of common values. The sense of being a particular nation of drinkers is always emphasized as a cultural specificity. Drinking wine in France leads to the quest for social re-embedding, but also to the proclamation of a nationalist versus a global ideology, depending on the political stance taken. The remaking of wine drinking culture is organized around local–global issues and concerns, and wine consumption with its corollary, taste, reflects these ideologies.

Going beyond the issue of membership of a group, French consumers have also integrated the importance of direct contact with the producer, seen as the authentic social experience. The figure of the wine grower has become the paragon of quality, and his visibility in the public debate and the media has reinforced his/her reputation as the only guarantor of an authentic product. Wine culture in France is created around this image to the detriment of the other actors in the wine sector, notably the wine merchants. With the development of the practice of *vente directe*, consumers now have the opportunity to meet the producer directly and to taste wines in the cellar. Frequently the tastings are conducted by the wives of the *vignerons*. At regional level, the wine industry is organized around visits to the producers, and the proliferation of wine guidebooks citing the best producers for each year has made them the centre of attention, transforming their clientele in the process. Memories associated with these visits are often recalled by consumers who are often able to cite all the producers they have visited over the years, describing their wines and the 'special' encounter with the producer. This characteristic is also mentioned by wine lovers who like to go through their list of producers citing their human qualities or the special time they had with them, and emphasizing that the wines produced by X or Y could only be very good. In fact, lots of interviewees have raised the point that very often the objectivity of the tasting organized in the club is compromised by their relationship to the producer, and some clubs have banned such relationships to make sure that they can judge wines objectively.

When examined from a broader perspective, the image of the French wine grower is one that conjures up images of the type of armchair nostalgia discussed by Appadurai.[46] These notions of tradition and authenticity are crucial to the commercial visibility of the product, serving the selling of consumer goods, using notions of history to provide a hint of panache.[47] French collective memory associated with wine consumption is articulated around the notion of space and regional diversity encapsulated in the notion of *terroir* and denomination of origin. In the global marketing war, *terroir* represents certain standards of quality often linked with artisanal principles of craftsmanship.[48] Moreover, *terroir* relates back to greater diversity in tastes by putting emphasis on the combination between places, producers and diversity, while New World wines concentrate on the standardization of tastes in relation to a specific grape and on modern production techniques that permit the production of a consistent quality of wine over the years. As gustatory sense is central to the creation of memory in our society, it is possible to argue that space and memory find ways of being articulated together at individual level through wine drinking. The French wine industry relies largely on these links between taste, place and denomination of origin to locate itself in the global wine market.

5. Taste, nation and globalization

Globalization has become one of the most commonly used and least understood of contemporary terms. If we adopt a definition that describes globalization as a multiple process of market economy, world governance and cultural delocalization, we also need to take into account the impact of the process. Yet all too often studies of globalization fail to consider the complex implications of its impact upon individuals, communities and even nations. In his documentary about the world of wine *Mondovino*, Jonathan Nossiter demonstrates quite convincingly how places, actors, families and narratives are intermeshed to create a global product localized and reinvented through familiar notions of authenticity, tradition and ancestry aimed at specific niches of the wine economy. Several representations of the product coexist and emerge, from one end of the spectrum represented by wine production to the other end, that of consumption. It is true that globalization validates the existence and the movement of the same production methods all over the world, leading in some instances to a process of cultural homogenization, as illustrated for example by the use of new oak in the various vineyards of America, Argentina or the 'old Europe'. However, it is possible to argue that globalization is a vector of differentiation as competition increases. Both processes of dissolution and reification seem to go together, and wine illustrates this tendency.[49] Globalization therefore provides us with a useful framework to rethink national drinking culture and to discuss to what extent the French respond to it.

Changes in wine consumption and culture have had a major impact on definitions of taste. At an international level, it has followed some of the major processes affecting the food sector more generally. Tensions between globalization and localism, frequently represented as a battle between homogenization and differentiation, are at the core of debates about wine consumption and taste. Firstly, the international wine industry has experienced a concentration at an economic level with ever larger companies whose size, branding, distribution channels and general marketing play an ever more important role in determining success. International companies are major players in the global wine sector, as was demonstrated by the recent episode of Mondavi (the largest American wine company) in Languedoc, where they were prevented from investing in vineyards by the local producers and politicians. The growth of multinational corporate enterprises is a powerful force for global convergence of values and behaviour, especially in relation to taste. Quality has almost certainly improved overall, with vast quantities of wine attaining consistent levels of quality. Yet for many, wine as a product has become bland, predictable and ultimately indistinguishable from any other mass-produced foodstuff.

Secondly, these economic transformations have permitted a substantial increase in the quantity and the quality of wines produced, and one of the effects of growing competition has been the transformation of wine into a high-quality product that is increasingly sold through chains or supermarkets. It is equally true to say that restaurants now have closer contacts with the wine industry through wholesalers and intermediaries, or even directly with the producers. The idea of access to a wider choice is an integral part of the tasting experience. As the multiple retailers must cater for the widest taste and achieve a high inventory turnover, the restaurant has to acknowledge the different needs of the modern consumer. The process of globalization has, however, privileged the market for premium wines which dominate the international wine sector, while it has become difficult for small producers to have access to that market. Yet French wine production is dominated by small producers, some of whom have succeeded in capturing international markets by emphasizing quality and artisanship and by seeking to provide an authentic social experience for consumers.

This opposition between *terroir* and brands refers to the opposition between modernity and tradition, and is at the core of any discussion about taste amongst wine lovers and consumers. According to the French scholars Chiva and Puisais, one of the consequences of standardization is an impoverishment of taste in food and wine which means that only three basic tastes are generally recognized (saltiness, sweetness, sharpness).[50] Taste (and its expressions for wine consumers) is not only about individualization. Belonging is created through the commensality of the exchanges taking place around wine consumption with the sense of sharing with people in similar circumstances a set of common standards and aspirations.

If following Billig we could argue that 'the nationally imagined identity is diminishing in importance, as compared with imagined "life-style" groups of consumers',[51] it is undeniable that a global wine culture has also played a major role in shaping French wine consumption. The result is that the processes of globalization, which are diminishing differences and spaces between nations, are also fragmenting the imagined unity within those nations. Yet a major process of reinvention and reconstruction is taking place headed by social actors, politicians, policy-makers and wine lovers. Today, consumption in France could be seen as a way of reshaping old ideologies, and it is certain that contradictory values are embedded in French wine drinking culture. The national dimension of wine culture no longer relies solely on consumption, but has more to do with specific emblematic values which are today in danger of disappearing. Attempts are constantly being made to restore, recreate or invent communities[52] and wine is today the object of such investment. The changing political, social and economic context has given rise to new expressions of local, regional and national identities based on differentiation and competition in the social sphere which are negotiated between individuals, groups and society as a whole. In this process, wine offers, through sociability and exchange, a collective and cohesive way of defining collective identities in the context of a changing society. As Warde has argued, the aspiration to culinary or drinking communion is exhibited in the language of tradition, the appeal of regional cuisines or regional wines, the validation of home cooking and home drinking, nostalgia for high-quality locally produced ingredients and wines, and endless reflection on the authenticity of these products.[53]

At the same time, the values embedded in wine consumption illustrate the attachment of French people to space, time, rural society, commensality and sociability, which are today challenged by globalization, modernity and multiculturalism. These values could be read as the traces of a surviving agrarian ideology, or they could be seen as an alternative type of consumption in an increasingly global society. For French people, despite the modernization of their society, wine remains a 'cultural exception' and in this context, it is part of the French specificity. Wine as a culture and as an object of consumption has always been used in different ways encapsulating different meanings but revealing its emblematic position as an element of French national identity.

Notes

1. Thomas M. Wilson (ed.), *Drinking Cultures: Alcohol and Identity* (Oxford and New York: Berg, 2005), p. 11.
2. Anthony D. Smith, *National Identity* (London: Penguin, 1991), p. 14.
3. For a discussion about the changes introduced by Anthony D. Smith to the definition of the nation see M. Montserrat Guiberneau, 'Anthony D. Smith on nations and national identity: a critical assessment', *Nations and Nationalism*, 10, 1/2 (2004), 125–41.
4. Ernest Gellner, *Nations and Nationalism* (Ithaca: Cornell University Press, 1983).
5. Benedict Anderson, *Imagined Communities: Reflections on the Origin and Spread of Nationalism* (London and New York: Verso, 1983).
6. By 'essentialist', I mean a constant and rooted element of French identity made up of a regional diversity presented as unchanged.
7. Sarah Howard, 'Selling wine to the French: official attempts to increase wine consumption, 1931–1936', *Food and Foodways*, 12 (2004), 205.
8. Ibid., 199.
9. Wilson, *Drinking Cultures*, p. 12.
10. Sarah Howard, *Les images de l'alcool en France, 1915–42* (Paris: CNRS, 2006).
11. See for example the work of Gilles Laferté, *La Bourgogne et ses vins. Image d'origine contr'lée* (Paris: Belin, 2006) and Marion Demossier, *Hommes et vins. Une anthropologie du vignoble bourguignon* (Dijon: EUD, 1999).
12. L.-A. Loubère, *The Wine Revolution in France: The Twentieth Century* (Princeton: Princeton University Press, 1990).
13. Didier Nourrison, *Le Buveur du dix-neuvième siècle* (Paris: Albin Michel, 1990).
14. Nourrisson, *Le Buveur du dix-neuvième siècle* and Thomas Brennan, *Public Drinking and Popular Culture in the Eighteenth Century* (Paris and Princeton: Princeton University Press, 1988), p. 74.
15. Brennan, *Public Drinking and Popular Culture in the Eighteenth Century*, p. 74.
16. Jean-Claude Bologne, *Histoire morale et culturelle de nos boissons* (Paris: Robert Laffont, 1991).
17. Nourrisson, *Le Buveur du dix-neuvième siècle*, p. 62.
18. Anne-Marie Thiesse, *La Création des identités nationales: Europe XVIIIe–XXe siècle* (Paris: Éditions du Seuil, 1999).
19. Loubère, *The Wine Revolution in France* and as quoted in Ulin, *Vintages and Traditions: An Ethnohistory of Southwest French Wine Cooperatives* (Washington: Smithsonian Institution Press, 1996), p. 523.
20. Kolleen M.Guy. *When Champagne Became French: Wine and the Making of a National Identity*, Johns Hopkins University Studies in Historical and Political Science, 121st Series (Baltimore: Johns Hopkins University Press, 2003).
21. Guy, *When Champagne Became French*, p. 30.

22 Gilles Laferté, *La Bourgogne et ses vins*.
23 É. M. Moentmann, 'The search for French identity in the regions: national versus local visions of France in the 1930s', *French History*, 17, 3 (2003), 307–27.
24 Herman Lebovics, *True France: The Wars over Cultural Identity, 1900–1945* (Ithaca: Cornell University Press, 1992) and Shanny Peer, *France on Display: Peasants, Provincials, and Folklore in the 1937 Paris World's Fair*, SUNY Series in National Identities (Albany: State University of New York Press. 1998).
25 Peter Scholliers (ed.), *Food, Drink and Identity: Cooking, Eating and Drinking in Europe since the Middle Ages* (Oxford: Berg, 2001).
26 Alan Warde, *Consumption, Food and Taste: Culinary Antinomies and Commodity Culture* (London: Sage, 1997).
27 Cited by Scholliers, *Food, Drink and Identity*, p. 8.
28 Wilson, *Drinking Cultures*, p. 13.
29 Warde, *Consumption, Food and Taste*, p. 7.
30 The book is the result of a study undertaken in 1963 and completed in 1968.
31 Jean-Pierre Albert, 'La nouvelle culture du vin', *Terrain*, 13 (1989), 117–24.
32 Warde, *Consumption, Food and Taste*, p. 10.
33 Ibid.
34 Marion Demossier, 'Consuming wine in France: the "wandering" drinker and the "vin-anomie"', in Wilson, *Drinking Cultures*, pp. 129–54.
35 Carole Counihan and Penny Van Esterik, *Food and Culture: A Reader* (London: Routledge, 1997), p. 1.
36 Counihan and Van Esterik, *Food and Culture*, p. 3.
37 Pekka Sulkunen, 'Drinking in France 1965–79: an analysis of household consumption data', *British Journal of Addiction*, 84 (1989), 61–72.
38 Thorstein Veblen, *The Theory of the Leisure Class* (Chicago: University of Chicago Press, 1899).
39 Mary Douglas, *Constructive Drinking: Perspectives on Drink from Anthropology* (Cambridge: Cambridge University Press, 1987), p. 9.
40 John Brewer and Frank Trentmann, *Consuming Cultures, Global Perspectives: Historical Trajectories, Transnational Exchanges* (Oxford and New York: Berg, 2006), p. 13.
41 Geneviève Teil, *De la coupe aux lèvres. Pratiques de la perception et mise en marché des vins de qualité* (Toulouse: Éditions Octarès, 2004); Jean-Luc Fernandez, *La critique vinicole en France. Pouvoir de prescription et construction de la confiance*, Logiques sociales (Paris: L'Harmattan, 2004); and Rachel Reckinger, *Les Pratiques discursives oenophiles, entre normativité et appropriation. Contribution à une sociologie des cultures alimentaires* (Thèse de doctorat, École des Hautes Études en Sciences Sociales, Marseille, 2 volumes, 2008). For a review of the works of Teil and Fernandez, see *http://aof.revues.org/sommaire37.html*.
42 By 'synaesthesia', I refer to the work of David E. Sutton on food and memory, *Remembrances of Repast: An Anthropology of Food and Memory*

(New York: Berg, 2001), p. 102. In his book, Sutton defines it as the crossing of different kinds of sensory experiences, as the basis for food being memorable and thus capable of evoking a larger whole.
43   Sutton, *Remembrances of Repast*, p. 102.
44   J.-D. Holtzman, 'Food and memory', *Annual Review of Anthropology*, 35 (2006), 361–78.
45   Warde, *Consumption, Food and Taste*, p. 13.
46   Arjun Appadurai, *Modernity at Large: Cultural Dimensions of Globalization* (Minneapolis: University of Minnesota Press, 1996), p. 78.
47   Holtzman, 'Food and Memory', 386.
48   David Bell and Gill Valentine, *Consuming Geographies: We Are What we Eat* (London and New York: Routledge, 1997).
49   I should like to thank my two colleagues Chantal Crenn and Isabelle Téchoueyres for contributing to the debate on the globalization of wine. See *http://edition.cens.cnrs.fr/revue/aofood/2004*.
50   Matty Chiva, *Le Doux et l'amer* (Paris: PUF, 1985) and Jacques Puisais, *Le Goût et l'enfant* (Paris: Flammarion, 1987).
51   Michael Billig, *Banal Nationalism* (London: Sage, 1995), p. 132.
52   Warde, *Consumption, Food and Taste*, p. 183.
53   Ibid., p. 184.

Chapter Two
Changes to a National Wine Drinking Culture

Wine has traditionally featured as the central beverage in French drinking culture. The French population, from childhood to adulthood, has, one day or another, been initiated into the art of wine drinking, and drinking wine has traditionally been a means of integrating social groups into national culture. Through its folklore, songs, publications, festivals, landscapes and architecture, wine culture inscribed in the region has been represented as an essential element of French national identity. Yet as wine consumption has declined, this rosy picture has begun to crumble and the mythical construction of a homogeneous wine drinking culture has been called into question. Young people today are said to have little or no knowledge of wine, and the image promoted by the media is that of a generational rupture.

However, wine drinking is about so much more than the simple alimentary act of quenching your thirst. First and foremost, it is a social activity which involves a group of individuals and has, amongst its aims, enjoyment, pleasure and, sometimes, intoxication. Secondly, wine drinking in France is supported by a culture which refers to a large body of knowledge surrounding the product, its producers and the wine market. It is presented as a sophisticated, complex and challenging activity, which involves both the acquisition of knowledge and memory and also the collective act of tasting and experiencing France in its geographical and rural diversity. The steady and apparently irreversible decline of wine consumption in France has been an economic fact since at least the 1950s and this decline in volume consumed has been accompanied by drastic changes in terms of what people drink, why, how, when and in which company.[1] Any study of wine drinking culture also has to take into account the production of wine, with its history of diversity, its actors, its cultural divisions and the claims that it is a cultural and social activity, a 'field for action' which is both competitive and defined by complex and changing rules.[2] The study of wine culture and consumption has to include production with the chain of intermediaries – *vignerons, coopératives, négociants* (wine merchants), the various professions – from the oenologist to the *sommelier* (wine waiter) and *caviste* (cellarman) and wine sellers – from supermarkets to wine bars – and the consumer, who arguably could be seen as an active, differentiated and creative category of actor. The many and diverse representations surrounding the product and its consumption are also essential to the understanding of wine drinking culture, from the choice of wine to the discourses surrounding its collective production and evaluation.

To understand the contemporary world of wine, it is necessary to place it in the context of a venerable tradition of French wine drinking culture. As in other fields, the past plays a key role in debates about contemporary issues, and as such is a site of intense competition for groups and individuals struggling to make their voices heard, particularly those that have traditionally been marginalized. It is why, when analysing the passions and issues behind its consumption, it is necessary to have a sense of the history of wine production and wine consumption, but also a history of French culture and society. The myth of a national French drinking culture has been so enduring that it is necessary to recall the tumultuous history behind its emergence. History has also become a commodity, and wine growers, merchants and others have sought to harness a sense of nostalgia for their present purposes.[3] The politics of nostalgia has also become an important strategy to be mobilized against the economic threat posed by globalization.

This chapter looks at the historical development of the concept of national drinking culture by focusing on three essential elements: firstly, the construction of a regulated economic space from the late nineteenth century onwards and the organization of national wine production upon the ideological foundations of the concept of *terroir* and AOC at a time of growing international demand for wine, agricultural modernization and urbanization; secondly, the consolidation of regional wine cultures and the parallel development of French gastronomic and oenological cultures in Paris and the French provinces, especially during the 1930s, and their importance in the diffusion of a specific model of consumption based upon the duality of region and nation; finally, the construction of the myth of French wine as an element of the national heritage and patrimony which has been part of a continuous process partly organized by the wine elites, partly regulated by the state.

The history of French wine drinking culture has been punctuated by crises that were frequently the catalysts for governmental measures seeking to protect a cherished industry from both international competition and the frauds which were such a common feature during the development of viticulture as an industry. Progress in science and technology, growing affluence associated with the expanding bourgeoisie and the reversal of government policy towards more control and regulation are amongst the principal characteristics of the twentieth century, and what Léo Loubère termed the 'wine revolution'.[4] The focus of this study is principally wine consumption and culture since 1945, but current issues need to be seen in the light of earlier developments affecting both production and consumption. Amongst them, the regulation of the wine market is a constant historical feature, notably following the law of 12 August 1905, which later provided the basis for the system of *appellations* which defined the geographical area and the 'local, loyal and consistent' customs of production (law of 6 May 1919). Revolts against these laws were common, and many legal cases were launched to broaden areas of production. It was the great economic recession, however, of the 1930s that forced the French government to seek a general legislative solution with the decree of 30 July 1935.

The AOC legislation of 1935 was completed in August 1945, with the recognition of VDQS (*Vins délimités de qualité supérieure*) which provided the basis for modern French viticulture and gave real impetus to the developing awareness of the need for quality.[5] It also provided recognition for the rising class of wine growers who had been able to acquire vineyards or consolidate their estates since the phylloxera crisis in regions such as Burgundy or Beaujolais. For the first time, wine growers, *négociants* and landowners were brought together and were given the opportunity to compete economically by producing AOC wines. The AOC established a strict and hierarchical classification of wines, from one region to the next and within each region, and consequently between growers based on the commercial reputation of their products. The concept of *terroir* was thus defined in relation to each vineyard and each variety of grape and there was also an explicit recognition of the *savoir-faire* (know-how) of the producer, which was seen as the guarantee of the *typicité* (local character) of the product according to the terms of the law.[6] It is noteworthy that decisions concerning the recognition of specific AOCs were originally initiated by *syndicats* or unions of producers in each geographical area who appealed to the courts in order to persuade the state to provide recognition through the establishment of the AOC.

These negotiations offer a clear example of the periphery/central authority process as they involved both the state and the local *syndicats* of the AOC.[7] As Loubère notes, from the late 1920s, wine growers repudiated the individualistic entrepreneur of earlier times as their model role and chose state regulation over traditional production and marketing, which could be explained by the growing internationalization of the wine market.[8] The centralized administrative organization of French vineyards illustrates some of the characteristics of the dual process of national/regional building of the French nation with a strong regional diversity and a wide range of professional interests and economic positions. The law of July 1935 established the Appellations d'origine contrôlées (AOC) combining the administrative, legal and professional aspects of the control of wine production. A public body the INAO (Institut National des Appellations d'Origine) was given the unique power of proposal to ministries through its committee body. This is the only institution of its kind in France. These regulations aimed to create a framework for the production of quality wine at a time of frauds and surplus production. The emphasis it placed on quality could arguably be seen as one of the greatest achievements of French viticulture during the first half of the twentieth century.

The shortages and economic disruption caused by the Second World War and the German occupation had a major impact on consumption patterns in the immediate post-war period. Wines, especially those with an established international reputation, were more or less protected by their status as defined in the *Code du vin* (1936). Yet the Germans took great care during the occupation to requisition them and organize their transit to Germany. This was also the period of Marshal Pétain's National Revolution and a conscious attempt to reconstruct national identity around the rural imaginary and an emphasis on artisanship, agrarian values and the myth of soil in which wine and vines symbolized a certain conception of Frenchness articulated by the Vichy propaganda machine.

The post-war period has been described by most commentators as a period of major transformation, as reconstruction and industrialization turned the country into a prosperous consumer society during a period that is still remembered in popular memory as the *Trente Glorieuses*. Economic transformation was accompanied by the emergence of a new middle class which benefited from economic progress as symbolized by the growing availability of consumer goods and leisure activities. This was also a period characterized by the mechanization of the agricultural sector, an era of progress symbolized by the growing presence of tractors in the fields as a symbol of modernity. French viticulture benefited greatly from these developments and from scientific advances, notably pesticides and oenological treatments which guaranteed better and more reliable harvests. The marketing of specific wines, often internationally, under the name of the local area started to become commonplace and no longer the preserve of a few high-quality wines. In Burgundy, for example, the majority of local wines adopted the name of the village where they were produced such as Puligny-Montrachet or Aloxe-Corton, identifying themselves with the more prestigious *premier cru* (Premium wine) or *grand cru* (higher quality of premium wine) of those names.

The 1970s also witnessed the first signs of a major transformation in the French diet as a consequence of rapid economic modernization and the flight from villages to the towns under the impact of the burgeoning prosperity of an increasingly liberalized society. The rise of an affluent bourgeoisie and the progressive decline of both the industrial and the rural proletariat marked the turning-point of these alimentary changes. In this context, wine was exposed to increasing competition from other types of beverages and even from the growing popularity of soft drugs, notably cannabis. It also began to be perceived as an emblem of the bourgeoisie, a symbol of pre-1968 France. From an alimentary product, wine became the object of intellectual investigation, and this shift was revealed by the attention of leading French intellectuals including Claude Levi-Strauss and Raymond Aron, who shed new light on the study of food. However, it was only in the 1980s and 1990s that a major decline in terms of total wine consumption was recorded, and this development was accompanied by a parallel revival of wine drinking culture with a proliferation of clubs, activities and discourses devoted to this passion.

1. Defining a national drinking culture

In 1957, Roland Barthes published his seminal work, *Mythologies*, which transformed the study of food in France. In it, he argued: 'To believe in wine is a restricting collective act; the French who might want to move away from the myth will have to face some problems, especially in terms of integration, the first of which would be to have to explain yourself.'[9] For Barthes, drinking wine remained a national technique with its associated sociability, self-control and culture of moderation, defining an important part of what it meant to be French. The series of articles he published collectively in *Mythologies* had been written between 1954 and 1956, and were originally published in a variety of newspapers and periodicals (*Esprit, France Observateur* and *Lettres Nouvelles*).[10] Interestingly enough, the chapter devoted to wine and milk was written under a new government headed by Prime Minister Pierre Mendès-France (1954), which was restricting the privilege of home distillers, promoting milk to replace wine during national political meetings and setting up the Haut Comité d'Etude et d'Information sur l'Alcoolisme (High Committee for Study and Information on Alcoholism).[11] The period coincided with a clear attack on alcohol drinking, and several commentators argued that wine had to be protected as a national industry.

The emblematic nature of wine drinking culture, which has inspired writers for centuries, remains deeply rooted in French identity, which helps to explain why few dare to challenge its origins, its content, its validity or even its transformations.[12] Most of the massive corpus of French literature published on the subject of wine that has appeared since the nineteenth century has been written by folklorists, notables (wealthy bourgeois) and politicians, historians, geographers, social scientists and connoisseurs, most of whom continue to peddle the myth of a homogeneous drinking culture as a formative element of French national identity.[13] According to Durand, 'Vine and wine give to our culture [I underline French culture] the constant mark of a familiar and ceremonious reference.'[14] It is clear that the myth surrounding wine in French society has struck a receptive chord, contributing to the external representation of French grandeur abroad as much as the internal construction of Frenchness. 'The French cockerel is a cockerel who drinks wine … It is a courageous cockerel singing loud and clear.'[15]

In an age of growing concern about excessive alcohol consumption, many British commentators seem to believe that being French seems to confer an almost magical capacity to acquire a certain connoisseurship. This idealized view is no less strongly rooted in France, and French arrogance about wine drinking culture is very often summarized with the expression: 'Here, we have the best vineyards and the best wines in the world', accentuating the ties between a territory and a product. For many French people, wine, or more precisely the love of good wines, characterizes Frenchness in much the same way as being born in France, fighting for liberty or speaking French.[16] It is part of the collective values underlining the transmission of a cultural and national memory. Here again, we glimpse what is in reality an idealized image of national harmony because wine drinking culture has always been characterized by its great regional diversity and its hierarchical nature. Whatever the theory, drinking a glass of Burgundy is not the same experience as drinking red plonk from the South. Nor can it be said that Bretons, Normans or Picards have the same relationship to wine as Burgundians or Gascons. Yet if the idea of a homogeneous wine culture is a myth, it is one with real power nevertheless, not least as a means of defending a cherished and significant industry against the challenges of globalization, Europeanization and economic liberalization. The history of wine, like any other alimentary product, demonstrates how social structures and cultural patterns have changed continuously over many centuries, not just as a result of outside influences, but also because of internal dynamics of their own.[17]

Whether real or imagined, the concept of a national drinking culture refers to the relationship in terms of consumption and production between one single and dominant drink – wine in this instance – and the majority of the members of the nation. The sense of belonging to this nation is mediated through the production and consumption of this particular drink, or the meanings associated with it as a collective good. French wine, on the one hand, could be defined as a single national alcoholic drink, 'a national treasure'[18] and, on the other hand, because of its geographic element, as a plural drink, supporting the expression of several identities. The geographic distribution of wine production has been the primary factor of identification since wine was first sold as a commodity identified with a specific place (Bordeaux or Burgundy).[19] The regional and territorial element is therefore constitutive of the national drink. The main strengths of wine drinking culture is to have combined a strong traditional diversity, represented by regional cultures, with the powerful image of wine as an icon of the nation, despite a patchwork of local economies, regional interests and a history of social reforms attacking alcohol consumption. These paradoxes are still clearly at the centre of contemporary debates, even if their content has changed. As Guy has argued, wine was 'an integral part of the argument around "a personality" of France built upon the seemingly unique blend of geography and history of each of its regions'.[20] This mythical and essentialist construction was made possible because the nineteenth century was a period of great expansion in wine consumption. This construction has over the years followed the main fluctuations of political, economic and social life, but it has also become the focus of various tensions and negotiations between different groups of actors, including ministers and other politicians, producers, landowners, *négociants* and experts.

Yet France was never characterized by a unified pattern of wine consumption.[21] During the nineteenth century, alcohol consumption altered substantially under the influence of a variety of factors, including wider access to wine and other alcohols associated with the general growth of popular purchasing power, relayed by the progress of viticulture and the improvement of transport networks via the railway and maritime routes.[22] Industrialization, and its attendant urbanization, was seen by some conservative commentators as a blight on society. In this context, the nation needed to be moralized. Amongst the social scourges identified as requiring reform, the excessive drinker stood out and was the object of governmental scrutiny and the focus of attention for an emerging temperance movement. Yet it would have been all but impossible for any government to attack wine production with any real force, given its economic importance.

The First World War, as in so many other fields, acted as a catalyst on national perceptions of wine, with the nation fighting for its survival and experiencing the cruel and long-lasting effects of the carnage on the western front. French soldiers (known as the *poilus*) were given rations of wine substitute to keep them going. Wine's powerful imaginary in France was thus reinforced because of the way in which *le pinard* had been identified with French soldiers during the Great War.[23] Patriotism and wine went hand in hand

and, despite growing concern over alcohol consumption, wine was seen by social commentators as a symbol of French civilization. The *poilus* were thus identified with wine through many of their songs like *La Madelon, Pinard de la victoire* and *Vive le pinard*. However, national identity was also constructed around the image of the French as moderate and knowledgeable drinkers of wine, an ideal constructed on regional models of gastronomy and the ideals of the affluent bourgeois who cultivated wine drinking as a cultural activity and almost an art form. Their dominant position in the social fabric and their discourse about wine drinking meant that any excess was very much tolerated by the rest of French society.[24] There are many iconographic examples of Alsatian, Bordelais and Burgundian wine drinkers depicted as sophisticated tasters holding a glass of wine in hand. It is undeniable that bourgeois and other notables, through folkloric societies and confraternities, played a major role in shaping the image of the wine drinker as an educated taster, a connoisseur, and as controlling patterns of drinking during festive and gastronomic occasions.[25] In non-wine-producing regions like Brittany, however, the image of the excessive drinker as a social scourge dominated public debate, while in Provence, there was not so strong an identification with wine drinking despite its being an area of large-scale production. This could be partly explained by the lack of a strong wine drinking culture associated with the absence of a famous, dominant and already established vineyard, and also by different economic and social power structures, the majority of these wines being consumed locally. Yet the national dimension was central to the rhetoric on wine.

One of the French wine industry's greatest achievements has been to persuade the public and politicians that wine was a national drink, sanctified by the work of generations of wine growers toiling on a sacred *terroir*. The work of Gilles Laferté on Burgundian elites demonstrates the complex processes at the core of this construction between regional and national levels.[26] Their strategy was, in part, a highly successful means of distancing wine from other alcoholic drinks such as Calvados and absinthe, which were the unwanted ghosts at their feast. Wine could therefore be represented positively connected to the various social and medical ills that so concerned the temperance movement, social reformers and conservative moralists.

According to Ulin, the organization and protection of a national and hierarchical productive space into a bounded, exclusive, regulated and limited perimeter, defined by tradition and artisanship, has provided the basis and the originality of French wines worldwide.[27] He argues: 'the effort to preserve an artisanal past, even one that is invented, especially on the part of wine growers in elite wine-growing regions, is interesting in its own right, given Marx's contention that industrial capitalism would eventually destroy craft production.'[28] The ideology of the *terroir* and its corollary, the AOC, results from the progressive evolution of the local relationship involving various social actors, mainly landowners, *négociants* and wine growers, who were part of the same productive sphere.[29] However, they shared radically different approaches to the product. Susan Terrio argues that the French state has consistently tended to regard artisans as backward and an obstacle to industrial progress, especially in the post-Second World War period when a rapidly growing service sector favoured white-collar workers and the professionally trained.[30] The artisans did not accept their subaltern position with resignation, but instead invented a collective discourse that associated artisans with the 'true' France, a France characterized by a traditional work ethic, family values, community cohesion and the non-competitive practices of the small-business sector.[31]

The emergence of the concept of quality in wine production at the beginning of the twentieth century was intrinsically bound up with the wider debates surrounding the definition of what was meant by 'wine', provoked by the emergence of a new discipline, that of oenology.[32] The growing regulations affecting wine production were designed above all to put an end to the increasing number of scandals involving frauds and abuses. It has been estimated that in 1900, 5 million hectolitres of wines were imported from abroad, a further 5 million hectolitres entered France from its colony Algeria, 8 million hectolitres of wines were artificially 'made' (from dried raisins or sugar) and 2 or 3 million hectolitres of homemade plonks produced by individuals.[33] In total, in the region of 20 million hectolitres were added to the annual production of 80 million hectolitres, of which only two-thirds were consumed by French people. The situation was complicated by the hierarchical nature of the wine sector, which was marked by serious social tensions. The merchants and *négociants* were the main buyers for these imported and foreign wines, as they were able to blend them and to produce cheaper plonk than the wine growers. Most of the wine growers, however, were still dependent on the *négociants*, as they were the principal commercial outlet for their wines. This economic dependency led the wine growers to resort to violence, especially in 1907 with the so-called 'Revolt of Languedoc' and in 1911 during the Champagne wine growers' 'outcry'.[34] Despite a series of government regulations, fraud proved difficult to eradicate. However, real progress was made with the drafting of the new AOC legislation in 1935.

These negotiations, at local level, were part of a vast movement affecting regional cultures, at a time when tourism, of both French and foreign nationals, and new forms of consumption provided the resources to reposition the regions into a national model through history, geography and rural images. The construction of a regional and national wine culture accompanied the construction of this vast, unique, economic and patriotic space in what Guy describes as 'something exceptionally French, to be protected against global marketing shifts'.[35] It was supported by a popular shift in ideologies. Herman Lebovics and Shanny Peer have shown that among cultural leaders in Paris, the French regions were crucial to this understanding of an authentic France. By the 1930s, across the political spectrum, the diverse regional cultures had come to represent a heterogeneous, but deep-rooted national identity, as opposed to the seemingly monotonous, industrialized and distant modern culture.[36] For Lebovics, the notables played a major role in exercising a strong influence on local communities and, at national level, through agricultural societies or regional associations and local unions.[37] It is undeniable that, because of their role at national and regional level, they were the main political actors, able to ensure the mediation of a cultural paradigm constructed around agricultural production, gastronomy and *terroir*. In Burgundy, for example, the discussions around the recognition of the AOC at local level from the 1930s onwards were dominated by the influence of notables and wealthy landowners, and in many cases, they made sure that their parcel of land was the one recognized at the top of the hierarchy (as *grands crus*). Some of these socially dominant figures were the leaders in the long process of recognition of the AOC. The ownership patterns of each vineyard meant that these debates had a regional flavour with, for example, the collective spirit of the South clashing with the individualist nature of Burgundy. They played an intermediary role between the communal syndicates and the national federation or interministerial organizations.[38]

For Laferté, the establishment of a new image of viticulture was intrinsically connected to the marketing of the region.[39] This process involved landowners who took over the pre-capitalist image of the wine grower and the community in order to promote an artisanal myth – around the wine grower, the village and the quality of wines – which in turn, contributed to a new reading of the Burgundian as a gastronome and wine amateur. In the wine industry, during the 1930s, folklore became a commodity facilitating social integration of newcomers and the selling of the products in a competitive context. But it was also a way to create a strong and coherent image of a very divided and socially heterogeneous world.[40] Folklore played a major role in shaping the image of the wine grower as a natural and authentic figure in an expanding industry, who was opposed to the *négociants*, his modern and urban counterpart. According to Guy, another development took place in the nearby and competitive region of Champagne. For Guy, the dominant discourse amongst *vignerons* was less about class than about protecting the *patrie* and the rural community.[41] In their battle, the *vignerons* succeeded in ensuring the recognition of their wines. However, the *folklorization* of Champagne was not constituted around the image of the wine grower and of a peasant culture as in Burgundy, but was instead constructed around Paris, with an emphasis on the development of a dining and drinking style, the emergence of an international wealthy class of drinkers from the USA and Europe who placed champagne at the heart of their festivities. This patchwork of regional drinking cultures illustrates the variety of models offered by the nation to the increasingly differentiated consumer of yesterday.

2. War and rupture

The shortages and economic disruption caused by the Second World War and the German occupation had a major impact on consumption patterns in the immediate post-war period. Compared with other types of products, wine, and especially premium wines, enjoyed a quite peculiar position as they were subject to close control of production, distribution and consumption by the occupying Germans.[42] Indeed, when the Second World War broke out, ordinary wine was immediately identified as a possible remedy for the epidemics and sufferings of the soldiers. According to one commentator, 'Wine is a good companion of soldiers. It gives them courage.'[43] Meanwhile local associations, such as that of producers in Languedoc, joined up with local charities to ensure that hot wine was served to the soldiers who travelled to the front.[44] During the war, soldiers were in theory entitled to one litre of wine a day as it was seen as a nutritious beverage. Yet for many ex-servicemen drinking a bottle of wine was a rare experience, and some recall drinking only two or three bottles in total during the period of the war as a whole.[45] Far from drinking what we might think of as an acceptable wine, most of the soldiers had to drink a substitute, wine with bromide, which was denounced after the war for its quality by the French press.[46] From 1940, wine was rationed to two litres per week per inhabitant, and then was reserved to the adult male population. Yet the situation regarding food and wine differed greatly, from one region to another, from rural to urban areas, or from one group to another. During the war, wine became the object of intense commercial competition as it was rationed and hard to obtain even on the black market: 'For Henry Jayer of Vosne-Romanée in Burgundy, it meant trading his wine for food, so his family would have enough to eat.'[47] Given the economic value of wine, wine-growing regions enjoyed an especially privileged and economically advantageous position during the occupation.

Until the publication of Kladstrup and Kladstrup *Wine and War: The French, the Nazis and the Battle for France's Greatest Treasure* in 2002, little was known about the status of wine during the Second World War. What their work illustrates is the position of wine as a national treasure, an object of exchange and favours, and as a protected good cherished by both the Vichy government (1940–4) and the Germans, but for very different reasons. For the Vichy government, wine was an essential element of the National Revolution, but it also became the object of several decrees and controls.[48] As in the First World War, wines carrying the distinction of an AOC continued to enjoy a practically free market[49] as they were not included in the viticulture statute which aimed at regulating the market.[50] For the Germans in Paris and elsewhere in France, wine offered a means of demonstrating their status as occupiers. With the drawing of the demarcation line, most of France's best vineyards – the *grands crus* – came under German control, and the authorities wasted no time in letting wine growers know who was in charge.[51] More than 2.5 million hectolitres of wine, the equivalent of 320 million bottles, were shipped to Germany each year. Millions of bottles were also drunk in Paris and in French restaurants as part of the entertainment of German soldiers and the German elites. In his diary of the occupation, Henri Drouot, a prominent historian living in Dijon, noted, at regular intervals, the encounters between German soldiers and local wines and alcohols.[52] He describes German soldiers as always drunk in the evenings. After 1941, the shortage of wine became striking, while in 1942 and 1943 more than 10 million bottles of wine were sold illegally on the black market, leading to tightened controls by the Vichy government.

Yet wine continued to occupy a special position in the French national ideology. The war did not mark a radical break with the previous period; it merely reinforced it, especially as far as the AOC was concerned. For a Vichy regime influenced by fascist and conservative ideologies stressing the virtues of blood and soil and claiming to represent a national revolution, the *vigneron* was the ideal symbol of the peasant in his *terroir*. Celebrated for his hard work and the agrarian values defining his community, the *vigneron* was at the centre of the National Revolution, at least until 1942. In a speech given to the Hospices de Beaune to thank them for the plot of land named after him, Marshal Pétain gave expression to these sentiments when he declared: 'You have flattered a personal passion of mine, my love for the soil and my instinct as a wine grower.'[53] The rationalization, especially of gastronomy (and I emphasize wine), commemorated the attributes of the new order: the defence of the family, the authority of the father, the domestic service of the mother, the regulated functions of tradition through work and respect of the hierarchy, the place of regions as a source of agricultural production as an echo of an agrarian Golden Age.[54]

Wine was only one of the elements on which the Vichy regime constructed its propaganda. It also rehabilitated dialects and *patois*, encouraged local cultures by expressing their sense of regional identity through history, geography, folklore, music, costumes, dances and museums with the aim of glorifying them. Georges Rouquier, a celebrated film-maker during the Vichy regime, won the first prize for the best French documentary made in 1943 with his film *Le Tonnelier* (The Cooper). His success illustrates the political emphasis of the National Revolution, which sought to celebrate artisanship and the traditional values of such professions. Jean Vigreux has argued that the plot of Burgundian vines named the Clos du maréchal Pétain, offered to Pétain by the region and the Hospices de Beaune in 1942, symbolized the ideal of provincial rural France, an ideal which never entirely disappeared from the Vichy cultural project.[55] At the time, this gesture was part of a wider government propaganda campaign diffusing a regionalist and traditional discourse, in tune with the National Revolution. According to Faure, the popularity of the Vichy government is in fact encapsulated in the shift operated between 'regional' and 'regionalism'. Through this representation of the peasant and his community,[56] the ideology of Vichy found some support from social groups in crisis.[57]

As Julian Jackson has noted, the history of Vichy is full of complexity and contradictions, as the example of Champagne makes clear.[58] In April 1941, de Vogüe, one of the principal actors in the local wine industry, called together producers and wine growers to set up an organization that would represent the interests of everyone in the region. His initiative gave birth to the CIVC (Comité Interprofessionnel des Vins de Champagne) and provided a model for future lobby groups and for representation of the profession at regional and national levels. Speaking as a unified front and with a single voice, the CIVC tried to negotiate with the Germans in the context of massive requisitioning and, at the same time, tried to protect its own interests. This particular episode illustrates that very often the French wine industry remained rooted in its regional dimension. It was only in the face of adversity that local and professional preoccupations converged and formed a general consensus. This primacy of regional leadership over a national consensus would be repeated regularly thereafter and the diversity of the wine industry remained one of the principal obstacles to the representation of the wine profession as a whole.

3. Wine and mass consumption

The modernization of the French economy contributed substantially to the further transformation of the role of wine in French society and culture after the Second World War. The affluence brought about by unprecedented and sustained economic growth (averaging 5 per cent of GDP per annum) ushered in a new age of mass consumption and leisure.[59] According to Ross, the speed with which French society was transformed after the war from a rural, empire-orientated, Catholic country into a fully industrialized, decolonized and urban one meant that modernization was thrown upon a society that still cherished traditional outlooks with all the force, excitement, disruption and horror of the genuinely new.[60] The private and domestic spheres were certainly greatly affected by these changes. French economic expansion in this period was based on a sustained growth in demand for consumer durables such as household appliances and motor vehicles. In 1960, food consumption represented one third of the average household budget, compared to around 18 per cent today.[61] Somewhat paradoxically, the kitchen and the domestic sphere were very much at the centre of this consumer revolution, both in terms of commodities and in their representation in the press, on the radio and television at a time when women were joining the labour force in ever larger numbers.

Indeed economic modernization was accompanied by a process of social fragmentation which was particularly visible in the sphere of leisure and consumption.[62] A dual concentration of the urban and tertiary sectors was responsible for changes in social stratification and in employment patterns. The increasing number of working women was one of the major transformations as their traditional role, confined to the kitchen and children's education, was radically challenged. This modernization illustrating the birth of consumer society and the growing industrialization of food production resulted in the opening of the first French supermarket in 1949 by Édouard Leclerc in Landernau, followed, in 1960, by that of the Carrefour in Annecy. These changes, which were a feature of the *Trente Glorieuses* (1945–75) were accompanied by a major expansion of the number of French holiday-makers, who increased from 8 million in 1951 to 20 million in 1966, a movement encouraged by the reduction in the average number of annual working weeks in both 1956 and 1969. Mass consumption and diversification were amongst the dominant features of these changes affecting tourism in this period, and it could be argued that the traditional social cleavages between the bourgeoisie and the working classes began to blur, while new spatial and professional divisions emerged. For instance, farmers were still the profession least likely to take holidays, as they remained bound by the traditional rhythms of harvest and markets. Perhaps not surprisingly, it was the increasingly affluent inhabitants of the suburbs of Paris who were to the fore in the new holiday and leisure market.[63] When it came to their choice of destinations, French people undoubtedly privileged the South of France and camping sites. However, the creation of regional parks, the rise of holiday villages (for instance in 1958 with the creation of the Village Vacances Familles association (VVF)) and the spread of campsites contributed to the expansion of French regional tourism. The rise of the leisure and tourist industries in the decades following the Second World War led to a revival of interest in regional culture and heritage, and the wine industry was particularly well placed to take advantage of this phenomenon.

For the wine industry, this period was marked by what Gilbert Garrier has called 'a triumph of generalized progress', as viticulture modernized alongside other sectors of French agriculture. In 1947, the establishment of the INAO (Institut National des Appellations d'Origine) meant that all of the major representatives of the actors involved in wine production met together with the affected ministries. The INAO provided the institutional basis and structure for the development of the AOC system, which was then expanded in the 1950s. Wine producers were also receiving more professional training, they were more educated and they started comparing their products. During the 1950s, French viticulture entered a new stage of adaptation associated with the development of the Common Market and the new European regulations it produced. It also had to face a new competitive context with the entry of Italy and later Spain. In quantity and as well quality, French wines have dramatically improved over the last fifty years, and French vineyards have experienced a major transformation of both their landscapes and their conditions of production. In some areas, such as Languedoc, substantial numbers of vineyards were uprooted in the 1960s and 1970s, while slopes abandoned a century before were planted with good-quality grapes such as grenache, mourvèdre or syrah.[64]

The emergence of a new wine culture was accompanied by the rapid diffusion of oenological knowledge and expertise in both academia and public discourse. Together they provided the impetus for what might be termed a second 'wine revolution', with newspapers, television and other media helping to diffuse oenological knowledge at the same time as the promotion of the latest gastronomical fashions. The publication of *Traité d'Oenologie* by professor Jean Ribéreau-Gayon in 1947 was a key turning-point as wine tasting became part of the broader scientific discipline of chemistry and was defined as the science of wine tasting by universities and the

Ministry of Education. The development of oenology as a new academic discipline gave a legitimacy to wine tasting as an objective and scientific activity.

Yet this development was not confined to chemists and intellectuals, and writers also contributed substantially to the establishment of wine drinking culture. In 1947, the gastronome Maurice Edmund Sailland Curnonsky, who wanted to explain the reasons for his likes and dislikes began editing a new culinary journal *Cuisine de France*, which later became *Cuisine et Vins de France*, with an impressive editorial committee featuring the novelist Colette, the publisher Charles Flammarion, the president of the national Assembly, Édouard Herriot, and the writer Jules Romains of the Académie Française.[65] The period following the Second World War was characterized by the prosperity of the bourgeois model of cuisine in which wine occupied a central position. This model was now becoming the norm for all sections of French society, and gastronomy and wine became the two key ingredients in the construction of a sociable and festive gathering. Food consumption and its attendant drinking culture were marked by a sharp division of gender roles. The bottle and the cellar were both seen as the prerogatives of the male in the domestic sphere, and this could still be said to be the case. All the rituals surrounding wine consumption were mastered by the host, while the housewife was in charge of the cooking. In 1954, for example, Raymond Oliver (owner of the legendary Parisian restaurant, the Grand Véfour), assisted by Catherine Langeais, presented his recipes for the first time on television. Wines were discussed by a wine waiter, and most of the programme focused on the chef, while his partner Catherine Langeais was confined to the role of helper dealing with the management of the kitchen. Television and celebrity culture boosted the adoption of this model with grand chef transformed into an icon of this period of economic expansion and leisure. After years of food shortages, eating and drinking became the signs of a new prosperity, encouraged greatly by the development of tourism in France.

However, the period was also influenced by the revival of temperance preoccupations, as demonstrated by the creation in 1954 of the Haut Comité d'Etude et d'Information sur l'Alcoolisme. Among its major objectives were attempts to measure the attitude of French public opinion towards alcohol consumption and to promote the virtues of moderation.[66] As a response to governmental pressures and to the changing nature of the market, growers and merchants emphasized quality, advertising to attract educated and discriminating readers and using all the latest marketing techniques. The concern with moderate drinking was, of course, somewhat at odds with the fiscal interests of a state long enriched by taxes on alcohol. Successive governments were also conscious of the political pressure that could be exerted by the wine lobby, and they had periodically sponsored campaigns encouraging wine consumption. As a compromise between government pressures and the economic interests of the wine growers, they all aimed at favouring a reasonable consumption of good wine while emphasizing that 'reasonable' meant moderation in the use of alcohol. It reflected conflicting opinions, with the Ministries of Agriculture and of Finance supporting consumption, while the Ministry of Public Health stressed the need for sobriety and the benefits of mineral water.[67] The debate is still intense between these ministries, as the wine profession and wine lovers seek to dissociate wine from other types of alcoholic products, while sections of the medical profession refuse to classify wine separately from other alcohols.

The publication in English of *Drinking in French Culture* in 1965 by the Rutgers Center of Alcohol Studies reflected the ambiguous position of alcohol in French society and the growing debate on alcoholism.[68] Until recently, the study of alcohol and wine consumption in France was never regarded as a serious topic of investigation and its status was always ambivalent. Most of the French studies used as the basis of the Rutgers Center's synthesis have therefore not been widely diffused. They provide us, nevertheless, with an interesting picture of wine and alcohol consumption in France during the period 1950–60.

According to Sadoun, Lolli and Silverman, the authors of *Drinking in French Culture*, wine and alcohol consumption had already been affected by a number of changes in attitudes and representations. Long seen as a healthy, nutritious and masculine beverage, the alleged benefits of wine were by 1960 being treated with growing scepticism. The French were progressively changing their attitudes to excessive drinking, even if wine drinking remained, for a great majority, a way to affirm their personality, and it was still common to praise a man 'who can hold his drink'. The aim of the study was to ascertain the precise place of wine drinking in French society. The results of the survey, conducted on a larger scale than any other before on wine drinking, emphasized the importance of social, regional and gender differences. By taking a snapshot of wine consumption in a twenty-four-hour period, they discovered that 70 per cent of the adults, 82 per cent of men and 60 per cent of women consumed wine. On average, men drank three times as much wine as women. The highest percentage of wine consumers was found amongst those from the more affluent and educated groups.

The largest per capita alcohol consumption, especially amongst men, was reported by those with the least education, while college-educated men drank the smallest quantities. When they examined drinkers from a regional perspective, it became clear that wine consumption was approximately the same throughout most of southern and central France, while in the north-east – in Artois, Picardy, Alsace and Moselle – it was replaced to a larger extent by beer and in the north-west, in Normandy and Brittany, by cider. If wine was usually consumed at home, drinking between meals accounted for a substantial portion of French alcohol intake, especially for farmers and manual workers. The authors concluded that wine remained the alcohol of choice for the poor, with farmers and manual workers consuming more than managers and white-collar workers. But this division, as their study points out, was already in transition, with several signs indicating that social fragmentation was beginning to appear.

The bourgeois model of wine drinking as moderate, ritualized and status-orientated consumption started to impose itself to the detriment of the popular and working-class model of drinking. This shift was confirmed by the work of Pierre Bourdieu, the French sociologist, in his book *La Distinction*, published in 1979. In his study of everyday life in France, Bourdieu took into account the multitude of social factors that played a part in the choice of clothing, furniture, leisure activities, dinner menus for guests and many other matters of taste. Focusing on the bourgeoisie, he argued that the social world functions simultaneously as a system of power relations and as a symbolic system in which minute distinctions of taste become the basis for social judgement. Yet Bourdieu remained largely silent about wine, presumably because it was not at the time an object of social 'distinction' for the bourgeoisie.[69] The 1970s would transform the status of wine from an alimentary product to an object of cultural and aesthetic meanings. Wine, because of its symbolic and culturally emblematic status, became, like gastronomy, a new field for identity marked by social differentiation, fragmentation and the quest for new forms of power and social relations.

4. Food, wine and a new era

The socio-cultural upheaval of 1968 and the subsequent economic shock of the 1973 oil crisis together marked the beginning of the end of a society which seemed to be based on traditionally fixed class distinctions. For some French commentators, such as Pascal Ory, the postmodern era was seen primarily as a demolition of old ideologies and hierarchies, both social and aesthetic. The 1968 crisis crystallized the contradictory values of traditional and modern French society, as age and class became strong cultural markers of the period. The socio-economic and demographic changes which took place in the previous decade gave birth to contradictory trends characterized by a growing heterogeneity and by the emergence of marked group identities with specific lifestyles.[70] The rise of individualism in French society accompanied this process of social transformation, in parallel with the shift from work time to free time,[71] a process which continued to develop more recently with the introduction of the thirty-five-hour week. In cultural terms, new values like ecology and consumerism started to emerge, headed by the 1968 generation as a reaction and denunciation of the old order embodied in the Gaullist regime. It gave way later to a new pessimism which was obsessed with individualism and sexual liberation, as illustrated by Marco Ferreri in his 1973 film *La Grande Bouffe*, a cruel fable of the corruption of the old world where food and wine are represented as icons of this decadent consumption.

Ferreri's film in many ways caricatured a world already in rapid decline, and the 1970s witnessed a reaction against the dominant style of gastronomy typified by Escoffier, restaurateur and culinary writer, codifier of the French *haute cuisine* with its traditional menus and gargantuan dishes.[72] In its place emerged a movement inspired by alternative cultural models, notably the Japanese, and the work of pioneering chefs such as Christian Millau and Paul Bocuse. Nouvelle cuisine,[73] described as 'a vast movement of culinary freedom',[74] was a term first applied in the 1960s by Henri and Christian Millau to the new style of cookery they found in the work of chefs such as Bocuse, Jean and Pierre Troigros, Michel Guérard,

Roger Vergé and Raymond Oliver.[75] No necessary complications, reduced cooking time, *cuisine du marché* (fresh food from the market), shorter menus, fresh game, elimination of excessive and rich sauces, an emphasis on regional cuisine, ultra-modern equipment and inventiveness were the ingredients of this new culinary genre which was aimed principally at urban groups with higher incomes. The publication of *La Grande Cuisine minceur* in 1976 by Michel Guérard illustrates this movement. What these chefs also had in common was the fact that they owned their restaurants, which gave them the freedom to experiment.

Wine, on the other hand, took longer to respond to the changes affecting gastronomy. Progress in winemaking and wine knowledge had already been made and more producers were trying to adapt their production to current patterns and trends of consumption. The fragmentation of taste and production methods facilitated a greater stability. With the emergence of nouvelle cuisine, better-quality wines did not enjoy the same status as before. Consumed in smaller quantities and facing increasing competition from other types of beverages, wine had to adapt to changes happening in the culinary scene. As Pascal Ory has argued, in parallel with nouvelle cuisine and the new status of the chef owning his restaurant, the same movement of owner-occupation occurred in French vineyards, and this represented for the first time in both worlds a fusion of competence and capital.[76]

As the chef became a star in his restaurant and increasingly a presence in the dining room, the function of maître d'hôtel declined, to be taken over by the professional function of *sommelier*, a powerful symbol of the new independent status enjoyed by wine. This profession, which has developed significantly since the 1970s, has transformed the place of wine in the public space of the restaurant. This important change had major implications for wine drinking culture, which became a separate social activity mediated by the presence of an expert, creating in turn a competitive field. The wine list was transformed into an exercise of knowledge and individual taste. Next to the chef, the *sommelier* had to ensure that wines complemented the food on offer and the profession of *sommelier* has over the last twenty-five years won full recognition, with the titles of *Meilleur Sommelier de France* or *Meilleur Sommelier du Monde* guaranteeing fame and fortune for those such as Philippe Faure-Brac who have become the stars of the profession.

Oenology was another profess[ion in the] formation of wine and wine cultur[e as an] object of consumption. First estab[lished in the 19th] century, it was revived and populariz[ed when universities] started teaching it to wine producers i[n the 1950s. Émile Peynaud] published his best-selling book on win[e tasting with titles] such as *Le Goût du vin* (The Taste of Win[e) in 1980.] Peynaud, following in the footsteps of [Ulysse] Gayon, imposed the oenologist as the onl[y expert in wine] tasting. In writing *Le Goût du vin*, Peynaud [gave access to] wine. Peynaud's career did not take off imm[ediately. F]rom 1949, the Station Oenologique (Oenological Office) of Bordeaux organized a course in wine tasting, and it was at the time unique in its study of gustatory sensations and olfaction. It became successful later in the 1970s, and generations of Bordelais were trained to taste wines, most of them becoming professionals. The same development occurred in Burgundy, where Max Léglise was the initiator of a similar revolution, which was initially confined to circles of professionals and wine lovers. Today oenology is the scientific branch of the profession, and generations of wine growers and wine makers have been formed in Bordeaux, Dijon and elsewhere. It has also become one of the major cultural activities by which consumers and wine lovers learn about the art of wine tasting. The impact has been incontestable at national and international level, with television programmes such as *Apostrophes* run by Bernard Pivot, himself a wine lover who owns a vineyard in the Beaujolais, and a proliferation of references in the other media devoted to wines. This democratization of wine has led to the phenomenon of celebrities such as Gérard Depardieu or Carole Bouquet buying vineyards, thus combining their passion with a lucrative investment. Yet it is worth noting that for Émile Peynaud, wine tasting and wine drinking were not synonymous, and that he did not personally like wine very much.[77]

Another major element in the changes affecting food and wine consumption in the 1980s was the burgeoning interest in the concept of *terroir* and the emphasis on nature and quality food in response to the alleged 'McDonaldization' of French society. In everyday life, the diet of French people was becoming more urbanized and industrialized, and this was especially true for younger generations, for whom fast and frozen pre-cooked ready-made food

...ce. This contributed to a greater division between ...ublic space, leading the restaurant to become a festive ...tional space, as opposed to the domestic and daily ...mption of the private home. In reaction, the media celebrity ...an-Pierre Coffe began his campaign in favour of local food and regional markets, while Maité and Micheline, the 'two fat ladies' of the Gers butchered a beef carcass on television. This renewal of interest in regional cuisines formed part of a wider trend affecting consumption, which privileged natural, authentic and rural products. The 1990s crystallized most of these changes with the emergence of new ecological issues, the BSE crisis and the general concern with quality for reasons of health and diet. Food and wine consumption were greatly affected by these changes, which continue to resonate today. However, in all of these changes, the position of wine still remains distinctive and unique.

As part of the wider developments of tourism and of cultural heritage and regionalization, a new form of wine tourism has emerged progressively since the 1970s. This wine tourism placed a special emphasis on the importance of direct contact with the producer and the geographic discovery of the wine regions and their gastronomic heritage. It has taken place against the background of a post-industrial society which has seen growing demand for ecologically orientated forms of leisure. The proliferation of wine routes offers a good example of these developments, as they provide a signposted itinerary through a well-defined area, be it the region, the province or the denomination area, offering a new way to discover France, its products, the producers and the activities associated with wine production, such as festivals and museums. This form of eco-tourism has greatly expanded in response to the crisis in the post-war model of agricultural regulation and the need to fight rural depopulation and unemployment. It was also part of a response to social transformations affecting French society with new forms of individualism and hedonism. New forms of divergence and convergence have emerged as the mass media and the domestic leisure industries have created both a degree of homogenization and different forms of stratification which have more to do with age than class.[78]

The French path towards modernization has a strong cultural content, and mass consumption, individualism and urbanization are combined with seemingly conflicting values such as differentiation, traditionalism and ruralism. This forms the background against which wine consumption has evolved. According to the historian Jean-Pierre Rioux, contemporary France is associated with a new form of ruralism, which is dominated by the influence of the urban population.[79] The issue of *ruralité* has recently emerged as a new object of intense contestation, owing partly to its evolving nature and to the changing relationship between 'countryside' and 'town'.[80] The boundaries between these two worlds have blurred, and consequently 'agricultural' is no longer synonymous with 'rural', and wider issues are at stake. Long-distance commuting, widespread retirement to the countryside, the proliferation of *résidences secondaires* (holiday houses) and the growing popularity of rural tourism are amongst the cherished commodities increasingly consumed by urban dwellers. This new context has helped to reposition wine as a cultural object of consumption, supported by the wave of *ruralisme* that has been a feature of French life for at least the last twenty years.

This brief historical account of the major changes affecting French wine culture and consumption since 1945 has highlighted some of the issues affecting French wine culture and consumption today. Some of these changes refer to the increasingly fragmented and dualistic consumption – that is to say mass consumption with an individualistic component and an ideological content. Others are related to enduring values which are reinvented, transformed and adapted to fit the new social configuration, the growing *face à face* between rural and urban worlds. Amongst other values, the past, with its associated tradition, the authenticity with the producer and the product, the true and real social experience with friendship and sharing are at the core of this new wine culture and consumption.

Notes

1 L.-A. Loubère, *The Wine Revolution in France: The Twentieth Century* (Princeton: Princeton University Press, 1990), p. 165.
2 Mary Douglas, *Constructive Drinking: Perspectives on Drink from Anthropology* (Cambridge: Cambridge University Press, 1987).
3 Sarah Blowen, Marion Demossier and Jeanine Picard, *Recollections of France: Memories, Identities and Heritage in Contemporary France* (Oxford and New York: Berghahn, 2000).
4 Loubère, *The Wine Revolution in France*.
5 After the Second World War, there was a desire for some kind of identity in the South, and in December 1944 it led to the creation of

the VDQS, formely a badge of high degree of nobility. AOC wines were replaced by *vins de pays* (country or regional wine) and VDQS (*vins délimités de qualité supérieure*).

6   Most of the classifications were, in part, inspired by earlier works of ranking conducted in the nineteenth century following the Universal Exhibition of 1855 and were based on the commercial value of the products.

7   Kolleen M. Guy. *When Champagne Became French: Wine and the Making of a National Identity* (Johns Hopkins University Studies in Historical and Political Science 121st Series Baltimore: Johns Hopkins University Press, 2003), pp. 128, 185.

8   Loubère, *The Wine Revolution in France*, p. 261.

9   Both Claude Lévi-Strauss and Roland Barthes reacted against the quantitative and material approach to food studies developed by generations of French food historians, who sought methods of examining food as an economic matter.

10 *Esprit*, founded in 1932, is an intellectual journal supported by a militant internal network. Its history can be consulted online, while *France Observateur* (1954) is the ancestor of *Le Nouvel Observateur*. Barthes wrote fifty-four studies between 1952 and 1956, which formed the basis of his *Mythologies* and the related discipline, semiology.

11 In 1954, Pierre Mendès-France, the prime minister, created the High Committee for the Study and Information on Alcoholism. For more details, see J.-C. Sournia, *Histoire de l'alcoolisme* (Paris: Flammarion, 1986), p. 257.

12 For examples of the wide range of literary supports, see the excellent book by Gilbert Garrier, *Histoire sociale et culturelle du vin* (Paris: Bordas Cultures, 1995; 1998).

13 Parallels could be drawn between literature on wine and gastronomic literature. For an excellent analysis of the gastronomic literature, see Pascal Ory, *Le Discours gastronomique français des origines à nos jours* (Paris: Gallimard/Juillard, 1998).

14 Georges Durand, 'La vigne et le vin', in Nora, *Les Lieux de mémoire*, vol. 2: *Les Traditions*, p. 803 : 'Vigne et Vin impriment à notre culture la marque constante d'une référence à la fois familière et solennelle'. (The translation in the text is mine.)

15 Jacqueline Lalouette, 'La consommation de vin et d'alcool au cours du dix-neuvième et au début du vingtième siècle', *Ethnologie Française*, 10, 3 (1980), 288.

16 See the survey conducted by the historian Jean-Pierre Rioux in *l'Histoire*, 100 (May, 1987).

17 Stephen Mennell, *All Manners of Food* (Oxford: Blackwell Science, 1985).

18 Robert C. Ulin, *Vintages and Traditions: An Ethnohistory of Southwest French Wine Cooperatives* (Washington: Smithsonian Institution Press, 1996), p. 524.

19 See for example the work of archaeologists in 'Archéologie de la

vigne et du vin', *Actes du Colloque 28–29 Mai 1988, Université de Tours* (Paris: Boccard, 1990).
20 Kolleen M. Guy. *When Champagne Became French*, pp. 136–7.
21 Didier Nourrisson, *Le Buveur du dix-neuvième siècle* (Paris: Albin Michel, 1990).
22 Ibid., p. 140.
23 Sarah Howard, 'Selling wine to the French: official attempts to increase wine consumption, 1931–1936', *Food and Foodways*, 12, 4 (2004), 205.
24 Thierry Fillaut, Véronique Nahoum-Grappe and Myriam Tsikounas, *Histoire et alcool*, Collection Logiques sociales (Paris: L'Harmattan, 1999), p. 115.
25 M. Demossier (1996), 'Une anthropologie de l'ébriété et de la fête en Bourgogne: "Séparer le bon vin de l'ivresse"', *Actes du Colloque "Les Vignerons du Moyen Âge au phylloxéra", tenu à Lyon les 18 et 19 octobre 1996*, École des Hautes Études en Sciences Sociales de Paris (EHESS), Centre Interuniversitaire d'Histoire et d'Archéologie Médiévale de Lyon (CIHAM), Centre Pierre Léon d'Histoire Économique et Sociale.
26 Gilles Laferté, *La Bourgogne et ses vins. Image d'origine contrôlée* (Paris: Belin, 2006).
27 For a detailed discussion of the concept of artisans in French viticulture, see R. C. Ulin, 'Work as cultural production: labor and self-identity among southwest French wine growers', *Journal of the Royal Anthropological Institute*, 8, 4 (2001), 691–712.
28 Ulin, *Vintages and Traditions*, p. 699.
29 See for example in Burgundy where a collective action has seen the light for the establishment of AOC despite a rigid social structure dividing the *vignerons*, the *propriétaires* (landowners) and the *négociants*. See the useful contribution of Olivier Jacquet, 'Les AOC à l'épreuve des fraudes en Bourgogne. Le négoce dans la tourmente', *Cahiers de l'Institut d'Histoire Contemporaine*, 6 (Dijon: EUD, 2001), 25–39 and more recently Olivier Jacquet, *Un Siècle de construction du vignoble bourguignon. Les organisations vitivinicoles de 1884 aux AOC* (Dijon: EUD, 2009).
30 Susan Terrio, *Crafting the Culture and History of French Chocolate* (Berkeley: University of California Press, 2000).
31 Ibid., p. 151.
32 Alessandro Stanziani, *La Qualité des produits en France, XVIIIe–XXe siècle* (Paris: Belin, 2003).
33 Garrier, *Histoire sociale et culturelle du vin*.
34 For more details, see Marcel Lachiver, *Vins, vignes et vignerons. Histoire du vignoble français* (Paris: Fayard, 1988), pp. 461–506.
35 Guy, *When Champagne Became French*, p. 188.
36 E. M. Moentmann, 'The search for French identity in the regions: national versus local visions of France in the 1930s', *French History*, 17, 3 (2003), 307–27.
37 Herman Lebovics, *True France: The Wars over Cultural Identity, 1900–1945* (Ithaca: Cornell University Press, 1992), p. 140.

38 Jacquet, *Un Siècle de construction du vignoble* and Laferté, *La Bourgogne et ses vins*.
39 Laferté, *La Bourgogne et ses vins*, pp. 435–42.
40 What is missing from his analysis is the crucial relationship between various classes of owners, especially the forgotten rising class of new landowners with cultural capital who had benefited from the phylloxera crisis. Laferté also ignores the contribution of wine growers to the process of *folklorization* (festivals, museums, publications of folklorist societies) during the 1930s, which are left silent in his analysis. Even if it is undeniable that the exchange was conducted on a non reciprocal basis, they were part of the world of wine and ought to be discussed.
41 Guy, *When Champagne Became French*, p. 181.
42 In 1945, French people consumed as much as 170 litres of wine per inhabitant per year.
43 Don Kladstrup and Petie Kladstrup, *Wine and War: The French, the Nazis, and the Battle for France's Greatest Treasure* (London: Hodder & Stoughton, 2002), p. 10.
44 Dominique Veillon, *Vivre et survivre en France, 1939–1947* (Paris: Histoire Payot, 1995), p. 31.
45 See for instance the testimony of Émile Peynaud published by Michel Guillard (1995). At the beginning of the war, soldiers were sent utensils and recipes for making hot wine at the front (Kladstrup and Kladstrup, *Wine and War*, p. 10).
46 Garrier, *Histoire sociale et culturelle du vin*, p. 272.
47 Kladstrup and Kladstrup, *Wine and War*, p. 10.
48 The Vichy regime strictly controlled the production and circulation of alcoholic drinks and practically prohibited any forms of publicity in favour of alcohol. See for example Garrier, *Histoire sociale et culturelle du vin*, the decrees of July 1939, March 1940, July 1940, August 1940 and the Code of Drinks.
49 Loubère, *The Wine Revolution in France*, p. 32.
50 Also called *Statut du vin*. A series of laws were promulgated between 1931 and 1939 and were modified by decree later. They deal only with table wines and not AOC wines.
51 Kladstrup and Kladstrup, *Wine and War*, p. 45.
52 H. Drouot, *Notes d'un Dijonnais pendant l'occupation, 1940–1944* (Dijon: EUD, 1998).
53 Kladstrup and Kladstrup, *Wine and War*, p. 76.
54 Olivier Assouly, *Les Nourritures nostalgiques. Essai sur le mythe du terroir* (n.p.: Actes Sud, 2004).
55 Jean Vigreux, *La Vigne du maréchal Pétain ou un faire-valoir bourguignon de la Révolution Nationale* (Dijon: EUD, 2005).
56 A fine example of the representation of the *vigneron* in the national museography is the Museum of Wine in Beaune.
57 See the excellent work of Christian Faure, *Le Projet culturel de Vichy. Folklore et Révolution Nationale* (Lyon: Presses Universitaires de Lyon, Éditions du CNRS, 1989).

58 Julian Jackson, *France: The Dark Years, 1940–44* (Oxford: Oxford University Press, 2001).
59 Philip Dine, 'Leisure and consumption', in Malcolm Cook and Grace Davies, *Modern France: Society in Transition* (London: Routledge, 1998), p. 236.
60 Kristin Ross, *Fast Cars, Clean Bodies: Decolonization and the Reordering of French Culture* (Cambridge, MA: MIT Press, 1995), p. 4.
61 Jean-Robert Pitte, 'La table', in J.-P. Rioux and J.-F. Sirinelli, *La France d'un siècle à l'autre: 1914–2000. Dictionnaire critique* (Paris: Hachette Littératures, 1999), p. 330.
62 Dine, 'Leisure and consumption', p. 237.
63 Rioux and Sirinelli, *La France d'un siècle à l'autre*, pp. 346–59.
64 Pitte, 'La table', p. 234.
65 For an introduction to Curnonsky, see the publications of Pascal Ory.
66 Roland Sadoun, Giorgio Lolli and Milton Silverman, *Drinking in French Culture* (New Brunswick, NJ: Publications Division, Rutgers Center of Alcohol Studies, 1965).
67 Loubère, *The Wine Revolution in France*, p. 187.
68 Sadoun, Lolli and Silverman, *Drinking in French Culture*.
69 Jean-Pierre Albert, 'La nouvelle culture du vin', *Terrain*, 13 (1989), 117–24.
70 Dine, 'Leisure and consumption', p. 237.
71 According to Dine ('Leisure and consumption, p. 242), this was a progressive shift which could be initially defined in 1975 when free time rose from 24 hours 16 minutes in a week to 28 hours 28 minutes in 1985. It was followed in 1981 by the Socialists' extension of paid holidays (*congés payés*, obtained under the Popular Front) to five weeks per year and the reduction of the working week to thirty-nine hours.
72 For a biography of Escoffier (1847–1935), see Pascal Ory, *Le Discours gastronomique français*.
73 Nouvelle cuisine is a contemporary school of French cooking that seeks to bring out the natural flavours of foods and substitutes light, low-calorie sauces and stocks for the traditional heavy butter- and cream-based preparations.
74 Jean Neirinck and Jean-Pierre Poulain, *Histoire de la cuisine et des cuisiniers* (Cachan: Éditions Jacques Lanore, 2000), p. 116.
75 Jean-Robert Pitte, *Gastronomie française* (Paris: Fayard, 1991), pp. 154–7.
76 Ory, *Le Discours gastronomique français*, p. 153.
77 Émile Peynaud, *Oenologue dans le siècle* (Paris: La Table Ronde, 1995), p. 16.
78 Jill Forbes and Nick Hewlett, *Contemporary France: Essays and Texts on Politics, Economics and Society* (London: Longman, 1994).
79 Rioux and Sirinelli, *La France d'un siècle à l'autre*, p. 931.
80 Hugh Clout and Marion Demossier (eds), *Politics, tradition and modernity in rural France*, special issue of *Modern & Contemporary France*, 11, 3 (August 2003).

Chapter Three
A New Wine Drinking Culture?

The development of a new wine drinking culture in France since the 1970s is one of the most striking features of the changes affecting wine consumption.[1] The decline in per capita rates of alcohol and wine consumption in Mediterranean countries over the last thirty years is rarely discussed in relation to the rise of wine culture as a new global cultural object. This phenomenon has spread rapidly and has taken different forms, from schools of wines in Bordeaux, Paris, Tokyo and New York to the commercialization of games such as Trivial Pursuit for wine lovers or the proliferation of wine tours. Each wine-growing region has its own range of activities, places to visit and cultural events, while non-wine producing regions boast wine clubs, wine shops and festivities organized to promote wines. Media interest has grown dramatically, and almost every French magazine now has a special section devoted to wines. A new wine drinker, whom I have defined as the 'wandering drinker', has emerged in France and elsewhere and it seems that moderate consumption and a quest for variety are what defines him or her. The concept of 'wandering drinker' describes those men and women who consume wine occasionally, especially in specific festive contexts, and who have a limited knowledge of wine. Their consumption is fragmented and largely contextualized, and it can be explained by a combination of factors including age, social, professional and economic status. Wine culture is perceived by the 'wandering drinker' as a complex world with a great diversity of rules, and he or she does not usually have the knowledge or the confidence to engage with it in any depth. The transformation of drinking culture and the presence of the 'wandering drinker' is a broad international phenomenon, but it has certain distinct features in each individual country.

In France, the rise of this new wine culture is characterized by fragmentation and democratization, and there are almost as many discourses and images around wine as there are bottles. In this context, wine gurus, experts and journalists such as Robert Parker or Michel Bettane have each sought to impose their own views and rules in this fragmented and highly complex world. One of the most distinctive features of the French situation is the absence of a codified and normalized drinking culture. Wine discourses have been legitimized as much for their literary style, as for their scientific content, and oenologists as well as *sommeliers* have become icons for connoisseurs and wine lovers as well as consumers. Books such as *La Dégustation* (Wine Tasting) sit on the shelves besides tomes such as *Le Vin dans l'art* (Wine in Art) or *Le Vin pour les nuls* (An Idiot's Guide to Wine), illustrating the importance of wine in contemporary culture and discourse. The field of wine culture is still dominated by men, but wine and its production have become a ubiquitous feature of modern gastronomy, tourism and photography, and have even penetrated the cultural fields of cinema, television, museums and radio as well as gastronomic festivals.

As part of this process, a wide range of discourses surrounding the product have emerged. Wine growers, wine merchants, wine lovers, oenologists and *sommeliers* all have their distinctive way of describing the product. This rich and heterogeneous culture has transformed the traditional relationship that French people enjoyed with wine, that is to say the simple daily consumption of a product. Today wine has become an *objet d'art* for the middle class, a means of differentiation, a place for social judgement, a medium for the expression of new social identities and ties, the arena of new discourses and the place for contrasting identities.[2]

When analysing wine culture, it is first necessary to have a broader picture of the actors involved at every stage of the journey from production to consumption. It is also important to consider the many spatial and social contexts in which these actors meet and discourses about wine are produced. Figure 3.1 identifies the main actors involved in the chain of production – such as wine growers, *négociants* and co-operatives, the places associated with wine culture and consumption – including wine cellars, bars, restaurants and supermarkets, and also the broader category of consumers, from ordinary wine consumers to wine lovers, all of them having different relationships with the product.[3] Wine lovers, who are in the great majority men, could be described as individuals who have established a close contact with the product by devoting a great deal of

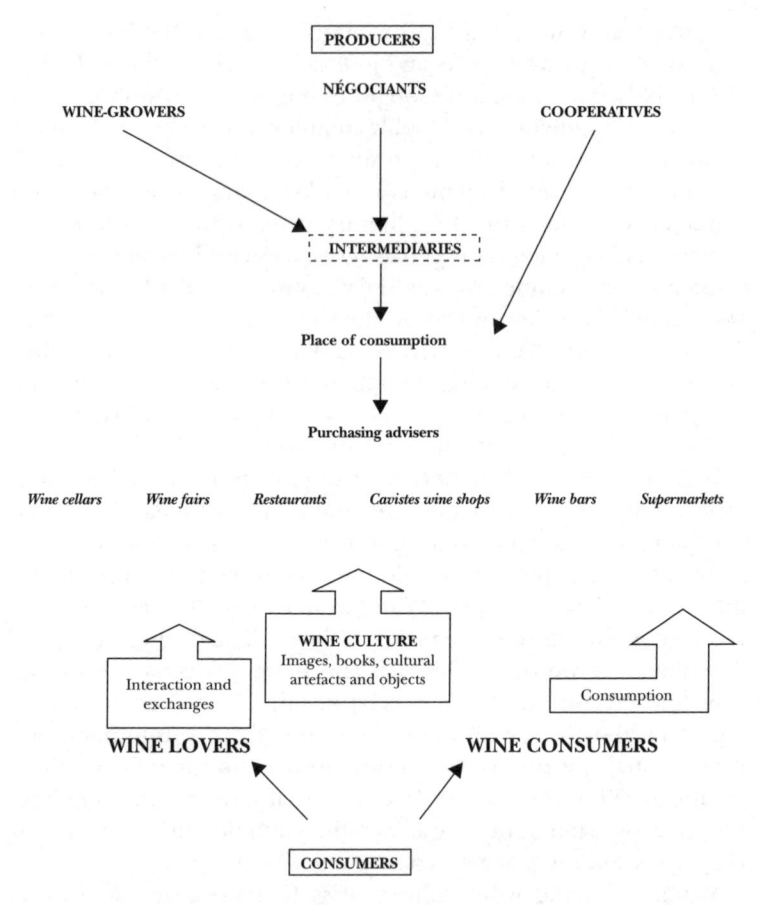

```
                        ┌─────────────┐
                        │  PRODUCERS  │
                        └─────────────┘
                           NÉGOCIANTS
   WINE-GROWERS                                    COOPERATIVES
             ╲              │                      ╱
              ╲             ▼                     ╱
               ▶  ┌ ─ ─ ─ ─ ─ ─ ─ ─ ─ ┐  ◀
                  │  INTERMEDIARIES   │
                  └ ─ ─ ─ ─ ─ ─ ─ ─ ─ ┘
                           │
                           ▼
                   Place of consumption
                           │
                           ▼
                   Purchasing advisers

  Wine cellars  Wine fairs  Restaurants  Cavistes wine shops  Wine bars  Supermarkets
```

Figure layout: WINE LOVERS ← Interaction and exchanges / WINE CULTURE (Images, books, cultural artefacts and objects) / Consumption → WINE CONSUMERS, both stemming from CONSUMERS.

Figure 3.1 Wine consumption and culture in France.

their time to the quest for wines under different guises, while the 'wandering drinker' in many ways represents the typical modern wine consumer. In order to explore the changes affecting wine consumption and wine culture and their relationship to expressions of national, regional and local identities, it is important to recall that wine drinking has become increasingly detached from the act of eating and has come to represent a distinct act of consumption in its own right. By shifting from an integrated element of the daily diet into an intrinsically hedonistic food, it has gained a highly complex set of meanings.

Attached to these new representations, wine tasting has also become an *affaire de goûts*, or a place of social discernment, hierarchy and power. Wine drinking has become drinking wines. Bourdieu famously argued that taste is socially constructed, and that traditionally the hierarchy of wines became identified with the social hierarchy.[4] The consumption of quality wine was a preserve of the bourgeoisie and was also historically associated with the emergence of the bourgeoisie and of restaurants in the course of the nineteenth century. Since the 1950s growing affluence has led to the democratization of eating out. New strategies were needed to differentiate groups of individuals from each other, and wine has offered one way of expressing this differentiation. When individuals make a statement such as 'I love Bordeaux', 'I do not like Burgundy', 'I prefer *vins de pays*', they are stating a claim to both economic and cultural distinction. This could be interpreted as mere snobbery, but in fact it refers also to a knowledge that reveals more about individual identity and preferences for a type of lifestyle.

The varied patterns of consumption are illustrated by the many discourses embedded in the cultural object of wine, and very often those who possess an understanding of wine are able to position themselves in relation to knowledge, distinction, empowerment and social domination.[5] Consequently there are various tensions between different types of consumers who are increasingly defining their identities through drinking wine or not, and through a complex set of consumption and cultural patterns. The connoisseur is defined by producers as the classic example of the educated male drinker for whom wine culture is about much more than drinking wine. One of his chief characteristics is his desire to empower himself and gain access to a better positioning in social terms through the social visibility of his consumption. He is very often described by other consumers and professionals as 'an arrogant drinker who knows everything'. At the other extreme, the 'wandering drinkers', a group that includes most male and female wine consumers, are experiencing a *vin-anomie*, that is to say that they are confronting so many rules that they are left with the anxiety of choosing the correct wine according to the imaginary pressure of society.

This research suggests that greater differentiation in social and economic terms means that individuals have acquired more freedom in their choices in the context of a greater diversity of products, occasions and meanings associated with wine drinking. Exploring different social situations in which wine drinking occurs enables us to understand the basis of the relationship between wine consumption and wine culture. Drinking is after all a social activity which involves a complex configuration of elements, representations and values.

Moreover, if wine drinking culture has grown in importance, it is also because wine consumption has declined. According to Sulkunen, the historical decline of wine and alcohol consumption cannot be explained by the fact that France had reached such a high consumption that the only way it could go was down.[6] For Sulkunen, as for other French commentators, the change was led by the growing middle classes, who were already drinking less than others. A modernization process explained this change, with differences between social classes acting as the motor of change. It is undeniable that wine has become one of the cherished objects of the new middle classes, enabling them to differentiate themselves from other social groups by adopting the ways of drinking that were once the preserve of the *haute bourgeoisie*. If social changes have played a major role, they cannot, however, fully explain the nature of the changes observed. Generational, regional and gender factors have also to be borne in mind. Other elements have contributed independently, but have been the result of complicated interplay between various social factors.

Five principal mechanisms have been advanced to explain the decline in European alcohol consumption: increasing advertising of beer and spirits, the entrance of new, mostly non-alcoholic beverages (called NAB), the rise of public health policies, economic factors such as high unemployment and EU policies that reduce production, and, finally, a change in public opinion that increasingly finds wine and spirits, but not beer, a health risk.[7] The French context combines some of these elements, but it has its own peculiarities as there has been a strong reaction from the wine industry through its powerful advertising campaigns. The so-called 'French paradox' which is based on the observation that the French suffer a relatively low incidence of coronary heart disease despite having a diet relatively rich in saturated fats, has also had a considerable impact, consolidating the image of wine as a healthy drink. In 1991, the French Dr Serge Renaud promoted the French paradox on an American television programme, *Sixty Minutes*.

The rise of the new wine culture needs therefore to be set against a complex and sometimes contradictory background of concerns about whether wine consumption is a positive or negative factor for public health. It could also be argued that the rise and development of this new wine culture shapes consumption in diverse ways as contradictory ideas still divide consumers around specific issues such as safe levels of alcohol consumption or the status of wine as an alcoholic product. As wine has been transformed into a complex cultural object surrounded by contrasting rituals and discourses, consumers confronted by a bewilderingly complex choice of wines tend increasingly to use wine consumption as a vehicle for conferring individual identity. Yet with the field of knowledge being so heterogeneous, most French consumers have difficulty in choosing from the range of wines on offer. This greater differentiation was only made possible because French wine production was also adapting to economic liberalization. Yet even today most French supermarkets have a small section devoted to wines from abroad and large expanses of advertising and floor space devoted to the sale of local products.

1. The crisis of French wine production

The agricultural and financial year 2003–4 was particularly difficult for French viticulture, which, under the pressure of growing international competition, saw a 9 per cent fall in the value of exports and a further decline in domestic consumption. Even the prestigious and usually wealthy Burgundian wine growers joined the demonstrations in March 2004 as an increasing number of producers and wine merchants were threatened with bankruptcy. The crisis was more than just a passing malaise, and one angry protester spoke for many when he declared:

> We are fed up. Wine is a cultural product. We have today to choose between a society based on the American model with junk food and Coca Cola, and our roots which have made France the land of gastronomy. Today wine is treated like a drug![8]

The French model of viticulture continues to exhibit distinctive and unique features, as it combines a very traditional outlook with an extreme diversity of products and producers, associated with a model of artisanship. Diversity, authenticity, history and 'quality' are amongst the values deliberately emphasized, constructed, marketed and promoted.[9] Yet it is impossible to deny the growing influence of the forces of modernization and standardization in all but the most privileged sectors of French viticulture.

The pressures of an increasingly international market are driving these changes, and as a result even the sacred model of the AOC, with its 450 appellations,[10] is under threat, with real conflict between the USA and the EU over the question of labelling. Protected and enjoying a practically free market since their creation, AOC wines have until recently been the principal beneficiaries of the revolution in wine consumption.[11] The concept of *terroir* has been fundamental to their definition and as Elizabeth Barham has argued: 'The historical concept of *terroir* viewed wine production as a complex dance with nature with the goal of interpreting or translating the local ecology, displaying its qualities to best advantage.'[12] These wines were defined as having been made from specified grapes cultivated in a given geographic space in accord with time-honoured methods. AOC wines were above all a collective property requiring constant discipline amongst growers in order to maintain standards. The *appellation* enabled wines that were once of low status to acquire a new standing and the economic and social advantages that accompanies it. Since the 1950s, however, an increasing number of wine growers have tried to obtain an AOC hoping to create more marketable products and to benefit from the advantages of a newly recognized area of production.[13] According to Loubère, the connection between geography and quality has become widely accepted and it is still the gospel of oenophiles.[14] Relying on geography and on geology, producers played the card of micro-diversity within the framework of the AOC system, expressing their individuality within a state-directed and controlled framework. This trend has also been observed in the case of co-operatives.[15] As Barham notes, 'Winemakers are striving to produce a wine that is special in the sense that it bears the "signature" of their style of *vinification* while not interfering with the "natural" taste that wines produced from that terrain should display.'[16]

This phenomenon has expanded, and there is no shortage of examples to demonstrate the growing expression of individuality amongst wine producers. Two producers, Denis Ferrer (an experienced *vigneron*) and Bruno Ribière (a wine-loving civil servant) from the Côtes du Roussillon AOC decided in 2001 to market a wine under the name CANA, and wrote on the label a poem with C-A-N-A as the initial letters of the four lines. It translates as 'Those who thirst for humanity and friendship will always be able to share a miracle that is born in the sky, the earth and the divine power of love.'[17] The mention of *vins de pays* was indicated on the back of the bottle. Because of its recognized quality, CANA was sold at no less than 20 euros a bottle, a price well in excess of its value as a *vin de pays*. Today the AOC and other labels such as *vin de pays* could be seen as valuable social and economic tools enabling individual producers to distinguish themselves from other producers within the same area of production. The system has developed to the extent that the *appellation* has been eroded as a form of social distinction.[18]

Indeed two broad criticisms have been directed at the system of the AOC. First, the institutionalization of AOC production has led to the creation of a *rente d'appellation* (a sort of private income related to the *appellation*) which is a form of corporatism by which professionals directly control the conditions and rules of their AOC.[19] This problem has been addressed by the INAO, the principal institution which governs the AOC. It was recently decided that a special committee of inspectors would be appointed with the aim of guaranteeing the rigorous application of the conditions of production by producers.[20] A second source of criticism has emerged from the fact that the majority of French consumers cannot distinguish between AOC and other *appellations* such as *vins de pays*. According to the ONIVINS, when interviewed on the subject of *appellations*, most French consumers gave the names of appellations such as Bordeaux, Côtes du Rhône, Beaujolais, Saint Émilion or Bourgogne without differentiating their position in the wine hierarchy.[21] Moreover, the survey pointed out that great confusion characterized their knowledge of the nature of the AOC. Comments such as 'there are some regional or local wines which have AOC', 'wine without an AOC labelled *propriétaire récoltants* [proprietor wine grower] is better ...' illustrate the confusion. Even wine lovers acknowledge the difficulty in trying to grasp the subtleties of the complex French wine market.

Another misunderstanding, according to the ONIVINS report of 2003, is the prevailing image of the wine grower as the paragon of quality-wine production for the average French consumer.

According to the ONIVINS, consumers continue to conceptualize wine as the result of the work of soil, nature and the wine grower, and there is no place for wine merchants or retailers to intervene at any stage of production. This analysis is largely explained by the growing and active involvement of wine growers in the direct marketing of their wines. In addition, many of the regional promotional marketing strategies such as tasting fairs, wine routes, the creation of spaces devoted to wine consumption like, for example, the Maison du Beaujolais (the House of Beaujolais) have focused on the wine grower. The wine grower is thus central to the promotional discourse to the detriment of any other forms of commercialization.

Another misconception becomes apparent when examining the perceptions of French consumers about wine production. The predominant discourses about wine growers are constructed around notions of authenticity, tradition and time-honoured methods. This traditional image is far from the actual reality of making and selling wine, and does not reflect the complexity of wine production or the quality of the product. Tremendous changes have occurred in the wine sector over the last fifty years. Many modern generations of producers have embraced all the advantages and techniques of modernity, playing the card of technological progress and international competition. More than ever before, winemakers have hastened to respond to changing fashions and perceptions of popular taste and their progressive integration into the economic and commercial sphere has meant that their wines are more influenced by outside factors than was the case with previous generations. Jean-Pierre Corbeau has argued that globalization has played a major role in transforming the tastes of the consumer, promoting the sale of wines that are sweet, fruity and easy to drink.[22] Many winemakers have responded to these changing fashions and have started producing wines that meet consumer demand. Indeed the majority of wine growers are dependent upon quality and reputation to access local/global markets and to maintain professional credibility.

Yet it is essential to emphasize the continuing diversity of wine production and the significance of geographic areas and socioeconomic positions. Growers of fine wines have perhaps understandably been slower to respond to the need for change than growers of *vins ordinaires*.[23] It was only when their economic situation worsened or when they had to prove something to the outside world after, for example a change of ownership, that they were ready to embrace new methods. Younger generations, especially women taking over the management of a vineyard, have often been the initiators of new styles in winemaking, taking more risks than their comfortably established rivals. The general trend, however, is towards a greater emphasis on quality.

So even if the card of tradition has been played in terms of image, the reality is more complex in terms of economic prosperity and modernization. The so-called traditional character of the methods used by contemporary wine growers has as much to do with social construction and perceptions of differences as with a real know-how associated with the product.[24] This has led to growing competition between wine growers who try to define their wines in relation to others by looking for distinctiveness and new marketing tools. This phenomenon has led to a crisis, as consumption has become the site of complex signs and contradictory meanings in a market where niches and tastes can be multiplied. On one level, wine marketing has become more difficult to read for consumers, while, on another, it is more straightforward, with the emphasis increasingly placed on categories of grapes, colour and geographic origin. The organization of the wine sector with the plurality of retailers and professionals, from specialist shops and supermarkets to wine shops, *cavistes* and wine merchants, is defined by greater diversity.[25] These places offer different expertises to the consumer and have had to respond to an increasingly sophisticated clientele, which has become more knowledgeable and interested in getting information about a particular wine or vintage.

Many of the specialized urban retail chains and outlets are managed by individuals who pride themselves on a detailed knowledge of wine, and their counsel is highly valued by their middle-class clientele. They are often asked to provide customers with advice about wine-tasting techniques and to pass on information about the specificity of particular wine-growing regions. Their activity has greatly expanded, with dinners organized around a specific theme, as was illustrated by a *caviste* in Saint-Médard-en-Jalles, near Bordeaux. He circulated the following menu (figure 3.2) by email to his list of clients and possible participants, both male and female (as very often couples register for the evening), placing emphasis on a region, Roussillon, and on red wines and on

> Bordeaux, le 21 avril 2004
> 30e « Repas Oenologique » du vendredi 7 mai à 20 h
> Thème : Les Vins rouges du Roussillon
> Chères Amatrices et chers Amateurs,
> Après les vins de l'Antiquité romaine, je vous propose une halte au bord de la Méditerranée. Au sud de Perpignan, se trouve une bande d'irréductibles vignerons qui s'accrochent à leur montagne. Le dépaysement sur le terrain et dans la bouteille est total. Le cépage « grenache » nous donne des arômes qui sont à la fois authentiques et séduisants … et oui, ça existe! Mais je garde les surprises pour la soirée.
> Dernière minute: si tout se passe bien, le viticulteur du Domaine de Ferrer Ribière, viendra du Roussillon, pour nous parler de sa philosophie!
> Domaine de Ferrer Ribière, 2002 Côtes du Roussillon
> « Le Plaisir » 2002, VDP des C'tes Catalanes de chez Mas Amiel
> Domaine de Ferrer Ribière, la Cuvée « Cana » 2002 C'tes du Roussillon
> Le menu qui accompagnera ces vins sera le suivant :
> Salade d'Asperges aux Légumes de Printemps et au Vinaigre Balsamique
> ooo
> Émincé de Magret de Canard au Poivre Vert
> ooo
> Fromage du Pays
> ooo
> Tarte au Citron Meringuée
> ooo
> Café
>
> Ces soirées ont lieu toutes les 6 semaines, mais elles peuvent aussi être personnalisées pour des groupes à partir de 12 personnes (entreprises, CE, associations, particuliers). Enfin vous pouvez aussi offrir (ou vous faire offrir) un « Repas Œnologique ».
> Recevez mes salutations gustatives et à bientôt!

Figure 3.2 An example of an oenological dinner (Bordeaux)

a selection of '*irréductibles [suprême] vignerons*'. The dinner party was presented as a celebration of the region of Roussillon. Each of the wines tasted is commented on by the wine grower, and he took great care to explain the vintage and his winemaking techniques. This is an interesting example of the sort of event punctuating the life of every city and small town in France. Very often, the wine grower presented has been discovered by the *caviste*, and their relationship is based on commercial reciprocity and personal friendship.

2. Wine consumption: fragmentation and anomie

If, as the historian Gilbert Garrier has argued, wine consumption has been democratized, it has also been transformed into a form of quest for individual identity in the context of an increasingly fragmented and postmodern society.[26] A greater variety of wines means more difficult choices for the average consumer. However, an overall decline in wine consumption has accompanied this process of democratization and has consequently made the wine sector unstable. It took producers a long time to realize the extent of the changes affecting wine, and it was only in the early 1980s that the main professional bodies of the industry became sufficiently concerned by their shrinking market to undertake serious statistical work on French wine consumption.[27] Between 1980 and 1985 the first surveys of consumption were conducted, and these enabled the interested parties to establish that frequency of consumption was one of the main factors in the changes taking place.[28] The analysis was based upon a sample of 4,000 people interviewed individually at home about their own drinking behaviour and that of the other members of the household. The results of these surveys provide an estimate for each individual of the annual number of days of wine consumption, while the actual observation of consumption during meals made it possible to calculate the average individual volume of consumption.[29]

Between 1980 and 1995, four five-year surveys were conducted and different samples of the population were selected for each survey, which had the unfortunate effect that no longitudinal, generational or consumer life-cycle data were generated. Other methodological problems have been identified, notably that the surveys could not be considered to constitute a continuous observation of consumer behaviour.[30] The quota method was used for the selection of the population, taking into account the following factors: gender, age, region of residence, type of household, occupational class and number of people sharing the household. From five modalities defining frequency, that is: every day; nearly every day; once or twice per week; more rarely; and never, three broad categories were constituted: regular consumers, who declare they drink wine every day or nearly every day; occasional consumers, who consume once or twice a week or more rarely; and non-consumers. For the authors of these surveys, an interpretative and empirical approach to these statistical data permitted an analysis of the major changes affecting wine consumption over a period of fifteen to twenty years.

The shifting character of wine consumption, and especially the fact that it changed over time and from place to place, modified the nature of the information collected. Moreover, if the surveys provide some general trends concerning wine consumption, these are limited by the fact that informants declared what they drank,

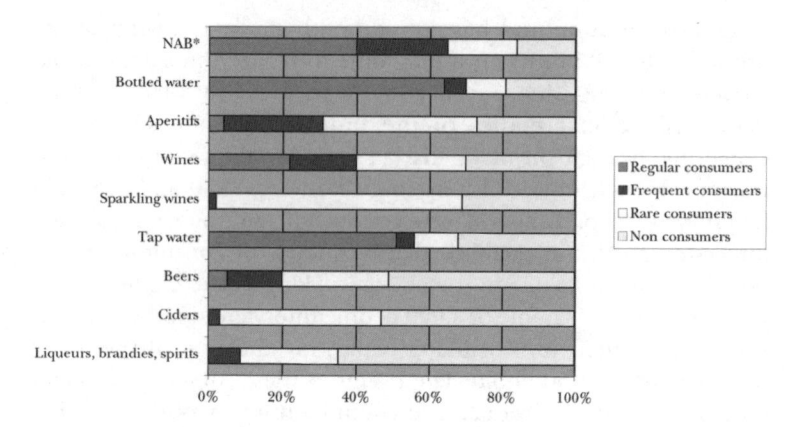

Figure 3.3 Frequency of beverages consumption
*NAB: Non-alcoholic beverages.
Source: ONIVINS, Infos, no. 91, March 2002.

but actual behaviour outside the home was not observed and could not be verified, especially where other members of the household are concerned. It should also be said that if these statistics provide us with a guide to wine consumption over a twenty-year period in terms of frequency, they nevertheless ignore the reasons for the changes observed, as the longitudinal factor is absent. Analysts are also unable to analyse the types of wine consumed. Indeed, the continuing persistence of regional identity in determining consumption has not been studied by these authors even though this has proved to be an observable fact of wine consumption. Thus the study of consumption is reduced to a simple matter of the volume of wine and alcohol consumed without considering its complex, changing and contextualized nature.

The research team nevertheless drew some interesting conclusions which provide a useful background to French wine consumption since the 1980s. One of the first major shifts which has been identified by other commentators studying alcohol consumption in Europe is the increasing competition between wine and other beverages in the context of daily consumption. Figure 3.3 illustrates that water and other non-alcoholic beverages have replaced wine as the dominant drink consumed during the majority of daily meals. If French sociologists recognize that despite the changes in diet, French people still perceive sharing a meal as a

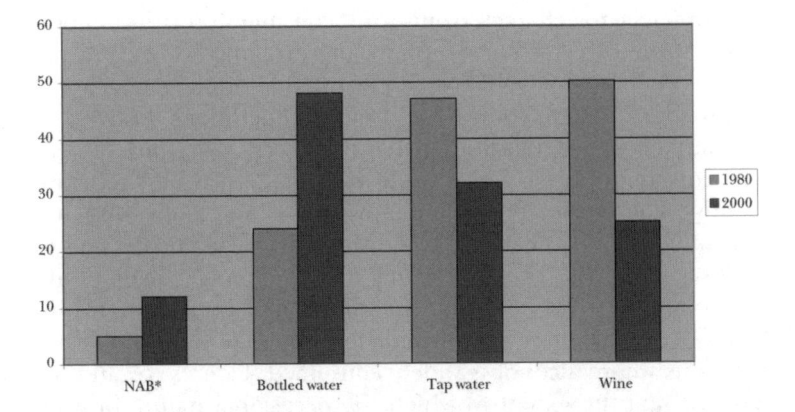

Figure 3.4 Evolution of drinks consumed during meals (percentage of consumers during the average meal)
*NAB: Non-alcoholic beverages.
Source: ONIVINS infos, no. 75, August 2000, p. 10.

major part of their lifestyle, they nevertheless acknowledge that wine is no longer consumed as a matter of course. Wine is now to a large extent associated with festive and special occasions, and the ONIVINS team has clearly pointed out that generational effect and life cycle contributed to these trends.

Amongst the many explanations provided for this shift, the health factor is very often put to the fore. Since the 1980s, publicity and health awareness campaigns, especially those aimed at women, have played a major role in shaping alcohol consumption. Yet contradictory tendencies emerge, such as the growing consumption of non-alcoholic beverages and the fact that the wine consumed today has a higher alcohol content than in the 1970s.[31] The traditional practice of diluting wine with water for example has all but disappeared. The emphasis on the role of health as a significant factor can, however, be overdone. The medical profession itself is divided between the advocates of moderate consumption and the partisans of abstinence, and as a result, public opinion is subject to a series of conflicting messages in relation to wine. Yet it is undeniable that water has become the drink associated with the everyday meal, attesting the rise of health concerns and the impact of anti-alcohol campaigns such as 'un verre ça va, deux verres bonjour les dégâts' (one glass of wine is OK; two glasses and hallo troubles).

Another factor characterizing wine consumption is the importance of the place of consumption, the drinking context. In the study conducted by ONIVINS, a clear divide opposes traditional and modern spaces, younger and older generations, festive and ordinary occasions, illustrating that the occasional nature of this new consumption has more to do with modernity and reflexive identity. The possibility of combining places, types of drinks and ways of consuming enables the individual to make choices and to multiply identities. This is certainly true for younger people who can combine periods of abstinence in alcohol consumption with family occasions where they drink a few glasses of wine and festive occasions where alcohol is widely consumed. Figures 3.5 and 3.6 demonstrate the extent to which the occasional nature of wine drinking defines an important part of this new alcohol consumption. While non-consumers and regular wine drinkers were the two dominant groups in 1990, ten years later the focus had shifted to occasional consumers and non-consumers, who represent 41 per cent against 38 per cent respectively in 2005. This phenomenon is certainly the most important change affecting wine consumption as wine is no longer part of the staple diet.

From the survey conducted in 2000 by ONIVINS, it seems that age is an important factor in determining the occasional or daily nature

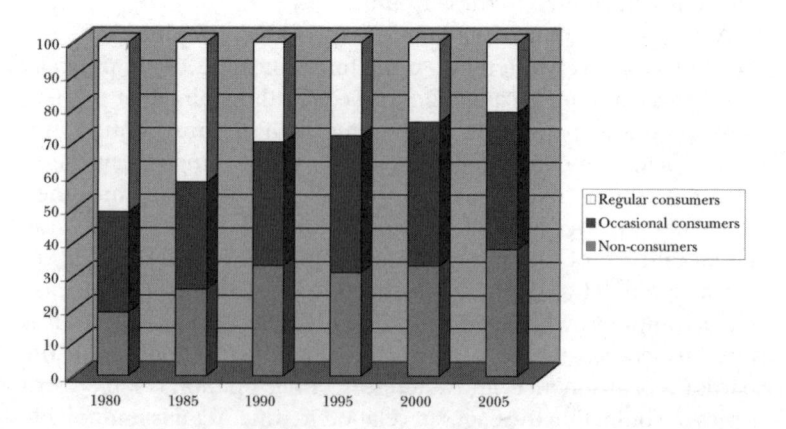

Figure 3.5 Evolution of the frequency of wine consumption amongst French people
Source: ONIVINS- INRA UM2 GRIECO Survey on wine consumption in France

of wine consumption. If we take the example of the age profile of daily or habitual consumers of wine it is perhaps not surprising that the older groups, especially those aged sixty or over, fit into this category. Here we have the generation raised on daily consumption in schools and at family mealtimes. Another element observed by the research team was that individuals are now starting to consume wine later in life, illustrating the rupture with wine culture often commented upon by the press. Yet recent surveys in 1998 and 2000 have been less convincing about this trend. Younger people who start consuming wine tend to do so occasionally, unlike older people who consume more regularly. These results argue in favour of a generational rupture confirmed by several studies focusing on other aspects of French society. The so-called generational division seems to have been very acute since the 1970s, but our fieldwork has proved that a growing number of young people are interested in wine and are eager to learn more. Their parents have assisted in the sense that in most of the interviews conducted with consumers, children have been described by their parents as being very open to wine culture.

When trying to define a clear profile of the new wine drinker, what I have called the occasional or 'wandering drinker', it is neces-

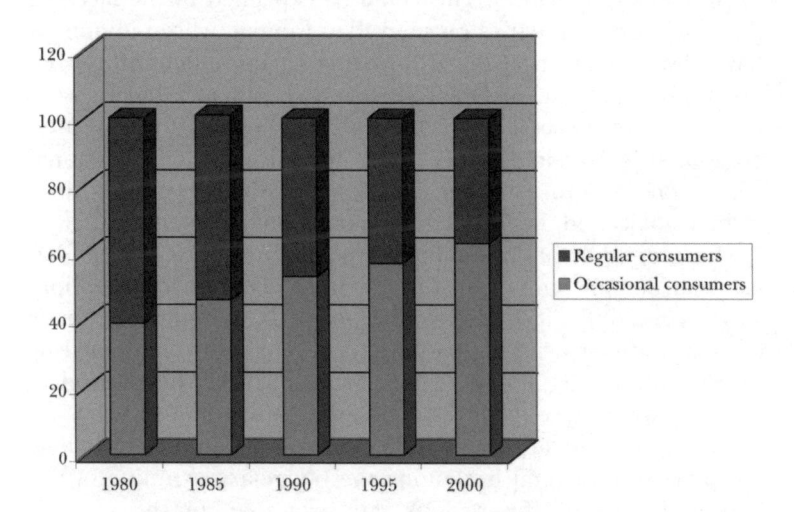

Figure 3.6 Frequency of wine consumption, regular consumption versus occasional consumption
Source: ONIVINS infos, no. 75, August 2000, p. 10.

sary to accept that in reality there is no such thing as the average French wine drinker, and it is doubtful if he/she ever existed. Instead we see an explosion of differentiated behaviours and needs reflecting a wide range of social groups that are more or less easily identifiable (adolescents, older people, women) and of networks of individuals, who at a given time of their life share ideas and patterns of behaviour towards a product that offers the possibility for both collective and individual expressions of identity. Yet there are still some enduring factors which allow us to make sense of wine consumption according to a specific field of representations. Amongst them, gender stands out as one of the key determining factors, and men and women have markedly different profiles where wine is concerned. Women have, in general, become wine consumers quite recently, but they have done so in a different way from men.[32] Despite the near-absence of women among wine connoisseurs and their underrepresentation in the wine sector, women have more or less followed the decline in regular wine consumption. As we might expect, the number of non-consumers remains higher among women than men (45 per cent against 28 per cent) and the proportion of regular consumers is again higher for the male population. This could be explained by the fact that there are fewer pressures on men than women, who traditionally have always been stigmatized for drinking too much. Moreover, women are more inclined to be sensitive to health and dietary issues than men and are constantly subject to social and cultural pressures. Somewhat surprisingly, there are 40 per cent of occasional consumers in both male and female categories, illustrating their rising visibility and the growing fragmentation of drinking patterns.

The geography of consumption is another important issue that has been largely ignored in the literature on wine consumption, and it is also difficult to have a clear picture of how ethnic origin or residence affects drinking patterns. A recent study conducted by Christine Boizot argues that regional traditions and types of production cannot fully explain the changes in the nature of wine consumption.[33] Yet according to her analysis, geographic variations can be observed when examining the budgetary spending of the household in specific regions. For example, in the case of Burgundy, she demonstrates that the budget devoted to VCC (*vins de consommation courante* or ordinary wines) is lower than in regions such as Aquitaine, Midi-Pyrénées, Auvergne and PACA (Provence,

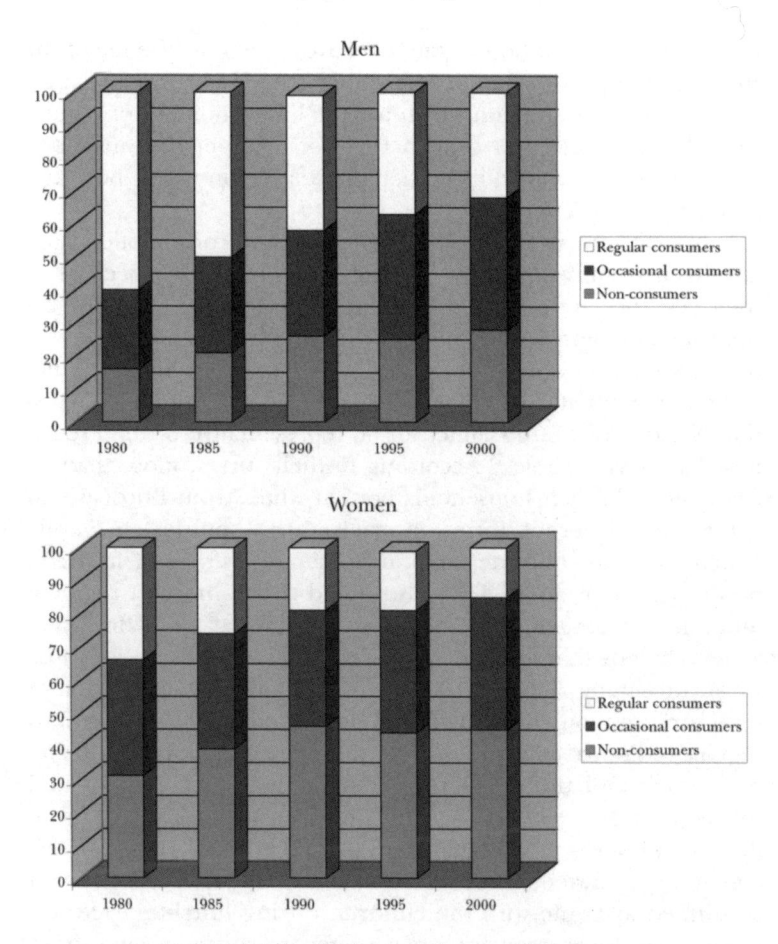

Figure 3.7 Frequency of wine consumption amongst French people over fourteen years of age and gender factor
Source: ONIVINS infos, no. 75, August 2000, p. 9.

Alpes, Côte d'Azur), where the production of such wines is more developed. Burgundians drink more AOC wines. The North, Alsace and Lorraine spend more money on beer, while in Haute-Normandie and Île de France strong alcohols occupied the major part of the budget. Another study conducted by ONIVINS concludes that despite a greater homogenization of drinking patterns between and within regions, there are still some regional differences between types of consumers – regular, occasional or non-consumers – and these patterns have experienced some of the trends noted previously, but at a slower pace.[34] For instance, they cite the North as a region which has the lowest number of regular wine drinkers (21.7 per cent in 1995 for 35.4 per cent in 1980), which seems to confirm its reputation as a region where beer and strong alcohol predominate.

Statistical surveys and opinion polls on wine consumption have also been commissioned by regional wine boards, but because of their cost they are restricted to the wine profession. Their conclusions remain vague and do not provide us with a clear sense of who drinks what in Burgundy or Bordeaux. For example, SECODIP has examined estimates of domestic spending for a sample of 5,000 households which are claimed to be representative of the French population as a whole.[35] According to their survey, more than 55 per cent of French households bought wines from Bordeaux in 2000, with different forms of packaging – bottles or plastic containers – to consume them at home, an average of fourteen bottles per household. They also noted that important regional differences emerged, with the North consuming more Bordeaux wines than any other region and Paris and its suburbs (*région parisienne*) consuming 38 per cent of the overall total. My observation of wine consumption during fieldwork conducted in 2003–4 in various regions of France confirms this growing fragmentation of drinking behaviours and the reordering at stake in French regions and between categories of drinkers. In cities such as Bordeaux or Lyon, the lunch hour is predominantly organized around a rapid *plat du jour* or a sandwich, while in rural areas, there is still a meal consumed at home with the children during lunchtime. It also reveals that the average consumer prefers to consume wines from his or her region of origin or residence unless he/she is a wine lover. Recent studies conducted by polling companies for ONIVINS even classify new types of wine drinkers such as the 'occasional by tradition' or the 'engaged hedonist, occasional' arguing that a wide range of categories describe the drinking habits of the French population.[36]

3. New drinkers, new places

By shifting from an integrated and staple element of the popular diet into a social object and a means of constructing an identity, wine has accumulated a highly complex set of meanings. Wine tasting still remains an *affaire de goûts* (question of taste), or a place of social discernment, hierarchy and power. Bourdieu has argued that taste is socially constructed and that, traditionally, the hierarchy of wines became identified with the social hierarchy.[37] Thus a complex hierarchy of wines reflects a similarly complex hierarchy of drinkers, which can be interpreted in terms of increasing social differentiation and competition. Today the middle classes form the largest group of wine consumers, and it is true that for many, wine is a means of defining status. By adopting an approach based on a combination of participant observation and an examination of life stories, it is possible to shed some light on the interaction between wine consumption and culture. The varied patterns of consumption are illustrated by the many discourses embedded in the cultural object of wine, and very often, the consumer finds him/herself lost in the profusion of expertises. Access to oenological/scientific discourse is thus, in part, a question of power, as very often people who are able to describe wines, and to differentiate between them, position themselves in relation to that knowledge, to establish a sense of distinction and social domination.

As a result, there are various tensions between different types of consumers such as the connoisseur and the 'wandering drinker', both of whom are defining identities through wine drinking and through a complex set of consumption and cultural patterns. As we have seen, the connoisseur could be defined as the classic type of educated drinker for whom wine culture is much more than drinking wine, while the wandering drinker might be defined as the average wine drinker who knows little about it and is experimenting through a process that can be described as a *vin-anomie*. There are also numerous examples of people making their professional careers out of the publication of their knowledge, and each wine-producing region can boast its own local culture and experts who seek to disseminate it.[38] New regional wine cultures have thus emerged in response to the decline of a largely mythical national wine drinking culture.

Yet the figure of the male wine connoisseur remains emblematic of French wine culture and consumption, and his pre-eminence in public discourses raises important questions for the anthropologist concerning the diffusion and spread of this new wine culture. A recent survey by Sofres has underlined the lack of basic oenological knowledge amongst the French, whose wine culture has often been represented as if it were homogeneous.[39] However, is the wine lover another mythical creature? The profile of the wine lover which is prominent in the vast literature on wines is seen as crucial to understanding the social processes and the values embedded in wine consumption and culture. The connoisseur emerged in the late eighteenth and nineteenth centuries as one of the figures of oenological culture.[40] Yet defining the connoisseur is not an easy task, and the recent proliferation and popularization of wine culture has, to some extent, contributed to the construction of the connoisseur as a repository of collective memory, who divides his time between drinking wine and buying books, guides and maps of wine-producing regions in order to make sense of a complex world. The re-emergence of the wine lover is connected to the constitution of a wine culture which has been democratized, professionalized and diffused through literature and the media, and has been fostered by the growing needs of this group represented mainly by the male urban middle class.

Yet the figure of the average drinker provides us with a different image of wine drinking culture. For some drinkers, wine has become an object of social tensions as they feel very often disarmed, lost or confused when confronted by the seemingly exclusive knowledge of the expert. For others, wine consumption has been transformed into a search for identities and differentiation, something that is demonstrated by the ethnography of various wine tastings, where individuals devote most of their time to socializing, communicating with others or just talking about current affairs. In Beaune, Bordeaux, Paris and elsewhere, wine tasting is not so much about wine, but more about yourself and the society you live in and the society you wish to live in incarnated as an 'ideal world'. It is worth noting that the cultural construction attached to wine drinking in France has started to crumble, as pointed out by the majority of our informers. From a private and domestic activity organized around the family meal, it has been transformed into a social, public and ritualized act around which the individual is constructing an 'ideal world', but at the same time is engaged in a complex process of reflexive identity building. All these different facets are today part of a complex process surrounding wine consumption in France and elsewhere.

As the expanding middle classes imitated the *haute bourgeoisie*, new strategies of social distinction were needed amongst these increasingly affluent groups to cultivate their sense of 'distinction'. Individuals have greater choice about what they want to drink, and in this regard complex processes of differentiation take place. There is a real tension between 'the wandering drinker', who reflects the fragmented type of wine consumption, and the 'connoisseur', who is seen as a dominant and perennial figure in wine culture and who likes a personal and loyal contact with the wine growers. The tensions between these two types of individuals illustrate the difficulty of any attempt to define French national wine drinking culture as a homogeneous object. Through wine consumption, individuals compete and construct their identity. The source of identity is the lifestyle image that individuals purposively appropriate or construct, and the shared normative orientations underlying their consumption. At the same time, the values embedded in wine consumption illustrate the attachment of French people to specific values of space, time, rural society, commensality and sociability, which are today challenged by globalization, modernity and multiculturalism. The values are activated through the regions and the idea of local products, ideologies largely encouraged by the state. These collective national values could be read as the traces of a surviving agrarian ideology or they could be seen as an alternative type of consumption in an increasingly global society. What could be concluded is that despite democratization and the fragmentation of wine consumption and wine culture, the access to this highly symbolic object representing the French nation is dependent on individual economic resources, knowledge and cultural capital, as wine is a world of its own.

4. The state against the drinker

Despite the continuous decline in per capita alcohol consumption in southern Europe, France remains amongst the countries with the highest consumption of alcohol (10.7 litres of pure alcohol annually per inhabitant).[41] Daily consumption has decreased, and there has been a move from traditional beverages (*vins de pays*) to quality wines and international brands of beers and spirits.[42] Yet despite this decline, alcohol and wine consumption remain a source of preoccupation for politicians and policy-makers. Recently, in the context of World Health Organization (WHO) initiatives in preventive medicine, alcohol consumption has come back to the fore in political priorities, and France has been one of the countries aimed at in alcohol policies.[43] Yet anti-alcohol rhetoric has always been an important element of French politics, but with a specific national twist due to the existence of the powerful lobby of the wine industry.

In historical terms, state policy towards alcohol consumption formed a complex story in which the position of wine relative to other types of alcoholic beverages has been constantly debated. As Sarah Howard has argued, during the inter-war period wine was central to the stability of national alcohol production and the core of a mythology linking notions of health, sociability, regionalism, tradition and patriotism.[44] If this mythological construction was part of a national discourse, it has come back to the fore in the context of recent changes affecting the wine sector. Yet it is facing a greater threat as modern consumers have to some extent turned away from wine. As a result a growing number of voices incarnated by the profession, wine lovers, wine experts and politicians are trying to respond to these drastic changes in consumption by contributing to the construction of a strong wine culture as a specific element of French cultural exception. In order to achieve this objective, they are resorting to some familiar notions of tradition, authenticity, regionalism, patriotism and health which they seek to apply to contemporary concerns.

In the years following the Second World War, when advances in medical knowledge concerning the effects of alcohol consumption increased, most French advertising was inspired by examples from the USA. The beverage distribution code decided, for example, to limit the advertisement of alcoholic drinks including wine. The Comité National de Défense contre l'Alcoolisme (National Committee of Defence against Alcoholism) joined in asking for more regulation of advertisements and limited access to alcohol.[45] However, despite increasing regulation and tighter licensing laws governing age limits, legal hours of sale, taxation and drink-driving, there was still strong resistance to a campaign in favour of abstinence amongst politicians, public opinion and the medical profession.[46] The presence of wine as a social lubricant remains at the core of social and professional relations, but because most of the alcohol regulations were aimed at alcohol products below 18 degrees of pure alcohol, wine was included.

The image of social degeneration associated with the drinker of the nineteenth century, immortalized in Émile Zola's *L'Assommoir*, was still prevalent in the 1950s when the Haut Comité d'Etude et d'Information sur l'Alcoolisme (High Committee for Study and Information on Alcoholism) emerged as one of the contemporary voices of the temperance movement. Founded in 1954 as a state organization by the centre-left government of Pierre Mendès-France, it was also supported by the conservative government headed by Michel Debré in 1959 with the aim of developing a public alcohol policy underpinned by an interministerial committee answerable to the prime minister.[47] A number of licensing laws were passed during the 1950s preventing the opening of premises in inappropriate locations, for instance near schools, and they set a maximum density of outlets in newly urbanized areas. The Haut Comité d'Etude et d'Information sur l'Alcoolisme sought, at the time, to improve quality of life by communicating information about matters of health and temperance or serenity and sobriety.[48] It deliberately focused on advocating moderate and informed consumption, and focused primarily on women and young people. During the 1950s these campaigns were conducted through the medium of posters, but by the 1970s radio, television and the press were all employed. In 1955 for example, posters were displayed in the Parisian tube and in buses as well as in twenty-seven provincial cities, on railway platforms and along some major road networks.[49] After 1970, most of the poster campaigns about the dangers of excessive alcohol consumption were organized at local and regional level as television and radio were now dominating the media. In the 1980s, the city of Brest pioneered a 'three days without drinking alcohol' campaign. Yet this regional fragmentation could be seen until recently as one of the major obstacles to an effective public health campaign. However since the Évin law of 1991 the controversy surrounding alcohol consumption has taken a new turn, putting drinking back on the national agenda. The ANPAA (Agence Nationale pour la Prévention en Alcoologie et en Addictologie (National Association for the Prevention in Alcoholism and Addictology)) funded by the association for road safety and various other ministerial bodies is trying to impose its presence in the public sphere.

Yet paradoxically this negative representation of alcohol has always coexisted side by side with a discourse on moderate drinking and with the image of wine as a healthy drink, dating back at least as far as Pasteur in the nineteenth century. This ambivalence about wine was a common feature of the French media and wider social and political discourse. In 1974, a French dietician denounced on television the presence of excessive amounts of sodium and lead in wine, which she argued were both harmful to public health, while just three years later another expert, Dr Maury, presented the opposite argument, again on television, claiming that wine posesses some remarkable medicinal properties. Between these two extremes, public opinion and the majority of the medical profession remain divided over the status of wine as distinct from other alcoholic beverages. Several examples of this juxtaposition of wine and health can still be found today in television programmes, the press and on websites such as *terroirs-France guide du vin*.[50] The French paradox is also part of this health-centred discourse on wine, and according to some experts such as Dr Craplet, if wine is presented by producers and the press as having a particular protective effect, it is also true of any other alcohol, as the nature of these drinks has been shown to have little importance.[51]

The creation of *Vinothérapie* in 2000 is a good example of the recent promotion of vines and wines as healthy products.[52] However it was the controversy sparked by the notorious Évin law of 10 January 1991 which illustrates the unique position of wine in the broader debate about alcohol consumption. Inspired partly by the previous discussions of the Haut Comité d'Etude and d'Information sur l'Alcoolisme[53] and following the attempt to establish a code of good practice between producers, merchants and the state, the Évin law modified the code governing the distribution of alcoholic beverages by forbidding all direct or indirect advertising for alcohol on television, film, at sports events, local associations for young people or ongoing education centres. Future advertising was restricted to a simple description of the product and was obliged to include a health-related message ('alcohol abuse is harmful to your health'). As one of the most restrictive laws of its type in Europe, the Évin law, since modified but still in place, limits the content of the messages on wines to the following: the degree of alcohol volume, the named origin, the composition, the name and address of the producer and a description of the product.

At the time of the vote, the Évin law provoked serious opposition from producers, and also from other categories or groups of actors such as doctors, gastronomic societies, wine experts and wine lovers. This opposition was, for instance, represented on French television by the doctor, André Parce, a chemist and wine grower in Perpignan, who argued that wine was not an alcoholic drink like the others. According to Parce and other apologists for the wine industry, moderate consumption has positive benefits. The wine lobby was using its network of wine connoisseurs to fight the state against a background of declining consumption. The lobby was also organized behind a group called 'Wine and Society' representing the wine sector with seven of the most powerful wine bodies such as ANIVIT (Association Nationale Interprofessionnelle des Vins de Table et des Vins de Pays) and CCVF (Confédération des Coopératives Vinicoles de France). The wine profession wanted, amongst other things, the recognition of wine as a food and as an object of cultural heritage, and it sought to amend the Évin law to its advantage. In May 2004, the French Senate finally voted an amendment to the law under pressure from the wine lobby, which permitted advertising of wine to refer to specific values and representations in relation to the sensorial and gustative characteristics of the product for the denomination of origin indications or AOC. This was ratified by the National Assembly, providing scope for more flexibility in advertising, with the possibility of using more descriptive terms in relation to *terroir*, but it still does not resolve the fundamental dilemma, namely that, whatever the claims of its apologists, wine remains an alcoholic product.[54]

The strong and largely traditional representation of wine as a healthy beverage was reinforced by a new medical discourse that emerged in the 1990s at global level, namely the so-called 'French paradox'. The French paradox was the name given to the apparently remarkable fact that people in France suffer a relatively low incidence of coronary heart disease, despite their diet being rich in saturated fat. It was suggested that France's high red wine consumption was a primary explanatory factor in this phenomenon. This theory was expanded on the influential American television show *60 Minutes* broadcast in 1992, which was subsequently publicized widely by the French media. Ever since, French doctors and other authorities have frequently argued in favour of the medicinal qualities of red wine, presented as the principal cause of the French paradox and as a possible protection against both coronary heart disease and Alzheimer's disease. Debates on television were often organized around a confused notion of moderate consumption and focused solely on wine as the unique cause of well-being.[55] In 1997, the media personality Professor Renaud, who defended the 'French paradox' on American television, was supported in France by Professor Fricker, who advocated a moderate consumption which was never clearly defined. The programme illustrated the confused definition of what constitutes moderate alcohol consumption. To take even the most obvious example, it was never made clear that people are not equal when it comes to determining a moderate level of consumption. The lack of a clear national governmental policy and of a well-defined campaign of information on the part of the medical profession contributed to the ambiguities raised by the various debates on alcohol drinking. However, in 1995, the French government, having adopted the principal recommendations of the WHO Alcohol Action Plan, started to mobilize the public through a national campaign based on three priority objectives: a decrease of 20 per cent in average alcohol consumption per capita; a reduction of damaging behaviour with health and social consequences; and a reduction of regional variations with the aim that all regions achieve the level of those with the lowest levels of consumption.[56] However, French attacks on excessive alcohol consumption are still very much atomized and lacking a clear focus, and the nation is still divided about wine.

The international nature of the debate concerning alcohol consumption and wine is, however, beginning to have an impact in France. The French position has started to shift in relation to social and economic changes and the balance of power between diverse sections of the population: consumers versus non-consumers, drinkers versus connoisseurs, water versus wine etc. The growing preoccupation of French people, and especially non-drinkers, with health issues and well-being has encouraged the state to take a more critical stance. Wine has also become a target as the campaign against advertising Bordeaux and Burgundy, led by the ANPAA in 2004, demonstrated.[57] However, the growing number of partisans in this new war of wine, which goes far beyond national interests, seems to counterbalance the content of the debate. As Alain Suguenot, one of the parliamentary deputies defending the wine industry proclaimed, 'This is an exceptional cultural product, an element of history [...] Do we have to deny our culture and to facilitate the penetration of this culture [he underlines American culture] which is already everywhere?' Wine consumption in France has thus been transformed into a front in a wider cultural struggle, and wine consumption has clearly become more than a simple economic activity and has been transformed into an ideological conflict with wine consumers lining up against the advocates of abstinence. By opting for the representation of wine as an element of cultural heritage or as a healthy drink, the wine industry is looking for an answer to the threat of declining consumption. Yet somewhat paradoxically this strategy is being employed at a time when the French are consuming less wine, but are arguably gaining more knowledge about the product. The idea that the majority of French people ever knew much about wine is debatable, to say the least. They used to drink more, but it was of the low quality represented by local plonks. Now they are more likely to experiment and to drink wine from other regions and even from Australia, New Zealand and elsewhere. As for the French state, it continues to be torn between the often conflicting objectives of fighting alcoholism through abstinence, while encouraging moderate alcohol consumption. The battle remains to be won and the opposition between these groups has yet to be solved.

Notes

1 Jean-Pierre Albert, 'La nouvelle culture du vin', *Terrain*, 13 (1989), 117–24. Wine culture as a cultural object is defined by the proliferation of objects, texts, discourses, images, artefacts and new places solely devoted to wine consumption.
2 For a discussion of the art status of wine, see Véronique Nahoum-Grappe and Odile Vincent (eds), *Le Goût des belles choses* (Paris: Éditions de la Maison des Sciences de l'Homme, 2004).
3 The concept of 'engagement' (involvement) has been defined by G. Teil, *De la coupe aux lèvres* (Toulouse: Éditions Octarès, 2004) and R. Reckinger, 'Les pratiques discursives' (thèse de doctorat, Marseille, 2008), and it encapsulates precisely the extent to which individuals engage with their passion. It is the dynamic character of the relationship which is underlined. Yet I believe from my study that it is more in terms of a constellation of consumers/drinkers coupled with the intensity of their passion that the sphere of wine drinking is to be defined.
4 Pierre Bourdieu, *La Distinction. Critique sociale du jugement* (Paris: Les Éditions de Minuit, 1979).
5 See chapter 7.
6 Pekka Sulkunen, 'Drinking in France 1965–79: an analysis of household consumption data', *British Journal of Addiction*, 84 (1989), 61–72.
7 Antoni Gual and Joan Colomb, 'Why has alcohol consumption declined in countries of southern Europe?', *Addiction*, 92, 1 (1997).

8   See 'Les viticulteurs bourguignons descendent dans la rue', *Le Journal du Palais de Bourgogne*, 21 (February 2004), 8.
9   'Quality' is put in quotation marks as it is defined as a social construction shared by different actors. See the excellent work of Geneviève Teil, *De la coupe aux lèvres*.
10 There were only seventy *appellations* when they were first conceived.
11 L.-A. Loubère, *The Wine Revolution in France: The Twentieth Century* (Princeton: Princeton University Press, 1990), p. 33.
12 Elizabeth Barham, 'Translating terroir: the global challenge of French AOC labeling', *Journal of Rural Studies*, 19, 1 (January 2003), 131.
13 See for example the recent case of Cahors presented in *Le Monde*, Sunday 25 and Monday 26 September 2001, p. 22.
14 Loubère, *The Wine Revolution in France*, p. 113.
15 See, for example, in the Minervois: Françoise Acquier, 'La qualité des vins à la croisée des terroirs et du territoire', *Revue d'Économie Méridionale*, 44, 176, 4 (1996), 53–71.
16 Elizabeth Barham, 'Translating terroir', 131.
17 They are presented as a typical example of the new wave of young southern French winemakers with low capital investment but exacting production values dedicated to making *vins de pays*, with a true expression of *terroir* from local grape varieties.
18 Marie-France Garcia-Parpet, 'Le terroir, le cépage et la marque. Stratégies de valorisation des vins dans un contexte mondial', *Cahiers d'Économie et Sociologie Rurales*, 60–1 (2001), 150–80, and her recent publication, *Le Marché de l'excellence. Les Grands Crus à l'épreuve de la mondialisation*, Collection Liber (Paris: Seuil, Collection Liber, 2009).
19 For a discussion of *rente d'appellation*, see the publications of Catherine Laporte and especially her thesis: '*Système d'information sur la qualité et profit. Le cas des vins d'appellation d'origine contrôlée de Bourgogne*', thèse d'économie, INRA-ENESAD, 2000.
20 *Le Figaro*, 'Les nouvelles règles des AOC', 30 April 2004, p. 19.
21 See ONIVINS report, *Le Vin, l'achat, la confiance et la marque. Le Cas du consommateur français*, Infos no. 105, July–August 2003.
22 Jean-Pierre Corbeau, 'Une affaire de goûts et de couleurs', GEO, special issue, *La Folie des vins du monde* (2007), 82–3.
23 Loubère, *The Wine Revolution in France*, p. 89.
24 Marion Demossier, *Hommes et Vins. Une anthropologie du vignoble bourguignon* (Dijon: EUD, 1999).
25 Loubère, *The Wine Revolution in France*, p. 181.
26 Gilbert Garrier, *Histoire sociale et culturelle du vin* (Paris: Bordas Cultures, 1995 ; new edition 1998), p. 249.
27 The first article was published in *Revue d'Économie Méridionale*, 39, 155–6, 3 and 4 (1991), 19–52 and was entitled 'La consommation du vin en France: Evolution tendancielle et diversité des comportements', by Patrick Aigrain, Daniel Boulet, Jean-Pierre Laporte and Jean Louis Lambert.
28 ONIVINS in collaboration with the Laboratoire d'Économie et de

Sociologie Rurales of Montpellier, a subsidiary of the INRA (Institut National de la Recherche Agronomique (National Institute of Agronomical Research)).

29 See Daniel Boulet and Jean-Pierre Laporte, 'Les comportements de consommation de vin en France', INRA, Sciences sociales, 3 (June 1997); personal communication.
30 Aigrain, Boulet, Laporte and Lambert , 'La consommation du vin en France'.
31 Wine growers interviewed on this topic recognize that it is historically difficult to argue the point, as the principal difference would be between the natural alcoholic degree of the grapes and the final degree of the wine after making wine. This difference according to them has drastically reduced because of the greater control over winemaking processes. The overall quality of wine has improved. There would also be major differences between wine regions and between types of wines. However, generally speaking, it is recognized by the professionals that the alcohol content has increased.
32 Jean-Pierre Corbeau, 'De la présentation dramatisée des aliments à la représentation de leurs consommateurs', in Ismène Giachetti (ed.), *Identités des mangeurs. Images des aliments* (Paris: Polytechniea, 1996), 175–98.
33 Christine Boizot, 'La demande de boissons des ménages: une estimation de la consommation à domicile', *Économie et Statistique*, 324–5, 4, 5 (1999), 143.
34 ONIVINS, *Les occasions de consommation de vin. La segmentation et l'évolution du marché intérieur des vins tranquilles*, Infos, no. 84 (June 2001).
35 See Marché des vins de Bordeaux, Commercialisation, Année 2001, CIVB, Bordeaux. I should like to thank the CIVB for these documents, especially Christophe Tupinier.
36 See, for example some of these surveys on the website of *Afivin* http://www.afivin.fr.
37 Bourdieu, *La Distinction*.
38 The success of a *sommelier* such as Philippe Faure-Brac, who gives interviews only on the phone for five minutes because of his heavy timetable, illustrates to what extent power and legitimacy are part of this new celebrity social status provided by knowledge of wine.
39 See http://www.tns-sofres.com/points–de–vue/opinion–style–de–vie/2006/?p=2 consulted on 24 April 2007.
40 Jean-Luc Fernandez, *La Critique vinicole en France. Pouvoir de prescription et construction de la confiance*, Logiques sociales (Paris: L'Harmattan, 2004), pp. 189–238.
41 For an overview report on alcohol, see http://www.eurocare.org/profiles/franceeupolicy.htm.
42 Michel Craplet, *A consommer avec modération* (Paris: Éditions Odile Jacob, 2005), p. 1398.
43 See for example the following link: http://www.euro.who.int/document/mediacentre/fs1005e.pdf.
44 Sarah Howard, 'Selling wine to the French: official attempts to

increase wine consumption, 1931–1936', *Food and Foodways*, 12, 4 (2004), 205.
45 Pierre Fouquet and Martine de Borde, *Histoire de l'alcool* (Paris: PUF, 1990), p. 85.
46 For a discussion of the representations associated with wine in the medical professions, see J. Rainaut and J.-L. Balmes, 'Genèse du discours médical', in *La Vigne et le vin. Les Enjeux pour demain* (Paris: Office International de la Vigne et du Vin, 1990), pp. 129–40.
47 Craplet, *A consommer avec modération*, p. 1401.
48 Thierry Fillaut, Jack Garçon and Muriel Bernardin, 'Les belles plantes ne s'arrosent pas à l'alcool. L'alcoolisme', *adsp*, 26 (March 1999), 20–2.
49 Ibid., 21.
50 See their website which presents the list of arguments in favour of wine as a healthy drink: *http://www.terroir-france.com/vin/sante.html*.
51 See *http://www.eurocare.org/profiles/france/paradox.html*, especially the bibliography.
52 The concept of this health centre based upon wines, vines and their medical properties has extended from Bordeaux to California and is now to be established in Italy. It is supported by an extensive traditional and local literature using grapes and wine as a medical product.
53 Fouquet and de Borde, *Histoire de l'alcool*, p. 88.
54 It also makes the law compatible with community law. When allowed, the message must be informative and limit itself to the following indications: degree of alcohol, origin, naming, composition and preparation of the product.
55 This was not medically demonstrated, as other factors could have played a part in the French paradox.
56 For a regional study of alcoholism, see the excellent work of Jean-Pierre Castelain, *Manières de vivre, manières de boire. Alcool et sociabilité sur le port* (Paris: Imago, 1989).
57 It has 1,200 salaried employees and a budget of 44 million euros, and is 90 per cent funded by the French state.

Chapter Four
Contemporary Discourses and Representations

In recent decades, the French public has been the target of an ever-increasing number of printed books, television programmes, exhibitions and public discourses on wine. The phenomenon has been well documented and is linked to the expansion of an affluent middle class, which has led to a democratization of wine drinking culture and consequently the transformation of the wine industry. These changes form part of the larger process of construction of a complex public culture involving media, tourism and leisure, but it also reveals artefacts of culture in the making.[1] The textualization of the wine drinking realm has been a recent process and, when contrasted with the decline in wine consumption, it offers an interesting platform from which to explore other aspects of the debates on national identity and globalization.

Discourses, texts, representations and images of wine in France have proliferated since the 1970s in the context of the modernization of the wine industry and its progressive integration into a liberalized market economy, which, in turn, shaped the production and consumption of wine. Yet the predominant message conveyed by the images, texts and publicity sponsored by the wine industry clashes with the internationalization of the wine market and the socio-economic realities of wine-growing communities. The continued emphasis placed upon 'tradition', 'community', 'authenticity' and 'quality' in local and professional discourse attests the success of dominant groups and professional bodies such as the INAO in imposing a conservative image of French wines. In a context of increasing competition and crisis, there has been a growing challenge to this classic representation of French viticulture, creating tensions amongst both producers and professional organizations. By examining these images at both regional and national levels, it is possible to analyse the process of social production of discourses and to investigate the interplay of power and identity. Focusing on some of the key cultural issues underpinning these representations and on the actors behind these processes enables us to examine the construction of wine culture. This discursive field illustrates some of the contradictions of what it means to be French, through the display of a national wine culture. If we take, for example, the state in the form of the Ministry of Agriculture, it is clear that wine professionals have played a significant, even determining role in the orchestration of this French response to global competition, while the Ministry of Health, on the other hand, has taken a critical stance relative to alcohol consumption, much to the disgust of the wine lobby. Yet economic liberalization has given a new flavour to the crisis. Competition between various levels of identification and between regions, groups and actors in the wine sector makes it more difficult to find common ground on which to respond to the threat of economic crisis. This chapter explores the complex and often conflicting nature of public and professional public discourse, using evidence drawn from the French media with the aim of demonstrating the ways in which it reflects competing definitions of wine culture.

1. The origins of oenological writings

Etymologically, 'oenology' is derived from Greek *oinos* (wine) and *logos* (discourse). By 'oenological literature', I mean the corpus of French writings, which includes all forms of literary expression, devoted to wines and vines, including the major transformations affecting the wine sector from the 1960s, inspired by the scientific revolution in wine production and the emergence of new and legitimized categories of intermediaries and actors in the wine sector such as the oenologist, the *caviste* (independent wine retailer) and the *sommelier*.[2]

With wine drinking accepted as an integral part of French sociability, pervading all aspects of social life and associated with patriotism and the defence of the nation, alcohol drinking was rarely considered worthy of study or even serious academic discussion before the 1950s. All that began to change with the highly original and pioneering essay written by Roland Barthes in *Les Mythologies* during the post-war period. In a chapter entitled 'Le vin et le lait' (Wine and Milk), Barthes analysed the significance of wine to the French. According to his interpretation, wine was of symbolic importance to the French expression of conviviality, of virility and, more importantly, of national identity. Nothing could be more expressive of an essential Frenchness than a *ballon de rouge* (glass of red wine). Yet it was not a truly *national* culture in that, for Barthes, wine drinking and its culture were very much the preserve of the bourgeoisie. Barthes deconstructs the mythological associations of wine by making explicit its real status as just another commodity produced for profit. Yet, as underlined previously, wine in 1950 was not yet an object of social distinction for the new bourgeoisie, as was the case with theatre or opera.[3]

Barthes aside, several other reasons could be invoked to explain the relative silence in regard to wine drinking in intellectual and academic circles. Firstly, gastronomic literature and its construction as a literary genre dominated and largely eclipsed the establishment of a separate genre of oenological literature. Secondly, historians were traditionally reluctant to study the field of drinking and alcohol. Indeed as Myriam Tsikounas argued in a collective book *Histoire de l'alcool* published with Thierry Fillaud and Véronique Nahoum-Grappe, 'Earlier French historians ignored drinking and drunkenness and their conception of history was unfavourable to the systematic study of drinking'.[4] Even the *Annales* School of French historians, who had from an early stage made the study of mentalities an object of investigation, tended to ignore drinking even when they turned their attention to food consumption during the 1970s. The few historians who chose to write about wine, such as Roger Dion, a historian and geographer, who published a major study on wine, did so from the perspective of the origins of viticulture, arguing that commercial prospects were the key factor in the creation of French vineyards. Wine consumption remained a taboo topic until the 1990s with the publication of the works of the historians Nourrisson and Garrier, dealing respectively with the drinker in the nineteenth century and a social and cultural history of wine.[5] It is true that the study of alcoholism as a medical disease and sociocultural phenomenon has attracted considerable scholarly interest. But the history of wine and the cultures of its consumption are clearly distinct from the study of alcoholism.

In his study of gastronomic literature, Pascal Ory traces the origins of gastronomic writings back to three main genres which are common to the literature on drinking and which can still be found today under various guises: dietary, poetic and technical/scientific discourse.[6] These three types of discourse offer a window onto the wider contemporary public discourse around wine. First, the dietary discourse refers to the medical and temperance rhetoric, which, in the case of wine, discusses the therapeutic functions or virtues of the product. A good example is provided by the work of Dr Maury, who argued that 'wine is the best medicine'.[7] There have been many such studies over the centuries, very often written by local notables, bourgeois, professionals or doctors seeking to demonstrate that wine is a distinct and specific type of alcoholic drink, possessing unique medicinal virtues. This is part of a long-established tradition linking the medical profession to local confraternities and gastronomic or regionalist associations and it is true that doctors have traditionally occupied a dominant position as consumers and cultural mediators. Many references to wine consumption and its supposed medicinal benefits can be traced back to the writings of classical authors such as Pliny the elder.

This dietary discourse continues to find supporters today, with many claiming that moderate consumption of wine is better for health than complete abstinence. The medical profession remains deeply divided over the question of alcohol consumption, particularly when it comes to defining moderate consumption, and various thresholds are recommended – from one glass to three glasses a day. The dietary discourse has come back to the fore in the context of recent health campaigns and especially in response to Nicolas Sarkozy's campaign against drink-driving. The revival of interest in the alleged medicinal properties of wine has coincided with the growing modern obsession with health and well-being. As we have seen, interest has focused upon what has been termed the 'French paradox', which argues that high red wine consumption helps to explain the relatively low incidence of coronary heart disease in France, despite the national diet being rich in saturated fat. In 2000, another medical development, the concept of *Vinothérapie* was created in the Bordelais to promote the medicinal virtues of wine. Inspired by the model of the spa, which has come back into fashion, a new concept of health and wine has been created with *Les Sources de Caudalie*. This spa, which treats patients with wine and its by-products, recently became internationalized, establishing itself in Italy and America. A series of publications bears witness to this revival of interest, be they *La Cure de raisin* (A Diet of Grapes) by Johanna

Brand (2000) or *Le Vin aliment de santé* (Wine a Healthy Food) by Jean-Marc Carité (1999), arguing that wine, and in particular red wine, is part of a healthy lifestyle associated with the French diet.

The poetic genre is also common to both gastronomic and oenological literature and it has been characterized by the permanent presence of folkloric writings associated with elitist wine societies or *sociétés de caveaux* (wine clubs).[8] This literary form, which has as its focus the sensual experience attached to alcohol drinking, is a feature of the folkloric regional wine culture which developed in the nineteenth century. Annibal de Monchanut's, *Vieil Hypocras au vin de Beaune* stands out as one of the earliest examples of what would become a prolific genre. More than a century later, in 1916, at the height of the First World War, Jean Bastia wrote a play *Le Pinard* (Plonk) which was performed with great popular success in Paris and in regional theatres, offering another example of the ties between wine and patriotism. By displaying different aspects of regional culture and its folklore, the literary genre helped to celebrate both the region and the nation by using humour and by debating current events. Folkloric writings are still a dominant feature of the regionalist discourse on wine, and Pierre Poupon, a Burgundian wine merchant, and Jean-François Bazin, a local politician, exemplify through their many publications this relationship between poetic genre and oenological discourse, offering a regional stance on wine and literary writings.[9]

Finally the technical or scientific genre represents the third type of literary work dealing with wine as well as with viticulture. There is a venerable literary tradition of agricultural writings of this type and titles such as *Traité sur la nature et sur la culture de la vigne, sur le vin, sur la façon de le faire et la manière de bien le gouverner* (Treatise on the Nature and Culture of the Vine, on Wine, its Production and its Good Husbandry) published in 1759 by Nicolas Bidet, *sommelier* at the court, and Edme Béguillet and his *Œnologie ou discours sur la meilleure méthode de faire le vin et de cultiver la vigne* (Oenology, or Discourse on the Best Method Used to Make Wine and to Cultivate the Vine) written in 1770 for an agricultural show organized by the Académie of Metz belong to this discursive field. These works were the ancestors of a technical literature which has progressively differentiated the art of drinking from that of cultivating vines. According to Fernandez, the foundations of a modern oenological culture were laid between the inter-war years and the early 1960s.[10] This development accompanied a transformation of gastronomic norms as the complementarity of wine and food became established alongside the emergence of an oenophile avant-garde committed to making wine tasting a recognized part of wine drinking culture. The development of oenology as a recognized scientific discipline, a branch of chemistry, played a major role in the diffusion of oenological culture and the growth of wine tasting as a separate literary field, particularly once oenological ideas and principles were diffused via the media and literary publications.

This mediatization of oenology came long after its original recognition as a science, which at the time had provoked a radical rupture in the prevailing discourses on wine. This first rupture was linked to the advance of scientific knowledge about the processes involved in the ageing of wines, but it was also connected to the advances in scientific knowledge, with the work of Louis Pasteur having a particularly profound impact. Oenological discourse acquired respect in scientific circles through the works of Ulysse Gayon, a student of Pasteur, who in 1916 created a national diploma in oenology at the University of Bordeaux. The tradition was subsequently maintained with the appointment of leading figures such as Professor Ribereau-Gayon and, later, Dr Emile Peynaud, whose publications played a major role in winning recognition for oenology as a branch of chemistry, but also as a scientific method popularized for analysing wine.[11] Many works had been published about wine tasting, but it was only with the institutional recognition provided by the University of Bordeaux in the field of sensorial analysis and its subsequent diffusion in professional circles, for example by Max Léglise in Burgundy (at the Station Oenologique de Beaune) and Émile Peynaud at Bordeaux, that a veritable oenological revolution took root. This silent revolution, which began in the 1960s, crystallized in the 1980s with the publication of Peynaud's best-selling work, *Le Goût du vin* (The Taste of Wine), which was widely read not only by professionals, but also by an increasingly numerous wine-loving middle class.

A comparison of Léglise and Peynaud, two particularly well-known figures from the world of wine in post-war France, illustrates the lack of a coherent national discourse at the time in relation to wine tasting and its techniques. Émile Peynaud, recognizing the lack of a common standard for wine tastings, cited at least five different methods used to analyse wines, namely commercial, technical, comparative, hedonistic and analytical wine tasting, demonstrating the heterogeneous nature of the technique, leading him to argue in favour of a single common approach such as sensorial analysis.[12] To put his ideas into context, it is helpful to recall that before the 1960s most French wine growers had never tasted wines from other wine growers. As a prominent Burgundian wine merchant remarked, 'When I organized the first wine tasting between wine growers in 1975, they were shocked by the idea of drinking wine from other competitors in the same region.' He was not alone in seeking to educate wine consumers, and Steven Spurrier, an Englishman living in France, promoted similar tastings with the opening of the Caves de la Madeleine in 1973 and later the Académie du Vin in Paris.

Both Peynaud and Léglise were skilled disseminators of their respective messages, and they were capable of talking and writing about wine and wine tasting in a clear and accessible fashion inspired by their scientific training. Their publications are amongst the most prominent and commonly displayed tomes in the libraries of wine lovers, attesting the real impact they had on wine culture as a whole. They are also on display in every French library. For instance, Léglise's *Initiation à la dégustation des grands vins* (Initiation to the Tasting of Great Wines, 1984) and Peynaud's *Le Goût du vin* have contributed to the popularization of wine tasting and its methods. For Léglise (*Initiation*, p. 15; my own translation), 'There was a time when nothing was written on wine tasting without using superlatives, exclamation marks, hyperboles or flowery images.' With the sensorial analysis and the methods used by Peynaud, wine tasting became a more respected scientific activity, a branch of chemistry. Generations of young wine professionals were educated at Bordeaux, and today oenology has gained international recognition. Peynaud considered the ability to taste accurately to be as essential to good winemaking as a thorough grasp of oenology. In *Le Goût du vin*, he wrote: 'I am not sure whether I have contributed more by making tasting an introduction to oenology or oenology an introduction to tasting.' Both wine production and consumption were affected by this scientific revolution, and before the end of the 1960s wine tasting became common practice amongst the majority of young wine producers. Wine merchants and *courtiers* (brokers), on the other hand, had always tasted widely, but monopolized a specialized expertise on wines.

2. Wine discourses and modernity

Oenological discourse under its diverse current forms is thus a recent creation that needs to be contextualized in relation not only to the history of gastronomic writing, but also to the emergence of a new wine culture.[13] The emergence of the oenologist as a critical voice in the 1970s was demonstrated by the appearance of a series of new publications devoted entirely to wine. This development was accompanied by the emergence at the end of the 1960s of the figure of the wine critic alongside the oenologist, the *vigneron* and the *sommelier*, who were all becoming increasingly visible categories of actors in the wine sector and in the wider public media. At the same time, there was a reorganization of the journalistic landscape: the magazine *Cuisines de France* became *Cuisines et Vins de France* in 1950, but it is only since the 1970s, that a specialized oenological press has become established with the *Revue des Vins de France* (*RVF*) in 1970 and *L'Amateur de Bordeaux* (1981).[14] Perhaps surprisingly, given the overwhelmingly masculine nature of wine culture, the media have also targeted women. Magazines such as *Elle* began publishing Christmas specials devoted to a selection of wines chosen to accompany the festive meal from as early as 1958, and from 17 November 1980 devoted an entire weekly section to 'Your wine guide', which subsequently was renamed 'Vin en vrac', and then 'Wine and friendship'.[15] In 1984, Jon Winroth launched a new weekly column in *Elle* entitled 'Bottle of the week', although this initiative was short-lived despite growing evidence of interest in wine amongst women.

The profusion of discourses on wine and the confusing messages they convey has not been helped by the lack of professional expertise amongst the journalists concerned, many of whom possessed at best a knowledge of gastronomy or were trained on the job. Fernandez cites the examples of Michel Dovaz, Thierry Desseauve and Dominique Couvreur, all well-known French wine critics, who began their careers writing for gastronomic journals, but who followed different paths to become wine critics.[16] It was during the 1980s and 1990s that specialized publications on wine emerged and wine critics established a professional code based on an intense and critical practice of wine tasting and collective assessment. In these writings about wine, those who knew how to speak and write about wine, and had therefore mastered a normative language, occupied a privileged position. It could be argued that they share a literary style and a real knowledge of the world of wine. They have the power to make or break reputations. By contrast, I have often been surprised by the silence of the *vigneron*, compared with the loquacity of the critics or experts tasting his products. The two expertises, tasting and writing, are not always commonly found amongst the critics as they require several skills, and the oenological press has looked for the combination of cultural capital and competences in wine tasting.[17] When they combine both, they gain access to a greater legitimacy in professional circles and their networks of expertise ensure that their judgements on producers are collectively regulated.[18]

The development of this specialized wine press and of wine guides was part of a global trend which had its roots in the Anglo-Saxon world. Here too publications responding to the lifestyle and expectations of a growing and affluent middle class anxious for advice about their choice of wines enjoyed immense success. Some of these guides such as *Parker's Wine Buyer's Guide* or Hugh Johnson's *Worldwide Wine Guide* have been translated for the French market and are commonly used for reference by French wine lovers. As Garcia-Parpet has argued, greater variety and range of publications is a distinctive feature of the French market.[19] This trend confirms the fragmentation of French wine drinking culture. In 1999, the *Guide Hachette* sold 150,000 copies, while the guide by wine guru Robert Parker registered 60,000 copies. According to Mme Montalbetti, editor of the *Guide Hachette*, 'Both guides aim at different publics: Parker's book is the work of a man with a school of thought [specific expectations in terms of wine's taste] and a very personal approach to wine. It is what we called an art book, while the *Guide Hachette* does not have an *esprit d'école* [school of thought].' Another characteristic of the *Guide Hachette* is the diversity of consumers it wishes to reach: 'To prescribe a quest and a diversity of taste is how I see its main role,' insisted Mme Montalbetti on several occasions during our interview. It could nevertheless be argued that in reality the *Guide Hachette* reproduces the AOC edifice and is far from an exhaustive and partial guide.

If the works of Robert Parker or the *Guide Hachette* are the international stars of the genre, many other personalities from the world of wine have been contributing to the trend, for example Dovaz or Bettane, both journalists, publishing their own guides and Ribereau-Gayon, an oenologist, writing a *Guide pratique des vins de*

France. What is telling about these guides is that each of them contributes a specific perspective on wine with a distinct language and format, emphasizing either the status of the author in the wine profession as a reputed or objective taster or the systematic organization behind the wine tastings of the products they compare. They also reflect the various discourses around wine as an object of consumption. Their respective views about the world of wine are contingent on the objectives they have set for their guide and to their position in the wine profession relative to the market. For instance, the *Guide Hachette* is more focused on the consumer, and as a consequence achieving recognition in its pages is something that is particularly valuable for young or new wine growers developing *vente directe* and in need of publicity. The guide co-edited by Dovaz and Bettane focuses more on high-quality wines that are already well known in the international market, and thus compete with the Anglo-Saxon gurus.

The world of both wine guides and connoisseurs in France is constructed on the foundations laid by the ideology of the AOC, which was created after the First World War and has now spread to foodstuffs and other traditional products, both in France and elsewhere in Europe. The literary field reflects the ideology of the AOC, as each guide is structured around regions, denomination of origin, villages, wine growers and co-operatives. If we take the example of the *Guide Hachette*, its tasting is organized in line with the regions and denominations authorized by the AOC. During the tastings that I observed in Beaune in 1999, the wines from different AOCs were tasted together. The whole exercise was controlled by professionals and the experts, who aimed to classify and rank the various producers within the same AOC, which underlines the fact that competition remains constructed at a local rather than at a national level. Their judgement, which is presented as being as 'objective and professional' as possible, is rarely unanimous.

In France, definitions of the quality of wine could be said to be 'an affair of specialists', and recent studies have argued that quality is a subjective issue and that the legitimacy of the process of decision-making in the wine-tasting committees relies upon a consensual and negotiated process rather than on an objective evaluation of the product.[20] The interviews that I have conducted over the last ten years with various actors in the wine industry confirm this analysis. They also show very clearly that different professions in the wine industry, from wine waiters to oenologists, use different languages to describe the same product. The growing wine literature underlines this lack of a unified and collective language as far as wine tasting is concerned; it also confirms the fragmented nature of wine drinking culture. Through the use of specific language, rituals and practices, issues of power are at stake as groups of individuals seek to dominate others, which calls to mind Giddens's argument that power is regarded as generated in and through the reproduction of structures of domination.[21] Clearly, in an area where the French state is still very active, new groups headed by the specialized press and a vocal lobby of producers have sought to empower themselves through their publications. Yet the process remains heterogeneous and lacking any strong sense of national coherence.

The wine sector is undeniably defined by a wide range of actors intervening at different points of the chain of production, and each profession is defined by a particular jargon and discourse, although two discursive fields are very often presented in opposition. For the oenologist who has a scientific training, wine is approached by a range of descriptive elements, which makes it a technical, highly impersonal and scientific commodity, while for the *sommelier*, wine is often seen as a symbolic, poetic and sensorial product. In *Le Goût du vin*, Peynaud warns the reader against indiscriminate use of the entire wine vocabulary, adding that the oenologist has the duty to contribute to the perfection of the art by defining what is meant behind the use of specific words: 'Tasting is their sphere, their speciality and where wine knowledge is concerned they preserve their expertise ... it is now up to oenologists to annexe and develop the field of tasting.'[22]

The spectrum used for describing wine from very precise correlates of chemical, vegetal and mineral components to an array of vague and idiosyncratic metaphorical constructions reflects the tensions facing oenologists, and for Peynaud, the constitution of a specific vocabulary was part of the establishment of the discipline as a branch of chemistry.

His comments call to mind the argument of Claude Fischler, who suggested that there are commonly two types of drinking cultures, illustrating the tensions underlined earlier between the oenologist and the *sommelier*, between *'boire froid* [drinking cold] characterized by a technical approach that dissects, analyses and finds defects, and *boire chaud* [drinking warm], which dreams, imagines, remembers, feels and eventually gets intoxicated with sensations'.[23] The American anthropologist Robert Ulin has used this dichotomy in his analysis of the vineyards of south-west France, opposing two different conceptions of the worlds dividing the profession, one technical and the other cultural, describing the differences between the scientists and the artisans in the world of wine.[24] While the scientific dimension has taken over the professional arena, the human or hedonistic dimension has growing popular appeal, with wine consumers and wine lovers, dominating the literary field.

3. Wine and contemporary writings: 'True France'

The emergence of an oenological discourse after 1970 took place in the context of the development of a new gastronomic discourse, the revival of regional identity and the transformations of the wine sector through the impact of the establishment of *métiers de la vigne et du vin*. The 1980s saw reforms of the educational system with a development of professional training, and in this context the food and wine sector acquired more visibility in its own right as professions such as *sommeliers* achieved recognition. At the same time, wine became a cultural object and the focus of passionate debate about its place in French society. Far from being consensual, these debates reveal the changes and tensions at the heart of French cultural identity in the context of a country that could be said to be obsessed with nostalgia.[25] If one thinks of the ongoing conflicts between *terroir* and brands, artisanship and industrialization, rural and urban, liberalism and protectionism, the position of the oenological discourse as defined above has been one of tradition, with emphasis upon local identity, authenticity and regionalism. This vision has developed in parallel with the progressive take-over by the *vignerons* of the whole chain of production through increased landownership, the development of *vente directe* (direct sale to consumers) and the mediatization of the profession as the unique guarantor of quality and safety. The 'authentic' producer, his family history and artisanship offer an extremely marketable dimension to wine production, which can be presented as guaranteeing a well-defined quality product in an era of industrialization and anonymity.

This ideal of wine production as a traditional craft has emerged in parallel with the rise of the oenologist, whose technical and scientific certainties have earned the sobriquet of 'wine doctor' or, in extreme cases, 'guru of wine'. There are clearly real conflicts between discourses that on the one hand preach the virtues of the unchanging, artisanal craft of the *vigneron*, while simultaneously extolling the expertise of the 'scientific' oenologist. That said, it is the *vigneron* who dominates the scene as the main actor of regional identities and *terroir*, figuring at the crossroads of various other discourses on *ruralité*, artisanship, tourism, leisure and local identity. Amongst the many publications that illustrate this tendency, the examples of wine growers publishing their memoirs as the accounts of a laborious life working in the vineyards stand out.[26] Yet it is interesting that no wine grower has directly contributed to the literature on wine tasting, tending instead to concentrate on stories telling their life rather than commenting on the overall quality of wines from their region.

The promotion of tourism based on the attractions of rurality and authenticity has facilitated the growing visibility of the *vigneron* as a leading actor in rural development. From the 1990s onwards, many regional administrations collaborated with the local *syndicats d'initiative* (tourist boards) to create wine tours, establishing networks of producers, *vignerons* and heritage sites to promote the discovery of rural France through the consumption of food and wine. In Burgundy, for example, the Hautes-Côtes region, which was given a specific AOC in 1961, promoted its wines by advertising the region as a distinct touristic and rural part of Burgundy, using initiatives such as the Maison des Hautes-Côtes (a local restaurant and a cultural centre which combined a cellar and a shop) and by compiling *routes des crus* (wine tours). Most of the project was organized by local political activists, notably Bernard Hudelot and the parliamentary deputy, Lucien Jacob, whose family had vineyards in the area and who was a leader of the campaign to put the Hautes-Côtes on the map of Burgundy.[27] The campaign to promote the Hautes-Côtes was a good example of what we might call microregionalism with a hitherto poor and rather neglected *vignoble* attaching itself to the Burgundian label, which gave it access to wider national and eventually global markets. As a result of this successful campaign, books were published on the region, its producers, folklore and cultural activities, a museum was created by Jean-François Bazin, himself a local politician and prolific author on the region and its wines.[28] New professional opportunities were opened up for a number of local wine specialists to obtain social recognition through the publication of their knowledge or expertise, contributing to the construction of regional and national wine culture.

Many examples could be given of specific trajectories illustrating the new ingredients of this regional revival. In Burgundy, the example of Jacky Rigaux, 'voice of the *terroir*', illustrates this growing visibility of wine specialists in France. Named by the press, the '*écrivin*' (a play on words about wine writing) of *terroirs*, he has published extensively on Burgundy wines with books such as *Odes aux grands vins de Bourgogne* (1997) or *Le terroir et le vigneron* (2006), and has had several of his books translated into English. Rigaux is responsible for teaching a diploma entitled 'Wine and culture' at the University of Dijon and for organizing wine-tasting sessions around the various *terroirs*. In this sense, he follows in the footsteps of the legendary Gaston Roupnel, who from the 1920s onwards was at the forefront of the Burgundian regionalist folklore movement.[29] Interestingly, Rigaux also presents himself as a leading figure in the anti-globalization campaign supporting José Bové in his various campaigns and publishing against globalization. Rigaux's connections to the local university provide a veneer of legitimacy for his writings on wine and the region, repeating a strategy from the interwar period of creating a new regionalism based on the relationship between local economic interests and the university.

At a local level, the construction of social and political networks around the wine profession, combined with other activities such as farmers' markets, the heritage industry and restaurants or gastronomic fairs, offered a platform for the display of a regional culture by ensuring the dissemination of a variety of publications based on these webs of knowledge. The establishment of these regional networks has been mirrored at a national level through the works of critics, *sommeliers*, chefs and stars of the world of wine in Paris and other major culinary centres. These actors, by their respective contributions, have established a wider network around specific wine growers, consolidating their reputation in the development of a French wine drinking culture. Bernard Pivot, a literary critic who owns a vineyard in the Beaujolais and has for many years organized a literary review programme on French television, provides a good example of the broader wine culture. Pivot, host of the popular *Bouillon de culture*,[30] has regularly invited celebrities from the world of wine to participate on his programme. Superstars such as Gérard Depardieu and Carole Bouquet have also given a new status to wine production by making public their ownership of vineyards in France and Italy and popularizing the life of the wine grower as the paragon of the rural ideal.

In Bordeaux, Bernard Ginestet is another example of how the worlds of wine and celebrity mix. Before the economic crisis of 1973, the Ginestets had been one of the most powerful families of wine merchants in the Bordelais. With three unsold vintages in their cellars, they were forced to sell not just their business but the great symbol of their prestige, Château Margaux, perhaps the most beautiful of all the Bordeaux wine properties. Along with Lafite Rothschild, Mouton Rothschild, Latour and Haut Brion, Château Margaux is one of the premier Bordeaux vineyards. Perhaps Bernard Ginestet could have recovered along with the wine trade, but casting a wider net, he lived for writing, painting, music and politics. He wrote his first book, *Le Grand Dam*, a novel, when he was in his twenties. It was followed by *La Bouillie bordelaise*, a parody of the Bordeaux wine trade that gained him considerable attention and more than a few enemies. The title means 'Bordeaux Mixture' and refers to a copper sulphate spray used to protect vines from disease. Ginestet also turned his hand to more serious writing. Two books, one on the wines of Margaux – the *commune*, not just the château – and another on the neighbouring *commune* of Saint-Julien, evolved into a series known collectively as Le Grand Bernard. He wrote some of these and edited the others. At the last count there were about thirty volumes under the Grand Bernard title. Ginestet was passionate about all literature and was a regular guest on literary talk shows on French television. He even became mayor of Margaux for almost twenty years, spending a good part of every day in his office at the town hall. Seeking a wider role in politics, he ran several times, unsuccessfully, for a seat in the National Assembly.

In historical terms, this rhetoric of tradition, *terroir* and *vigneron* is heavily charged with historical, cultural and political significance and is clearly intended to associate wine production with the evocative concepts of authenticity, quality and tradition. These cultural and discursive strategies are designed to serve various interests, from a nostalgic consumption of wine to a commitment to an essentialist conception of France that is very often at the core of conservative and agrarian ideologies. Herman Lebovics in his work on French cultural identity analyses conventional discourses about the nature of identity of 'true France' as reactionary.[31] It is a view that is widely held, and it presents France as the source of reactionary political and social agendas.[32] Yet, as Whalen has demonstrated, resuscitated or newly created traditions serve to link regional interests to a French national political identity, and such rhetoric can serve different purposes today and cannot be analysed simply in political and ideological terms.[33] Some of these essentialist values have more to do with the position of France in the international and European spheres, arguing for a specific national position and cultural exception as part of a policy of economic protectionism for key sectors such as viticulture, but others refer to global values circulating at transnational level around the wine sector.

This construction of the wine grower as a key figure of the world of wine responds to new societal preoccupations. First, his representation as a male figure is that of the powerful, charismatic and 'noble' voice of a rural community which seems to have been empowered by its confrontation with modernity. The pace of social and economic modernization poses a challenge to traditional rural communities, and in this context wine growers have sought to represent themselves as the last bastion of a declining world. Yet the picture is more complex, as some drive around in their 4 x 4s, earning many times more than their predecessors, while others are struggling. Secondly, it is a response to internal changes which have transformed the position of the wine grower in the wine sector giving, it seems, more power to the oenologist, 'flying winemaker' or technician, all of whom can be seen as figures of modernity. Yet the average wine grower has benefited from this well-orchestrated construction headed by leading professionals and politicians. This is a crucial aspect of this construction, the wine grower as the last representative of tradition, the last bastion against modernity and economic liberalization.

4. Wine and television

If the literary production devoted to the world of wine has boomed since the 1990s, the treatment of wine in television broadcasting has been characterized by a more progressive and cyclical growth. My research on the treatment of wine and viticulture by French television broadcasters has concentrated on the audiovisual archives of the Institut National Audiovisuel (INA), established from 1944 until May 2004 and designed to answer questions such as 'How has French television dealt with the object "wine"?' and 'What were the main topics shown by French television?'[34] Overall, 3,721 programmes dealing with wine were broadcast on French television from the wine festival (*La Fête de la vigne*) (first programme 12 September 1941) to *Conseils les caves à vin* (last programme selected: 3 April 2004, advice on how to constitute a wine cellar). For each of the programmes we set a series of criteria for the analysis: year of programme, list of descriptive terms, such as type of programme (news or documentary) or key words established from a list constituted over the years and counting around 150 terms related to wine. Two very different databases were used to compile the corpus on 'wine', constituted from 1944 until today, including all of the archives of the INA from the beginnings of French television. This is described as a heterogeneous database, and it reflects the archival interest and not the diffusion. A second corpus created by the INA from 1995 corresponds to the legal deposit of all television programmes and is therefore more homogeneous in terms of its collection and description. The database on 'wine' has been constituted using Mediacorpus and a number of key words such as 'vine', 'oenologist', 'viticulture', 'tasting', and so on.[35] The Mediacorpus software enabled the selection of all programmes dealing with our object of analysis by using 'index key words' or 'index title' or 'general index', which refer to the description of the programme selected and its broadcast date.

Several topics have been chosen for the constitution of the database and have been cross-referenced to the corpus on 'wine'. They include the following keywords: oenologist, *sommelier*, wine lovers, women, festivals and confraternities, drinking and wine consumption, good wines and AOC, frauds, environmental issues, regions and wine-growing areas, Europe, colonies, international/exports, famous places/events or personalities associated with wine culture such as the Hospices de Beaune, Robert Parker and Vinexpo. Then the corpus constituted was cleaned and checked for any 'parasites' such as the same programme transmitted twice or topics with a low frequency (only once or twice shown over the period covered). If there are clearly some methodological limits attached to the corpus, it is nevertheless valuable to see which themes have been broadcast by French television from 1945 as wine culture forms a whole body of knowledge, images and representations which are at the heart of our discussions on consumption and national identity. For purposes of statistical analysis, the periods selected are organized by decades.

The history of wine has traditionally been divided between those who write about wine production and those who analyse its consumption, with the two usually being presented as two separate technical worlds: viticulture dealing with nature and its control (agronomy), viniculture dealing with the science of making wine (oenology). Although it could be argued that both of these form part of the whole, they have nevertheless always required different skills and competences, which were not always historically and geographically unified. The literary field has to a large extent mirrored this divide, and most publications have either focused on viticulture, nature, *terroir* or geography or have addressed either the art of making or the act of drinking wine.

If we adopt this line of demarcation to explore the ways in which television has favoured one or the other, it is interesting to note that in broadcasting terms both expanded substantially after 1960, with an initial slight bias in favour of viticulture. Graph 4.1 is presented by decade and demonstrates a continuous and steady increase of broadcasts for both fields during that period especially from the 1960s. Viticulture benefited most from this until the 1990s, as several perennial themes recurred associated with grape harvests, specific places or events (for example the wine auction of the Hospices de Beaune), festivals of wine growers (the Saint-Vincent Tournante) and issues related to agricultural matters or modern techniques such as the introduction of the mechanical grape harvester.[36] The focus of these programmes was very much on the region or the place of production, illustrating the changes taking place in viticultural techniques. Since the 1990s, there has been a slight decline in broadcasts, although it is likely that this has been reversed with recent controversies and the problems of growing international competition.

Looking at the details of the programmes broadcast during this period, they clearly respond to two major preoccupations for the French media: the series of activities related to wine at regional level, be they annual or exceptional, and the conjectural episodes affecting the wine industry. From the mid-1980s, wine seems to take the lead, with more programmes devoted to its consumption as illustrated in Figure 4.1.

If we examine broadcasting on an annual basis, it is clear that viticulture, like any other agricultural activity, is more likely to be cyclical, responding to the natural calendar. French television has certain perennial topics such as the start of the wine harvest, some key festivals and Beaujolais *nouveau*, but it also responds to economic crises, problems of wine sales, failed harvests or strikes. Periods of calm or even decline in interest, such as that from 1995, were quickly reversed when wine became newsworthy in 2003–4 after the clamp-down on drink-driving which had such serious implications for wine drinking.

Amongst the repository of broadcasts, there are several themes worth examining, either because they have disappeared after enjoying a period of success in broadcasting terms or because they have emerged as the direct result of the transformation of wine culture. Amongst the themes which have become unfashionable are what might be described as popular and working-class styles of wines associated with Paris and its *banlieue*, but also a sociable and café style of consumption that has been all but abandoned. Muscadet (white wine) or *petit vin blanc de Nogent* (typical white wine from Nogent in the suburbs of Paris), which were fashionable in the 1950s and 1960s, particularly with working-class consumers, provide

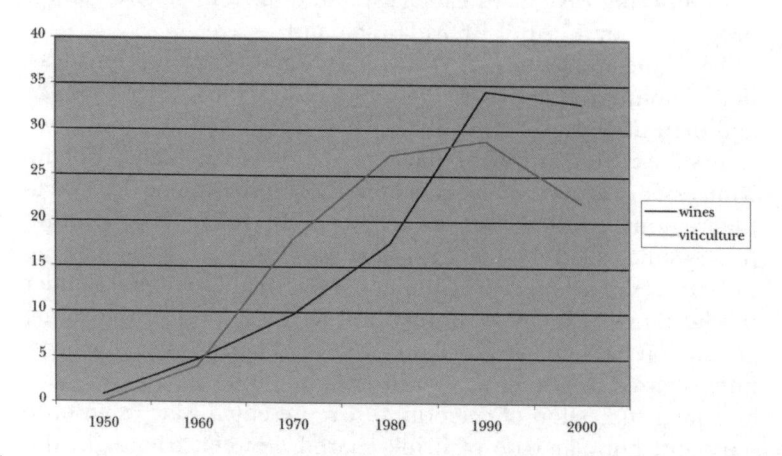

Figure 4.1 Broadcasting wine and vine by decades in French television

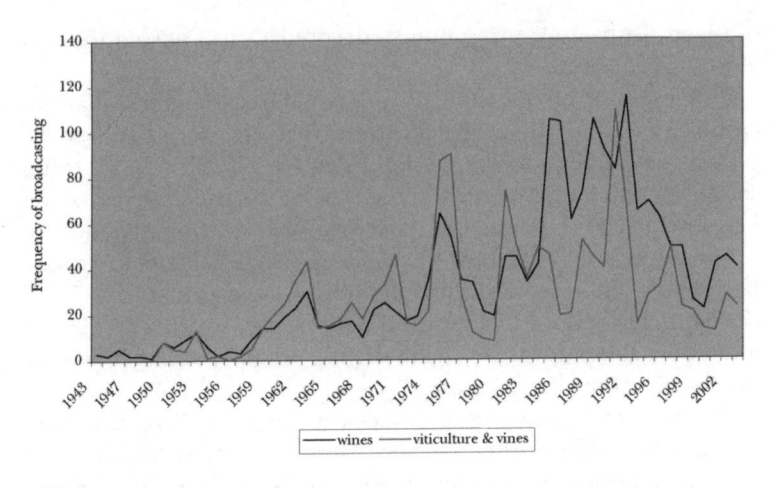

Figure 4.2 Broadcasting wine and vine in French television.

good examples. On 29 July 1948, a television programme was broadcast entitled *The Congress of Muscadet*, followed on 7 October 1969 by *The Harvester in Muscadet*, illustrating the marginal position of this type of wine in French society. It was not until 1989 that it returned to the screens, when it came back to attention in a nostalgic form with programmes under various rubrics, such as harvest, shortage, new Muscadet (like new Beaujolais) and history, to be given a final programme on 17 April 1997 (TF1, 8 p.m.).

The same applies to *Petit Vin blanc de Nogent*, which was broadcast in the months of June 1954, 1957, 1959, 1960, 1963, 1965, 1967–72, and then disappeared until 1985, when it returned as a result of a renewal of the festival of La Fête du petit vin blanc. Roland Nungesser et groupe de Nogent as part of a programme devoted to the regions entitled *Bonjour la France*. In June 1990, another programme called *Ah le petit vin blanc* was broadcast in the news up to 1995 by similar short programmes of less than two minutes under the headings of memory, history and festivals. Most of the young generation has never heard about *petit vin blanc de Nogent*, which was immortalized in a song written in 1943 and interpreted ever since by a long succession of celebrities. It represented wine as an ordinary and popular type of drink shared between friends in the *guingettes* (open-air cafés). These two examples reveal much about the processes taking place around the emergence of the new wine drinking culture, which established itself through a nostalgic relationship to the past. They demonstrate that elements of the past were used to promote a new wine culture made up of old topics as much as new elements in the dissemination of it.

Amongst new elements forming this wine culture in broadcasting that we already have discussed in relation to the literary field, 'women' and 'wine lovers' are particularly revealing. On 18 September 1973, a report of just two minutes entitled *Femme sommelier* was broadcast during the evening news followed by a short documentary, *Femmes et vins* on 29 October 1987, then on 9 September 1991 *Vins de femmes*, followed in 1994 by three different programmes on women and wines which became a standard feature on French television.[37] This growing interest in the relationship between women and wine is indicative of the way in which gender roles have been transformed in France, with women becoming significant both as producers and consumers for the first time.

'Wine lovers' is another topic covered only recently by French television. It is important to note that the use of the terms 'wine lovers' and 'good wines' emerged more or less in parallel up until 1990s. The first programme devoted to wine lovers was broadcast in March 1983 and was entitled *Temps libre aux amateurs de vins* (Leisure Time for Wine Amateurs), but it was not followed by another programme until 1998. In 1991, *Le Bon Vin et les autres* (Good Wines and the Others) was followed in 2002 by *Le Très Bon Vin à portée de tous* (Good Wines for All). More precisely, the term 'winemaking' corresponded to the debates around the rise of oenology and its recognition in the technical sphere, especially in the wine-growing community, while 'wine tasting' has been a continual topic of interest since the broadcast under the intriguing title of *Dégustations de bons vins à Londres* in 1961.

Another new term coined to describe some of the changes affecting wine drinking culture is 'oenology', which appeared for the first time in January 1982 under the title 'Ideas to Follow', and was then given three minutes in 1984 as part of *La Maison de TF1*. Several programmes were broadcast subsequently in 1987, 1993, 1994–5, 2002, 2003 and 2004. It is a good example of how the science of oenology has been incorporated into a wider popular activity illustrated by the timing of these programmes in the evening and aiming at new consumers and wine lovers. Oenology clearly forms an important part of the new wine drinking culture orientated more towards younger people and modern representations of wine. On 15 December 1995, a programme entitled *La Langue du vin, le vin sur la langue*, presented by Bernard Pivot in *Bouillon de culture*, documented the various languages and professions attached to the wine industry. The four professionals sat next to each other and then proceeded to offer completely different discourses on wine, synthesizing all the contradictions attached to wine drinking culture in terms of language acquisition.

The internationalization of the wine market is also an area of preoccupation for the media. A first period, from 1950 to 1980, saw a higher frequency of references to countries such as Germany and eastern Europe, followed by Portugal and Spain; The exception was Australia, first represented in 1962 with a report of the grape harvest carried out with machines. The creation of the Common Market in the 1950s meant that competition first from Italian and subsequently from Spanish producers was growing. From the 1980 onwards, rapid development of New World wines dominated broadcasting, followed by the various European partners joining the Common Market. It is striking that, historically speaking, broadcasting has focused on the growing number of competitors, with Argentina and South Africa amongst the latest.

Throughout the period the threat of foreign competition has therefore been the key theme, and France has always adopted a protectionist approach to its wine market with importation of foreign wines never encouraged. However, in 1976, Steven Spurrier, a wine merchant in Paris, organized a prestigious wine tasting in Paris known as the 'Judgement of Paris' which saw the victory of Californian wines over French Chardonnay such as Bâtard-Montrachet. This notorious Paris tasting took place on 24 May 1976 in the covered terrace at the Intercontinental Hotel. Spurrier, who owned a small wine shop in the city centre and a wine school next door, wanted to draw attention to some exceptional wines from California, then unknown in Paris. He brought together a panel of eleven judges, including Odette Kahn, editor of *La Revue des Vins de France*, Jean-Claude Vrinat and Raymond Oliver of the *Taillevent* and *Grand Véfour* restaurants, the *sommelier* Christian Vanneque of the *Tour d'Argent*, Aubert de Villaine of the Domaine de la Romanée-Conti, Pierre Tari of Château Giscours, Pierre Brejoux of the INAO, Michel Dovaz of the Wine Institute of France and Claude Dubois-Millot and Patricia Gallagher of the Académie du Vin. The results were so shocking that some of the tasters refused to admit that they had been on the jury. The media virtually ignored the story and *Le Monde* refused to publish it. Again this was not broadcast on television, demonstrating clearly that the French felt offended by the outcomes of the tasting.

The internationalization of the wine market has been intrinsically linked to the progressive process of European integration and successive reforms affecting viticulture in the Community. Europe as a term of broadcast has fluctuated, depending upon circumstances. If we examine references to the European Community, not surprisingly we find peaks associated with major crises. Amongst the most significant was that of 1983, when the Dublin agreements introduced a reduction of quotas for distillation that led to the wine war, and that of GATT (General Agreement on Tariffs and Trade) in 1992. On 5 December 1985, *Le Monde* commented on the agreement reached by the ten European member states two days earlier in Dublin on the reform of the common organization of the market in wine undertaken to facilitate the enlargement of the European Community to include Spain and Portugal. French television covered the negotiation in great detail with regular news items devoted to it.

Another topic of growing concern for broadcasters is the issue of wine and health, something that paradoxically has become ever more important despite declining alcohol consumption. The Évin law, which was the cause of intense debate, was presented by the French media as a national controversy with significant implications for French society. Following the adoption of the Évin law, the powerful wine lobby mobilized the regional bodies and their representatives from the wine sector in a bid to convince their deputies of its potentially disastrous consequences. In Burgundy, the adoption of the Évin law was said to have cost the local Socialist deputy, Claude Patriat, his seat for not responding energetically enough on behalf of the wine profession. Once elected, his successor was quick to seek appointment as the leader of the *Groupe d'Études Viticoles* (Viticulture Study Group) in the National Assembly. From 24 February 2005 when the Evin law was modified following the lobby organized by the wine sector, deputies and various personalities from the world of wine signed an agreement with the ANPAA (Association Nationale pour la Prévention en Alcoologie et en Addictologie) to incorporate an article mentioning the right to

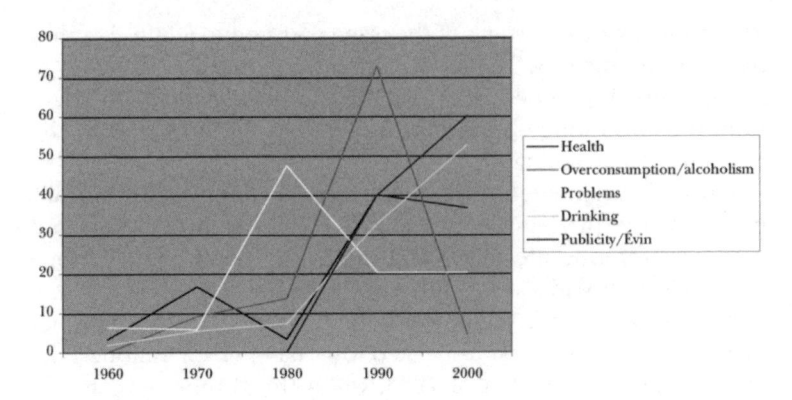

Figure 4.3 Health and Wine.

include in the publicity references to *terroir*, distinctions obtained and the denomination of origin. It also authorizes the use of objective references to colours, olfactory and gustatory characteristics of the product. French television reported at regular intervals the discussions and negotiations around the Évin law and covered most of the debates, for example, with nearly two minutes devoted to the law on 12 December 1990 at 1 p.m on national news.

One final area of note is the competition between wine-growing regions. Television broadcasts reflect historical and political processes as well as the competition between French wine regions as illustrated by figures 4.4 and 4.5. Behind each region, there are particular images and cultural references which are articulated, and in deciding to associate specific events with specific places, it could be argued that television contributes to the mapping of French vineyards in the public imagination. Figure 4.4 gives a more precise idea about the way the various wine-growing regions were represented on French television between 1950 and 2000.[38]

Figure 4.4 makes it very clear that competition has increased, with the number of regions involved rising from six in the 1950s to fifteen in 2000–4. The 1980s and 1990s marked a turning-point with new regions becoming visible on the French wine landscape. Some of them could be seen as peripheral to other famous regions (Aude or Côtes du Rhône), others reveal the major structural transformation taking place in some of the less prestigious vineyards (Hérault or Corbières). New vineyards are also coming to the fore under the impact of tourism, the rise of wine culture and regionalism.

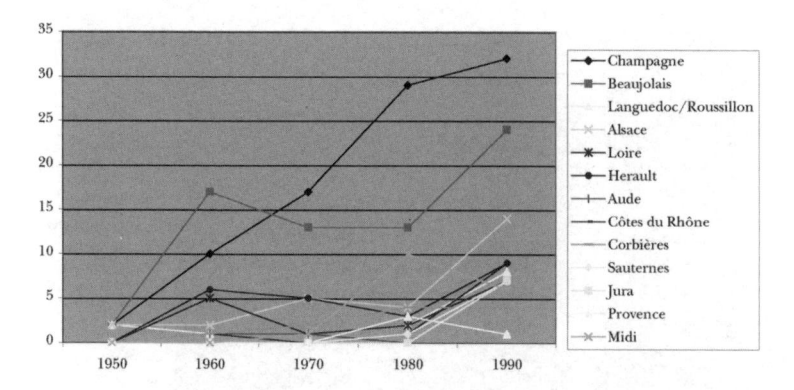

Figure 4.4 Wine regions and television broadcasts.

Amongst the various regions represented, there are at least three identifiable groups of wine-producing areas: one dominant and emblematic group formed by the oldest and most traditional vineyards with an established historical reputation, highly prestigious AOCs such as Burgundy, Champagne, Bordeaux and Beaujolais, which have been competing but remain in a powerful position in broadcasting terms, and another group of vineyards which are less well established and therefore have had a less visible screen presence, such as Alsace or Languedoc. A third group is formed by the smaller and less historically visible vineyards which have fallen behind in terms of media attention.

Figure 4.5 suggests, as we might expect, that the main competition has been between Burgundy and Bordeaux, while Champagne has always arguably occupied a unique position as it has been internationalized and commercialized in a much more organized and efficient way around the big companies such as Moët & Chandon or Mercier.[39] The image of Champagne as a luxurious, expensive, festive and international wine remains a powerful tool in the hands of the region and it explains to some extent the continuing appeal of the product. The case of Beaujolais is explained partly by its proximity to Burgundy, its association with the Beaujolais *nouveau* phenomenon and the urban and international character of its clientele, which was a feature of its success in both the 1950s and again in the 1980s.

Historically, Burgundy and Bordeaux dominated French vineyards, and their constant competition is a permanent element of

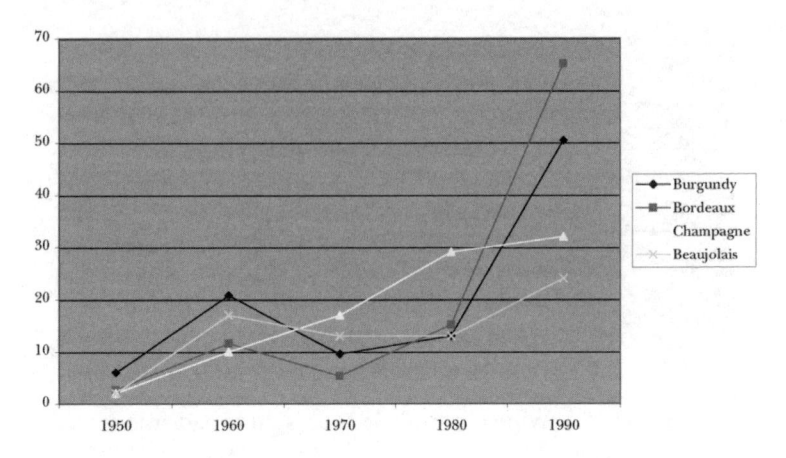

Figure 4.5 Broadcasting historical/traditional vineyards.

French national discourse. They represented the different ends of the spectrum of French vineyards, Bordeaux wines being associated with aristocratic and elitist clients while Burgundy has always been seen as the wine of a more rustic and bourgeois type of consumer. It is interesting that with the shift towards wine culture in broadcasting and the growing urbanization of French society, Bordeaux comes to the fore in terms of time devoted to it and frequency of broadcasts. In some ways it could be said to represent a modern icon of French society, famous for the rejuvenation of the city and an incarnation of the wine and oenological revolution that has occurred in recent years, leaving Burgundy in its wake. The competition between regional economies and local wine production through television contributes to the construction of a national wine community as part of the democratized discourse and its visual culture. Burgundy is represented by the Vente des Vins des Hospices de Beaune and the image of the peasant wine grower in his cellar, while Bordeaux is associated with the modernity of the cellars, architecture, art and the Rothschild family. It has to be said that the role of political actors, regional wine committees and the wine profession as a whole reinforces this mapping of regions. The fierce competition between them allows this national model to become more dynamic and to embrace the modernity of the wandering drinker as it enables him/her to travel through the regions mapped in the course of the programmes.

5. Wine discourses and identification

In the profusion of discourses and images surrounding wine, it is possible to identify a number of contradictions that lie at the heart of French drinking culture. Among them, technical progress versus artisanship, *vignerons* versus wine merchants, *terroir* versus brands, nation versus region, health versus alcohol consumption – all stand out as the ingredients of a heterogeneous culture that creates tensions between various social groups in French society. The explosion of discourses and debates about wine cannot disguise the fact that the new wine culture is dominated by middle-class, white professional males of thirty-five years or older. Yet if it is important to be aware of this fact, it is nevertheless significant that it is part of a broader social movement connected to the expansion of leisure culture facilitated by the extension of annual holiday periods, the lowering of the retirement age and the new thirty-five-hour week. Yet the international market and global pressures have strengthened the wine sector and have politicized wine as an element of the 'cultural exception'.[40] The process of economic liberalization is the common background behind the modernization of French society, and it has had a major impact on national drinking culture. The role played by culture in the expression of local and national identity and in the process whereby individuals engage with the past and build their future through the consumption of a wide range of cultural artefacts such as wine is telling.

Homogeneity has been replaced by diversity, stable identities have given way to salience, and culture is seen as fragmented. Traditional community values are perceived as eroded, and the links between people and their communities, real or imagined, have been altered. Wine culture, in this regard, constitutes for specific groups in French society one of the supports for the expression of individual and collective identification. Its construction reveals the social processes by which vocal and powerful groups such as wine growers are able to raise their voices to counteract wider processes of modernization. Yet, the balance between producers and consumers remains difficult to maintain. Far from being homogeneous, the construction reveals the shared normative orientations underlying wine consumption, but also its divisive features. It illustrates the values embedded in wine consumption and the attachment of French people to rural society, time, commensality and sociability, as well as their concerns for the future represented by the forces of globalization, modernity and multiculturalism, which are the new points of tension. All of these values act as markers of past identity or new ties in order to grasp and to make sense of the future.

Wine drinking culture in this new landscape is obviously far from being a homogeneous 'object' of study. This chapter has focused on wine drinking culture under its various guises, illustrating the heterogeneity of the discourses, representations and symbols around wine, all of which contribute to a form of integration, at one level, between specific groups of individuals, but may nevertheless at another more individual level mean different things to different people or create divisive tools to exclude or antagonize. In the case of France, the traditional cohesive functions still operate amongst specific groups of wine consumers or wine lovers, but the divisive functions seem to prevail, undermining some fundamental processes of common solidarity even amongst wine lovers. On the other hand, wine amateurs and the professional and regional elites have exercised a pervasive cultural influence spreading this new wine drinking culture in every direction and trying to re-establish what they see as one of the last bastions of French identity.

Notes

1 Arjun Appadurai, *The Social Life of Things* (Cambridge: Cambridge University Press, 1988).
2 By 'legitimized', I mean categories of actors who have been recognized in the literary field and have been published. They have also acquired a profile in the media.
3 Pierre Bourdieu, *La Distinction. Critique sociale du jugement* (Paris: Les Éditions de Minuit, 1979).
4 Thierry Fillaut, Véronique Nahoum-Grappe and Myriam Tsikounas, *Histoire et alcool*, Logiques sociales (Paris: L'Harmattan, 1999), p. 125.
5 Didier Nourrisson, *Le Buveur du dix-neuvième siècle* (Paris: Albin Michel, 1990) and Gilbert Garrier, *Histoire sociale et culturelle du vin* (Paris: Bordas Cultures, 1995; new edition 1998).
6 Pascal Ory, *Le Discours gastronomique français des origines à nos jours* (Paris: Gallimard/Juillard, 1998).
7 Dr Maury published in 1974; his work was reissued in 1992.
8 For an illustration of this development, see the article by Gilles Laferté, ' "Un folklore" pour journalistes: La confrérie des Chevaliers du Tastevin', *Ethnologies Comparées*, 8 (Spring 2005), 1–32.
9 For the modern usage of this type of writings, see for example the following website referring to Pierre Poupon's writings: *http://*

www.clubgrappe.com/indexeng.htm or his publications such as *Le Vin des souvenirs* and *La Fin d'un millésime*.
10 Jean-Luc Fernandez, *La critique vinicole en France. Pouvoir de prescription et construction de la confiance*, Logiques sociales (Paris: L'Harmattan, 2004), p. 191.
11 Ribereau-Gayon published in 1947 twenty pages on wine tasting in his 'Traité d'œnologie'.
12 Émile Peynaud, *Œnologue dans le siècle* (n.p., La Table Ronde, 1995).
13 Ory, *Le Discours gastronomique*, p. 46.
14 For a detailed and interesting analysis of the emergence of the oenological press see Fernandez, *La Critique vinicole*.
15 I should like to thank Magali Dechen and Hélène Hachenberger of the Bibliothèque Municipale de Dijon for providing me with the analysis of *Elle* in relation to wine.
16 Fernandez, *La Critique vinicole*, p. 50.
17 Ibid., p. 52.
18 Ibid., p. 50.
19 Marie-France Garcia-Parpet, 'Le terroir, le cépage et la marque. Stratégies de valorisation des vins dans un contexte mondial', *Cahiers d'Économie et Sociologie Rurales*, 60–1 (2001), 150–80. Her book, *Le Marché de l'excellence. Les Grands Crus à l'épreuve de la mondialisation*, Collection Liber (Paris: Seuil, 2009) is a useful contribution to some of the questions raised by the wine crisis in France.
20 See Gil Morrot, 'Peut-on améliorer les performances des dégustateurs?', *Vigne et Vin* (1999), 31–7 and François Casabianca and Christine de Sainte-Marie, 'L'évaluation sensorielle des produits typiques. Concevoir et instrumenter l'épreuve de typicité', in *The Socio-economics of Origin-Labelled Products in the Agro-food Supply Chain: Spatial, Institutional and Coordination Aspects*, 67th EAAE Seminar, le Mans, 28–30 October 1999.
21 Anthony Giddens, *A Contemporary Critique of Historical Materialism*, vol. 1: *Power, Property and the State* (London: Macmillan, 1981).
22 Émile Peynaud, *The Taste of Wine* (London: Macdonald Orbis, 1987), p. 12.
23 Claude Fischler, *Du vin* (Paris: Odile Jacob, 1999), p. 30.
24 Robert C. Ulin, 'Work as cultural production: labor and self-identity among southwest French wine growers', *Journal of the Royal Anthropological Institute*, 8, 4 (2001), 691–712.
25 Olivier Assouly, *Les Nourritures nostalgiques. Essai sur le mythe du terroir* (n.p., Actes Sud, 2004).
26 See for example, in Burgundy, Louis Chapuis and René Engel, who have both written about their families.
27 For more information see Marion Demossier, 'Territoires, produits et identités en mutation. Les Hautes-Côtes en Bourgogne', *Ruralia*, 8 (2001), pp. 141–58.
28 Among his wide range of publications, Jean-Francois Bazin has been in charge of the prestige series Le Grand Bernard des Vins de France, prestigious series and he has devoted his life to the promo-

tion of Burgundian wines. He is also a good example of one of the contemporary elites involved in the revival of wine culture and regionalism at local level.

29 For a discussion of Gaston Roupnel and his writings, see Marion Demossier, 'Entre littérature et objet ethnologique. "Nono" ou la construction du vigneron comme archétype de la culture locale', in A. Bleton-Ruget and P. Poirrier, *Le Temps des sciences humaines. Gaston Roupnel et les années trente* (Paris: Le Manuscrit, 2006), pp. 173–98.

30 The programme *Bouillon de culture*, whose scope he tried to broaden beyond books, was on television between 1991 and 2001.

31 Herman Lebovics, *True France: The Wars over Cultural Identity, 1900–1945* (Ithaca and London: Cornell University Press, 1992).

32 Philip Whalen, 'Burgundian regionalism and French republican commercial culture at the 1937 Paris International Exposition', *Cultural Analysis*, 6 (2007), 31–69.

33 Ibid.

34 The INA is a public organization with an industrial and commercial role that was set up through the reform of the audiovisual sector conducted in 1974 and finally implemented on 6 January 1975. Its aims are as follows:

   1. To preserve the national audiovisual heritage;
   2. to use this heritage to the full and make it more readily available;
   3. to keep abreast of changes in the audiovisual sector through its research, production and training activities.

   More than 80,000 hours of programmes are collected every year, half of which come within the framework of the legal deposit, with the remainder comprising documents contributed by public radio and television channels for professional archiving and, to a lesser extent, from private collections acquired or gathered by INA. INA collects production and/or broadcasting media together with documentary and legal data relating to the programmes contributed. The cataloguing and content description data are checked and enhanced by INA research assistants. This work means that the INA database can be fed and so the archives can be reused. More than 2 million documentary descriptive notes are now available. The television collection is divided up into three categories: national news, national programmes and regional news (this latter category has not been included in our research). INA's national newsreels collection includes television news broadcasts, programmes and political debates, information features, outside broadcasts, magazines and sports broadcasts. The collections come from the activities of RTF and ORTF (French radio and television) from 1949 to 1974 (about 200,000 topics), national broadcasters since 1975 with TF1 until 1992, Antenne 2 and FR3 until 1992, France 2 and France 3 until the present time (about 1 million topics) and the France 3 Paris Île-de-France collection from 1964 to 1986 (27,000 documents). National programmes: INA's 'Production' Collection covers all television genres: television films, series, serials, documentaries, entertainment broadcasts, TV games, cartoons, news feature and cultural programmes, drama, concerts etc. It is derived from the national production of RTF and ORTF from 1950 to 1974 (50,000 documents), production from national broadcasters since 1975, with TF1 until 1982, Antenne 2 and FR3 until 1992, France 2 and France 3 up to the present day (250,000 documents), la Cinq (part of the collection from 1987 to 1992 amounting to 3,000 documents), the Télé Emploi Collection (job news and vacancies) from 28 March to 17 April 1994 (400 documents) and broadcasts produced or jointly produced by INA since 1975 (Direction des Programmes de Création et de Recherche, Ina Entreprise) with some 1,600 documents.

35 Mediacorpus is a file manager associated with the Excel programme enabling researchers to conduct a statistical analysis of the corpus selected.

36 For more details on the Saint-Vincent Tournante, see Demossier, Producing tradition and managing social changes in the French vineyards: the circle of time in Burgundy', *Ethnologia Europea*, 27, 1 (Spring 1997), 29–47; and *Hommes et vins. Une anthropologie du vignoble bourguignon* (Dijon: EUD, 1999).

37 Jean-Pierre Corbeau, 'De la présentation dramatisée des aliments à la représentation de leurs consommateurs', in I. Giachetti, *Identités des mangeurs. Images des aliments* (Paris: Polytechnica, 1996), 175–98.

38 For each region, the figures indicated the percentage of broadcasting relative to the other regions mentioned. 1950s: Burgundy 36.84, Champagne 15.78, Bordeaux 15.78, Beaujolais 10.52, Languedoc 10.52, Alsace 10.52; 1960s: Burgundy 29.62, Beaujolais 20.98, Bordeaux 16.04, Champagne 12.34, Hérault 7.4, Loire 6.17, Alsace 2.46, Aude 1.23, Languedoc–Roussillon 1.23, Côtes du Rhône 1.23, Corbières 1.23; 1970s: Champagne 27.41, Beaujolais 20.96, Burgundy 17.74, Bordeaux 9.67, Alsace 8.06, Hérault 8.06, Corbières 3.22, Aude 1.61, Loire 1.23, Languedoc–Roussillon 1.23; 1980s: Champagne 24.48, Bordeaux 17.34, Burgundy 15.3, Beaujolais 13.26, Alsace 4.08, Corbières 4.08, Hérault 3.06, Provence 3.06, Loire 1.02, Côtes du Rhône 1.02, Sauternes 1.02, Midi 0.10; 1990s: Bordeaux 27.75, Burgundy 22.05, Champagne 12.16, Beaujolais 9.12, Alsace 4.94, Côtes du Rhône 3.42, Hérault 3.42, Languedoc–Roussillon 3.04, Sauternes 2.66, Loire 2.66, Jura 2.28, Aude 2.28, Midi 2.22, Corbières 1.52, Provence 0.38; 2000s: Bordeaux 35, Burgundy 14.16, Beaujolais 10.83, Champagne10, Aude 5.83, Languedoc–Roussillon 5, Alsace 5, Hérault 3.33, Jura 2.5, Loire 1.66, Côtes du Rhône 1.66, Sauternes 1.66, Provence 1.66, Midi 0.8, Corbières 0.83.

39 Aline Brochot, 'Champagne. Objet de culture, objet de lutte', in M. Rautenberg, A. Micoud, L. Bérard and P. Marchenay, *Campagnes de tous nos désirs* (Paris: Maison des Sciences de l'Homme, 2000), pp. 75–90.

40 Many producers, politicians and wine experts argue that wine cannot be perceived like any other alcohol product as in France it is embedded in a culture, a history and an industry; therefore it has to be seen as an element of national heritage, a cultural good.

Chapter Five
Ethnographies and Contexts[1]

This chapter offers a major selection of my fieldwork on wine consumption conducted over a six-year period from 1999 to 2005. Using a multi-sited ethnography, I selected a series of analytically relevant episodes or snapshots to shed light on the context in which stories about wines are narrated. My argument is that wine consumption goes beyond the act of drinking, and as each story demonstrates, individuals use wine and wine drinking to fulfil specific functions related to the creation, maintenance and negotiation of their personal identity. By telling the story of my encounter with wine consumption, I deliberately want to emphasize the complex nature of the act of drinking and the fact that any attempt to regulate such consumption may fail if the context is not taken into account. Each of the contexts analysed contributes to our understanding of the elaborate construction that is the world of wine in France. The idea of wine as an element of French national identity was always something of a myth, but the recent emergence of a wine drinking culture as a global phenomenon is attached to the modernization of our societies. The five episodes selected illustrate the complexity of this construction, the role of specific actors in the transmission and diffusion of wine culture, the role of institutions and politicians in its making, the way consumers relate to it in different contexts and finally the way a specific wine culture develops in a territory where French values are anchored in a re-interpretation of the past.

1. Ethnography 1 of the 1990 and 1999 *Guide Hachette* classification in Burgundy

In January 1990, I participated as a guest in a workshop on wine tasting organized by the BIVB (Interprofessional Office for

Burgundian Wines), during which I was invited to join the wine-tasting committee of the *Guide Hachette* which met some weeks later. Several round tables of 'experts' were formed and we were given the task of tasting specific samples of wines and then discussing them. My panel was composed of a famous female oenologist from one of the big wine merchants in Burgundy, three wine growers from the local area, one *courtier* (wine broker) and a businessman. The results of our deliberations had to be written up and submitted to the organizer of the panel. Intense discussion followed each tasting and very often the judgement of the female oenologist, seen as the expert, dominated the debate.

Years later, on 14 January 1999, I was invited again, this time in my capacity as an anthropologist, to a wine tasting organized by the *Guide Hachette* for the seventeenth edition of their wine guide. On this occasion, the editor of the Guide, Mme Montalbetti, was present to inaugurate the first wine-tasting session. In her speech, she announced: 'I would like to thank you for coming again this year, as it is our seventeenth year together and I would like to thank all the tasters who have worked with us over this period, tasters who come again and again for the pleasure of tasting and also for the rigour of the exercise.' The wine tasting was composed of more than 3,000 different wines and was spread over a period of three months. During this period, all the AOCs of Burgundy were tasted and classified by panels of experts selected for the various tastings. A local expert working for the local *protection des végétaux*, M. Bernard, was appointed to direct what Mme Montalbetti describes as this highly 'professional' and controlled event. Each year, M. Bernard is in charge of selecting the new or promising AOCs and he explained: 'I start with the Côte de Nuits. In fact, I open the wine tasting with Gevrey-Chambertin, and it also could be a Vosne-Romanée or a Chambolle-Musigny, which are very good AOCs, as much for their names as for the expectations they raise.'

In two of the wine-tasting rooms of the new BIVB, forty-three people, including six women, gathered together to taste fifteen wines from the village of Gevrey-Chambertin. They included sellers, wine merchants, *courtiers*, wine growers, oenologists, wine journalists, chefs and a small number of wine lovers recruited from all over Burgundy.[2] According to Mme Montalbetti, the quality of the *Guide Hachette* derives from the high level of expertise of the professionals involved, and in this context she emphasized the relative absence of wine lovers, with many judged as not sufficiently competent to participate. Each jury, composed of a minimum of three individuals, tasted fifteen different wines from the same AOC presented that day. Tasters are given a place with a separate desk, two INAO glasses and a technical slip which they have to fill in.[3] This slip refers to the description of the product tasted listing four main characteristics and asking for a general comment concerning the evaluation of the wine: type of wine (red, rosé, white; dry, soft, luscious; still or sparkling), eye (foam sparkle; colour, with intensity and clarity) and mouth (first impression; balance; dominant flavours; length). A mark is attributed from 0 to 5, 0 being a flawed wine not selected and 5 being an exceptional wine. In front of each taster, a sink and a tap enable them to drink water and to spit during the tasting. Each of the forty-three committee members tasted blindly (that is to say the bottles are presented with a black cover masking their origins); after the samples are given to them they try to put their sensorial experience into words.

These two ethnographic episodes separated by a period of nine years illustrate how professional wine culture changed during the 1990s. While wine consumption has declined continuously, a new wine culture – at national and regional level – has proliferated in a variety of ways, from television programmes and a specialized literature to wine experts and wine bars.[4] Most libraries now have a specific shelf devoted to wines as part of the cultural activities on offer, alongside travel guides and cookery books. In 1994, a specialist wine library known as L'Athéneum was launched in Beaune by Hachette in collaboration with a Burgundian wine merchant. The emergence of the wine expert accompanied this trend, and these experts have become some of the leading actors in the commercial sphere whose expertise has been legitimized as that of an 'objective taster'. The proliferation of guides and books devoted to wine are a good indication of this movement.

The *Guide Hachette* was created in 1984 and was aimed principally at helping the consumer to decide which wines to buy. According to Mme Montalbetti, 'The new consumer wants different things. The guide is a commercial adviser of discoveries and of diversity of tastes.' The first edition sold no less than 85,000 copies, and 5,000 wines were selected for inclusion from amongst 8,000 tasted. Over the years, the tasting has become more professional, often being organized by the *Interprofession* of each wine-growing region, which includes all the representatives of the wine sector. As Mme Montalbetti has said, 'Like other French publishers, Hachette was concerned, from its creation, with the democratization of knowledge and culture.' The development of a wine culture from the 1980s onwards was based upon a wider diffusion of knowledge, and a more scientific approach to wine and its consumption was the new leitmotif of several publishing houses.[5] It is undeniable that the *Guide Hachette* was the first to create a competitive and critical environment for the French wine growers who decided to submit their wines to expert scrutiny. Recognition by the *Guide Hachette* has been of great financial benefit to some producers, dramatically increasing sales of their wines, including those not actually listed in the guide. As a result, the *Guide Hachette* has created a more competitive culture amongst wine growers, who have a real economic incentive to win marks of esteem such as the prestigious *coup de cœur* (special favourite) label awarded by Hachette. Very often, as a result of such a recommendation, the wine grower will display this honorific recognition on the door of his cellar and will use it for commercial purposes.[6] From the 1980s, Hachette has published a range of other books designed to complement its guide. Specific specialized books such as *Connaître et choisir le vin* (To Know and Select Wines) illustrate this new culture of advisers emerging in French wine drinking culture. A major wine encyclopaedia is also being prepared under Hachette's supervision, but has not yet been published.

The world of both wine guides and wine lovers in France is constructed on the foundations laid by the AOC system, and the *Guide Hachette* itself is organized in line with the regions and denominations authorized by the AOC. As M. Bernard explained, 'The selection takes place in relation to the expectations we have of a specific AOC, the traditional typical taste.' During the tasting in Beaune in 1999, the wines from different AOCs were sampled together. The whole exercise was controlled by the panel, who aimed to classify and rank the various producers within the same AOC, which underlines the fact that competition remains constructed at a local rather than at a national level. Their judgement, which is presented as being as 'objective and professional' as possible, is rarely unanimous.

In France, the quality of wine could be defined as 'an affair of specialists' and it is clearly a subjective issue. The whole legitimacy of the process of decision-making in the wine-tasting committees relies upon a consensual and negotiated process more than on an objective evaluation of the product.[7] Even in the case of the *Guide Hachette*, M. Bernard admits that tasting is a subjective art and that there is no objective truth in wine tasting. The committees also demonstrate strikingly that different professions in the wine industry, from wine waiters to oenologists, use different languages to describe the same product and are not always in agreement about the same product tasted on different occasions. The growing wine literature underlines this lack of a unified and collective language; it also confirms the fragmented nature of wine drinking culture. Yet wine drinking culture in France is frequently presented as a monolithic objective body of knowledge and culture.

Amongst the parameters used for the description of the wine were considerations of the product based on whether or not it was already drinkable and which dishes could best complement it. Each group of three tasters shared the same samples, and from their judgement the local organizer, M. Bernard, had to produce 'a coherent and technical wine-tasting note', a task that was extremely challenging when the three tasters did not agree on the wine's qualities. Divergent opinions were even possible between two individuals sharing the same professional background, and to try and resolve the split, the wine was tasted again by other experts and a general consensus was established by M. Bernard. It is interesting to see that the judgements expressed by various professions, from oenologists to *courtiers*, could differ in their nature as each profession looks for different qualities when tasting wines. According to M. Bernard, the oenologist will be more technical while the *courtier* will look for more pleasant wines. The variety of opinions is nevertheless seen as a major sign of the professionalism of the guide.

Once the tastings were complete and the technical note had been written by M. Bernard, another local 'expert' was asked to rewrite each of the notes in a poetic and anecdotal manner: 'Finally, it is he that has all the importance, that is to say that it is up to him to look at the comments ... I suppose that he will be able to see what the experts mean or want to say' (M. Bernard). In this case, the 'expert' was a journalist and local politician (a previous head of the regional council) who is the prolific author of a series of best-selling books on the wine-growing villages of Burgundy, in which he adopts a literary stance, positioned between folklore and ethnology, as is illustrated by the following quotation from a work published on Saint-Romain in 2002:

> *Saint-Romain – Sous-la-Velle 2002*
> *From the hard work of a wine grower to the access to the status of landowner, from polyculture to monoculture, that is the story of this family during the second half of the twentieth century. Brilliant, their Chardonnay recalls fresh breadcrumbs, flint and vanilla. In the mouth, its taste is quite mineral with a slight sensation of bitterness. Its acidity will make it last. Sous Roche Rouge 2002, astringent, tasting slightly of animal and leather.*

It is worth noting that during the interview, Mme Montalbetti briefly mentioned the contribution of the literary expert, constantly praising the highly professional character of the guide. Her discourse aims at giving legitimacy to the *Guide Hachette* in relation to other competitors such as Robert Parker's publications or the *Guide de la Revue des Vins de France*. Her comments emphasized the objective context of the wine tasting which is clearly explained in the guide's introduction. The *Guide Hachette* offers a vast panorama of each wine-producing region, and through the editorial work conducted by the local 'expert', its publication integrates changes at a micro socio-economic level, recognizing good producers from one year to the next and shaping their reputations as a result. According to M. Bernard, when wine growers are not selected for inclusion in the *Guide Hachette*, they rarely come back to discuss the quality of their wines, confirming that some of them remain passive in the selling of their products. Most of the ones included refer to the continuity of their recognition throughout the years of the *Guide Hachette*.[8] Its essential role is to transform through its writings the technical evaluation of a wine into a literary description, which in turn contributes to the reputation and revival of a gastronomic regional identity through a folkloric and anecdotal presentation of each producer.

This literature is also part of a wider movement associated with a new form of gastronomic regionalism based on economic regeneration and local identity which contributes to the region's reputation beyond its own administrative boundaries.[9] It could be argued, following Robert Ulin's study of the south-west wine-producing regions, that a similar process of 'cultural production' and invention has taken place in the majority of French wine-growing areas.[10]

The guide appears as a fundamental tool in constructing reputations and, consequently, in consolidating economic positions. By 'democratizing wine consumption', as Mme Montalbetti has pointed out, the *Guide Hachette* provides a national framework for the expression of local and regional identities through a well-established national and regional politics of taste. This politics of taste is, according to the head of the *Guide Hachette*, a question of 'everyone expressing his or her difference. We live in a society which must be diverse. Each one has to tell his or her difference.' Yet it could be argued that by prescribing tastes, the guide also restricts them, especially when looking for the specificities of each *terroir*, as was suggested on numerous occasions by the organizers. The *Guide Hachette* becomes one of the tangible ways of consolidating the ideology of the *terroir*, as typicity is the main criterion emphasized during the tastings. Wine has therefore become a commodity to express differences and 'distinction', and in this respect the expert occupies a powerful position in the diffusion of culture. Its consumption however, relates back to social differentiation, questions of exclusion and, by the same token, issues of local and regional identity. It confirms the hegemonic position of some wine producers compared with others in this highly competitive sector. It also sheds light on the power of the written word in a society where new means of communication are now challenging the establishment personified by the *Guide Hachette*.

2. Ethnography 2 of the spring wine fair of the Caves Particulières in 1997

On 11 April 1997, I was invited to interview M. Jean Ezingeard, the president of the the Caves Particulières, in Paris, where they had organized their spring wine fair.[11] The spring fair is a public event organized by wine producers from all of the main wine-producing regions of France, enabling visitors to buy wine directly from the producer. The wine fairs, which have mushroomed all over France, are part of a wider economic process which has seen producers take direct control of the commercialization of their wines. Young wine growers and others struggling to establish their business reputations have used the fairs to promote their products. The wine fair has attracted growing interest over recent years. In 1994, 25,000 visitors attended, and by 1997 this figure had risen to 45,000. Most of the visitors are from cities and the majority of them from Paris. Twenty-two wine growers participated in 1994, a figure that rose astronomically to 910 in 1997, attesting the growing presence of individual wine growers in the commercial sphere and to their need to sell directly to customers. The modern building, with its glass and aluminium structure, was in stark contrast to the internal decoration of the fair, where artificial grapes, oak barrels, green and white displays, INAO glasses and a large red carpet dominated the scene.

At the reception, I asked for Mr Ezingeard and I was sent to his stand. A stocky *vigneron* welcomed me with a warm handshake and then proceeded to announce that he was 'the president of a place for authenticity and conviviality, and definitely not a fun fair', emphasizing the need to control excesses in wine drinking. The beginning of our discussion focused on the historical development of the wine fair, and his discourse emphasized the importance of the collective organization of southern French producers, established in the 1970s with the aim of taking over the commercialization of their wines. Their influence still dominates the organization of the fair, and from the various individual displays it is easy to guess where each producer comes from, as they seek to impose their own image through such techniques as displays of bottles and labels on the stand, their wine boxes or the presentation of the *Guide Hachette* conveniently opened to reveal their own personal entry. The sense of diversity and the informal nature of the fair, which is organized in a very haphazard fashion (it was easy to get lost because of the lack of a clear organization between the wine-growing regions), confirm the heterogeneous nature of both production and consumption.

In this open space, visitors wandered about in pursuit of their passions. Tasting and buying wine is clearly the main aim of their visit. Some people already had a definite idea of what they were looking for, announcing, for example, 'We want to buy twelve bottles of Château Margaux', while others were more curious and were searching for something new: 'White or red? Which AOC?' asked a producer. The publicity of the wine fair illustrated this tendency: 'Behind each of the bottles that you will meet on your travels, you will see a face, hear a personal story, taste a specific and unique *savoir-faire*.' Most of the visitors were Parisian men, but during the weekend more wine lovers arrived from all over France, having come especially for the occasion. The tribal and masculine nature of the crowd denoted that wine tasting remains a male collective activity, yet very often groups of men and women or couples come together to buy the wine. What strikes the anthropologist is the sharp contrast between urban (consumers from the cities) and rural worlds (the wine growers). The fair provides a social space for urban dwellers in quest of their rural roots. However, any clear sense of social differentiation between the visitors becomes very difficult to read. The profile of the connoisseur of wine in particular dominated the various conversations I had with those present. The wine producers interviewed during the fair confirmed that the connoisseur was their favourite customer, and that during this event they had made some interesting and memorable contacts. The producers made the point that the connoisseur was the customer they were looking for, a man of discernment who knows about wine and is not obsessed with labels and 'big names'. There was, however, a strong sense that wine tasting had to be controlled and limited. This distinctive pattern of moderation was encouraged by the organizers, and throughout the exhibition there were posters displaying a single half-empty glass of wine. Security guards were on the scene to assure cohesion and social order in the event of anyone failing to heed this subliminal message.

The success of such events, which have multiplied over the last thirty years, illustrates only one aspect of the changes affecting wine consumption. This is part of a new attraction for popular tastes of *vins de pays* or *vins plaisirs* (wine for pleasure), which illustrates again this new type of consumption dominated by occasional and urban drinkers. Recent surveys have confirmed the increase in the consumption of quality wine, which rose from around 4 million hectolitres in 1960 to 13 million in the 1990s. In response to this demand for good wines, the INAO has seen the number of applications for the official status of AOC (denomination of origin) soar dramatically over the last twenty years. A growing social differentiation has accompanied this trend. A certain degree of social disordering is going on reshaping social positions and issues of power. In this new social context, the figure of the connoisseur or wine lover as a regular consumer is blurred by that of the wandering drinker who seems to be used as a symbolic figure in the new wine-marketing campaigns.

The spring wine fair of the Caves Particulières offers a striking example of the many annual events organized around wine and food production. Each region and each month of the calendar is punctuated by these wine and food fairs, which have grown in importance since the 1980s as part of an expanding leisure culture. This new passion is part of a wider interest in local products and a quest for pleasure, combined with direct contact with producers from all over France. Several wine lovers encountered during my ethnography of the fair plan their year in advance in relation to this series of regional festivities and fairs. The wine fair enables them to explore new regional wine areas, taste new wines, discover new wine-growers and to privilege direct contact with the wine sector. This characteristic is particularly sought after by wine lovers as they are primarily urban dwellers with little or no contact with the world of wine. For others, fairs provide an opportunity to meet at regular intervals with the *vigneron* from whom they have bought wine in the past.

What is striking during these events is the presence of the *vigneron* as the symbol of resilience, compared with other agricultural professions, whose products have been industrialized since the 1950s (the milk industry for example). Tasting wines from the *vigneron*, and with the *vigneron*, is seen by most wine lovers and consumers as the ultimate in wine consumption. All the ingredients are thus displayed to enable this direct, real and authentic contact: wine is presented as a gift commodity, the wine grower comments on his products and on his know-how. Cultural and regional emblems displayed around the *vigneron* remind the consumer of the 'authentic' nature of the French wine industry. For the anxious and confused wine consumer, these wine fairs provide a more human and social method of buying than supermarkets with their piles of bottles presented, with different labels and AOCs. This social characteristic of the fair is a new and important aspect of wine consumption. Many of the wine lovers interviewed emphasize that their best memories around wine tasting are related to the presence of the producer, a presence which clouds the judgement and transforms the evaluation of the product into a highly human and emotional exchange. At the other extreme, some wine lovers fear that this human and emotional aspect of the tasting may represent an obstacle to their appreciation of the wine, and they prefer to avoid any collusion with the producer when evaluating his products.

Another element of the wine fair is the emphasis placed on authenticity and tradition. Philippe Chaudat has shown how supermarket chains refer to concepts of authenticity, *terroir*, tradition and regional identity to promote local wines from the Jura.[12] The *mise-en-scène* of these products makes sense for the consumer as it refers to their specific local and cultural context, and Chaudat notes that the publicity materials used by the supermarkets rely extensively upon the sense of belonging to both a national French heritage and to a regional identity. The same comments could be applied to the spring fair of the Caves Particulières, where regional identities coexist next to each other to form part of a wider French identity, a sense of what it means to be French. Authenticity and tradition are cultural markers which attach specific conceptions and imaginary values to the concept of the present. As Chaudat has argued:

> *Consuming authenticity will enable the consumption of the imaginary and of the past in order to produce the present, but will equally enable the creation of one's own identity, the appropriation of a geographical space, the interiorization of the image of what one drinks and the ability to become this image in return.*[13]

Consuming authenticity and tradition when drinking wine relates to the concept of time, in the context of a constantly changing society. French consumers are very much attached to the idea of authenticity and to the notion that products have to be more natural and less industrialized and processed. This could be partly explained by the anxiety created by our postmodern societies. In a survey on the oenological knowledge of French consumers, conducted by Ipsos-Insight Marketing, it was pointed out that consumers are aware of the technical changes affecting wines, but that they are against any complete modernization of the process of wine making: 'The idea of blending wine seems suspicious to them …'.[14]

Another aspect discussed in the Ipsos-Insight survey is the attachment of French people to the notion of *terroir*. The concept of *terroir* is almost untranslatable, but it refers to a traditional food or to the agricultural produce of a specific geographical region. It has become a term charged with meaning for French urban dwellers in search of their roots and an ideology acting as a support for the expression of social and economic divisions. For French consumers, *terroir* and AOC wines encapsulate two elements. First, they connote the qualities of the soil and the natural characteristics which made the wine and which classify it within the hierarchy of French wines.

Secondly, it is also about social distinction and economic position, as wine prices depend partly on their ranking. Various factors contribute to the position of each wine within the vast range on offer. Consuming wine, therefore, remains an act of differentiation, in which individuals position themselves in relation to others. In this quest for identities, old and traditional values coexist, and it is possible to say that wine has never been so modern.

3. Ethnography 3 of the Saint-Vincent Tournante. January 1991, Puligny-Montrachet, and 2004, Monthelie (Burgundy)

The Saint-Vincent Tournante, the principal regional wine festival of Burgundy, takes place on the first weekend following St Vincent's day, 22 January, in honour of the patron saint of wine growers. The right to host the Saint-Vincent Tournante rotates amongst the wine-growing villages of Burgundy and returns nearly every thirty years to its point of departure. In 1991, the village chosen for the event by the Confrérie des Chevaliers du Tastevin organized a procession attended by representatives of the seventy-five mutual-aid societies in the region, followed by a church service held in parallel with a free wine tasting and, finally, three banquets of honour.[15] Over the years, the festival had been transformed from a family and village gathering into a vast celebration which is open to the public for two days. In 1961, two Americans were invited by the local wine merchant to follow the small procession going to the church. In 1991, more than 100,000 people turned up, including visitors from Britain, Switzerland and the USA. Thirty thousand bottles of wine were drunk, three banquets were organized and the village made a profit of around 4 million French francs. By buying a glass for 25 francs, visitors were able to taste the wines for free.

Increasingly concerned by the risks and excesses associated with such a gathering, the Confrérie des Chevaliers du Tastevin decided in 2003 that the festival would return to its original form, a village festival for the wine growers. Vougeot and Monthelie started to set the example, and the wine-tasting part of the festival was abandoned to give way to a local and intimate type of gathering. Several explanations were advanced to explain the return to a more human size of this previously enormous tourist event. Problems of a financial nature, with the necessity for a small *commune* to balance the budget and to deal with issues of taxation, were cited, as were the difficulties involved in trying to control drunkenness and large numbers of people during the festival. Finally the image projected to the outside world began to cause concern and strengthened the argument for returning the festival to its more modest forms. The festival had initially been an occasion to drink good wines which were normally confined to prestigious wine tastings, without specific ritual and *mise-en-scène*. This side of the festival has disappeared except for one banquet which is still organized in Beaune every year to replace the village banquet. Previously three types of wine were consumed during the festival itself. The wine of the *cuvée* Saint-Vincent, which was drunk in a public space, was served from the bottle to the glass and was offered directly to the consumer without the ritual accompaniment traditionally attached to this type of wine. This wine was intended for the thousands of visitors who could, in theory, consume limitless quantities of a famous and not normally affordable wine. On the other hand, a hierarchy of bottles of good wines with labels (from other vintages or coming from other local vineyards or the cellars of renowned producers) was consumed in the more private and social space of the three banquets, organized by the *Confrérie*, the local priests and the wine growers of the host village. The latter included the wine-growers' clients and focused on an emblematic and highly ritualized type of wine consumption, which accompanied the elaborate meal prepared by a distinguished Burgundian chef. The Saint-Vincent Tournante thus provided an excellent example of how different social situations produce markedly different types of wine consumption for different drinkers and how the festival offers a medium for the expression and reception of a wide range of social identities.

The historical development of the festival illustrates the emergence of a new type of wine consumption and culture. In 1961, wine consumption was privately organized and structured by each family around the Sunday meal. By 1991 it had became a festive, public, less institutionalized and more fragmented type of consumption, shedding light on a new social hierarchy of drinkers and leading to more disturbances. In 2004, the festival went back to a family, professional style of gathering with a clear message of moderate consumption. It is worth noting that as wine consumption has become more public, festive and separated from eating (wine shops and wine bars have given a more visible and social status to wine consumption in French society), differentiation also became increasingly visible (as is revealed by the 1999 festival compared to 1961). The public and private dimensions of wine drinking have had to be renegotiated, and in line with this change the more public it has become the less consumption has been controlled. In 1961, nobody in the village was recorded as being publicly drunk during the festival, and most of the wine consumption was organized around the table, as part of a family meal. Yet the organizers of the festivals during the 1990s complained about the increasing problem of excessive drinking and tried to address the problem but were unsuccessful because of the growing popularity of the event, which attracted more and more young and excessive consumers. There were several cases of alcoholic comas at the Saint-Vincent Tournante of 1991, which was something the Burgundian wine growers did not want to see associated with their product.[16]

In 2004 and following Sarkozy's clamp-down on drink-driving, no obviously drunken behaviour was recorded by the organizers. This change could also be explained by the pressures put on the Confrérie and the wine producers to respond to growing concern about alcohol and public health. It is an issue that raises the difficult question of the relationship between young French people and alcohol. As one visitor in his twenties from Dijon commented to me in the 1990s: 'Wine is not as much a part of our culture; we are a different generation from our parents, a generation that consumes more alcohol than any other, but wine is not part of it.' Excessive consumption also underlined the extraordinary and festive character of the event. In this sense, 'festive' also meant 'occasional'. Another important development in the festival of the Saint-Vincent Tournante was the opening of the wine cellars, which have now completely disappeared from the festival. Instead of a family gathering, the tasting had become an opportunity to advertise the AOC and to publicize the name of the village and that of the region. Again, it was a common wish on the part of the producers to transform the rationale behind the festival and to respond to the current political climate.

The organization of the festival in 1991 emphasized the quality and reputation of local wines, giving the wine's name to different wine cellars, from the Folatières to the Clavoillon. The menus of each of the three banquets held during the festival also highlighted the various AOCs belonging to the village and enhanced the position of each wine in the local hierarchy of wines: 'If there is only one banquet today, the gastronomic culture is still at the core of its organization'; 'Lobsters go well with Bâtard-Montrachet (*grand cru*, white wine).' For most diners, moderate consumption was encouraged by the combination of distinction with taste. First and foremost, it becomes a stylish exercise of your tastes and a proof of your 'distinction'. Again by becoming public, wine consumption has become more ritualized and sophisticated under the increasing power of wine lovers (and not the wine growers). It is worth noticing that in the process, the group represented by the wine growers has declined, becoming marginal as wine tasting is increasingly recognized as a professional art.

The Saint-Vincent Tournante thus reveals a wider phenomenon. Visitors now come from all over France and many take the opportunity to visit the region and combine buying wine with tourism. The leisure culture, of which tourism is an important element, was given a boost in France by the lowering of the retirement age and the now abolished thirty-five-hour week introduced in the 1990s. The emergence of a new wine tourism has accompanied this trend, and almost every wine-growing region has its own wine route, and has encouraged the publication of regional guides about gastronomy and wines. The wine tour has contributed to the modernization of local infrastructures and tourist accommodation.[17] Numerous examples could be given to illustrate the general efforts of local governments and of the French state to promote French wines, both at home and abroad, such as the *Fête du Vin* held in June in Bordeaux along the Garonne. In this voyage of discovery of French wine-producing regions, the wine grower has emerged as the principal intermediary. In contrast to the supermarkets or the wine-merchant chains such as Nicolas, wine growers offer an alternative type of consumption based on a more personalized and authentic approach. The client has to contact them to make an appointment, and the meeting is organized around the tasting of new wines in barrels followed by bottles of the most recent vintages. Such a relationship can lead to the establishment of regular and personal contacts that each partner tries to maintain. The wine growers are well aware of the less faithful nature of their modern clientele and of their expectations as consumers. Thus they provide the 'wandering' drinker with a warm welcome and with a profusion of wines to help sales. Established and prestigious vineyards such as Bordeaux and Burgundy have been able to retain some of their traditional customers and to consolidate their clienteles. Consequently some of the most popular wine growers have such a high reputation that it remains impossible to visit them or to buy their products. Wine lovers, using some of their contacts with the professionals, are sometimes able to get some of these cherished wines.

The general craze for direct contact with the producer illustrates some of the principal features attached to the concept of the 'wandering drinker': occasional in his/her consumption, looking for a new discovery, a *coup de cœur*, passionate in his/her quest and basing the quest on the consumption of others. This approach, encapsulated in the representations of the wine grower, is an effective emblem of a so-called declining and disappearing rural France which in fact has shown itself to be more adaptable than previously thought. However, wine consumption is often more than a simple passion. For many individuals, wine drinking has become a means of defining their identity in an increasingly modern and fragmented world with consumption patterns acting as a way of demonstrating an individual's position and of expressing both personality and individuality.

4. Ethnography 4: Les Graves, December 2003

M. Deluc suggested that I arrive around six o'clock for a wine tasting followed by a meal shared with the principal members of the association, 'the core of the group', composed of the 'encyclopaedist', as he was presented to me, a young local wine grower, 'the best taster of the group', an oenologist from Bordeaux, and a couple of young and newly arrived wine growers. Mr. Deluc's daughter had warned me some months before about the highly professional character of her father's wine club and his passion for wine: 'He takes it very seriously and I am sure he will be happy to talk about it.' Mr Deluc's house was situated near Bordeaux, in the middle of the Graves vineyard, and when I arrived there following his directions, I discovered a beautiful house at the end of a country lane, surrounded by pine trees and a lovely garden with a swimming pool. Mr Deluc used to work for an insurance company and his wife is a retired teacher. I did not know exactly what to expect from this first meeting with *Tire-Bouchon Attitude* ('Corkscrew Attitude') and it took me the whole dinner to understand what they meant by this funny nickname.

I followed the path leading to the front of the house and despite the difficulty of finding the entrance door (which was not clearly indicated by any signs such as a bell or even a clear entrance), I decided to knock at both the kitchen window and the door next to it. A small, sixty-something man came to the door, introducing himself as M. Deluc and his companion, the oenologist of the association. It was clear that the meeting was above all dedicated to wine tasting as an art, a social performance and a *mise-en-scène* for testing my wine culture. I did not feel at ease as I had to drive back to Bordeaux (30 kilometres away) and felt the pressure of conforming to the arts of the table and of wine drinking. In the back of my mind was the shadow of Nicolas Sarkozy, and his energetic campaign against drink-driving. My position as a neutral and objective social anthropologist was going to be challenged as the organization of the dinner party and the various signs communicated to me by M. Deluc soon made clear. A huge white, elegantly furnished living room was on my right, occupied by a large, round and convivial dining table dressed for the occasion with a set of two glasses for each guest and magnificent tableware and cutlery. I did not feel at ease with the situation as I was expecting something more convivial, less grandiloquent and more rustic. My years of anthropological fieldwork with wine growers contrasted drastically with the new setting, and I was not sure who was at the centre of the performance: them or myself? The bourgeois atmosphere and the highly ritualized character of the meeting took me by surprise and I was not sure to have either the energy or even the inclination to comply with their rules of the game. But, perhaps I was imagining them?

Immediately after my arrival, we were taken to the living room to sit on a sofa facing a big chimney, surrounded by antiques. Two bottles accompanied by a couple of things to nibble (Bayonne ham served with melon and white onions on a stick) were offered to us. Starting with a glass of Blanquette de Limoux from the *cave coopérative*, the wine tasting (as it could be defined, considering that each wine drunk was commented on and analysed or discussed by the group) took several hours and we 'tasted' (drank and not spat out) no fewer than eight wines, finishing late in the night around one o'clock, when whisky started to be drunk. All of the guests (we were eight in total), mentioned the issue of drink-drinking, but as they were living nearby they did not see it as a major obstacle, which was not my case. Once all of the guests had arrived and had been identified in relation to the association, the local wine grower and finally the 'encyclopaedist' joined us for dinner. Conversation began about wine. M. Deluc was full of admiration for the expertises and knowledge of his two colleagues. For the occasion, I had brought a bottle of white wine from Burgundy, which was selected by my local *caviste* on the recommendation that it was a surprising bottle from the Mâconnais, tasting like a Meursault. Mr Deluc showed the bottle in the middle of the dinner emphasizing that it was a present and that the 'encyclopaedist' surely must know where it came from ... which he did, to my own surprise, identifying two possible names of producers.

The wine tasting was conducted around the meal prepared by M. Deluc's wife, which was composed of a vegetable *terrine* followed by a veal *ragout* with olives and oranges, cheeses and a local apple tart. Seven bottles were tasted, each followed by comments and criticisms, mainly expressed by the wine grower. In the middle of the dinner, there was some discussion between the encyclopaedist and the wine grower concerning one bottle which was not clearly identified:

> The encyclopaedist: *I am sure it is the cuvée (a special vintage) prestige ...*
> The wine grower: *No, I tell you it is not indicated on the label, and I have got some bottles in the cellar.*

The *Guide des Vins de France* was then consulted to clarify the issue, and even after that they were still in disagreement about it.[18] The whole evening turned into a social exercise of taste and knowledge, accompanied by a conversation turning around the French regional and national model of gastronomy and drinking. When we started to compare France with England, their opinions were firmly stated: 'The English are thirty years behind us in terms of taste. Here we have everything. We do not live far from the producers, we can visit them whenever we want, we can taste their products and we do it every day.' I did not feel at ease with the turn of the conversation, especially when the wine grower sitting next to me angrily declared: 'I do not want to welcome English people to my cellar any more; they taste everything and then they only buy one bottle. Better the Germans than the English.' It took me a bit of time to decide what was making me feel uncomfortable. Was it the whole exercise of performing socially and showing one's competence in wine, or was it the feeling that I felt personally attacked. During the entire evening, I attempted to have a minimal input into the conversation, to make sure that things happened naturally to some extent. But perhaps, the whole performance was above all for outsiders. At the end of the evening, they asked me why I was living in England and I told them that my husband was English, which made things worse – at least for them.

The evening was very rich in analysis, and numerous questions came to my mind: Was the world of amateurs a world of essentialists, showing off, power, control? How was I able to judge if they were right in their analysis of the wines? What was at stake during that evening? Some of the answers would be found later when juxtaposing all the various ethnographies which make the world of wine unique.

5. Ethnography 5: The JCE (Jeune Chambre Economique, Junior Chamber of Commerce), Nuits-Saint-Georges (Burgundy), February 2004[19]

I met Annie P., through one of my friends who was very involved in local development and gender equality and was working on a project with her. What I did not know when I phoned her to ask for an interview was that she was the same Annie that I already knew from my local choir. Annie is a friendly forty-something lady who is a very active civil servant. Divorced and a mother of two young girls in their twenties, she is involved in a number of associations and leisure groups, from the choir to wine club and yoga. As she emphasized during our first interview, she is the only woman in this very male group and she has always had to fight for her position. This informal wine club, which has no name and no particular status, is composed of nine individuals, one woman and eight men, who meet at regular intervals to taste wines and then share a meal. From my first encounter with them, they were the direct opposite of the *Tire-Bouchon Attitude*, the Bordelais wine club: informal, relaxed, very friendly, less obsessed with social status and knowledge about wine.

The purpose of their meetings was above all to continue their friendship established at the JCE and to learn more about wines. As Annie put it, 'Being a newcomer to the area, I very rapidly felt obliged to conform to the culture of the place, that is to say to drink and learn to talk about wines, if I wanted to be socially integrated.'

Wine was thus perceived as a social lubricant, and learning about the local wine culture was a way to be recognized and admitted into society. All the members of the group belonged to the JCE and lived in Nuits-Saint-Georges or nearby, which made their drinking less restricted than mine, as I had to drive back 10 kilometres. They are also all professionals (civil servant, chemist, teacher, oenologist and accountant), which explains in part the ability to finance their passion. They are all more or less related to the wine industry, at least according to them.[20] The rules of the club require that each of them, in turn, has to invite the others for dinner and to organize a wine tasting. In fact, Annie is the only one who cooks when receiving them, while all the others rely on their partners and wives do it for them. The world of wine is definitely a male universe, and as Annie is perceived as a single divorcée she is allowed to join the group, confirming the sexual nature of the gatherings even if they vehemently denied that courtship is also part of the experience. The club meets on a monthly basis, and each member brings a bottle related to the topic of the tasting, which could be wines from Spain, wines from a particular region of France or wines from a recent vacation.

The night they invited me to join them, the topic selected was Hautes-Côtes de Nuits and Côtes de Nuits whites, and I was advised by Annie to go to the local supermarket and choose a bottle of this area, which I did, opting for a Bourgogne Hautes-Côtes de Nuits white, a '*coup de cœur Guide Hachette*', for which I paid 8 *euros*. The party was organized that night by Didier, a teacher of English in his fifties, married to a dancing teacher who did not drink wine. Their town house was carefully restored and full of antiques. Annie and I arrived together and we both brought flowers and chocolates for our hostess who was in the kitchen actively preparing, what promised to be a very delicious meal. That night, only four other members of the group joined us, as most of the others were still on holiday except one, who did not want to attend after having had a heated discussion with Annie on politics and immigration at the previous meeting.

The tasting was held at the beginning of the evening, and they explained to me that they wanted to do it professionally, and therefore I was given a tasting-form to fill in. The five bottles to be tasted were ranked according to the AOC, then the year and finally the implicit knowledge they had of the reputation of the producer. My bottle came third by order of tasting and we started with a Hautes-Côtes de Nuits 2001, Domaine des Chambris. An implicit ranking was collectively chosen. During the tasting, I kept silent and asked them questions only if appropriate. One of the members, Dominique, who is also a municipal councillor and belongs to a family of wine growers (his brother runs a vineyard), dominated the discussion as the oenologist was not present to comment on each wine. Each member gave his/her opinion about the wine tasted, the visual aspect, the smell, the taste of it, and then conclusions were summarized by Dominique. The discussion about each wine was very open, and the whole exercise was very relaxed. All the members of the group drank their samples and it was very difficult for me to escape this collective libation.

The social pressure to drink wine was difficult to ignore, and I found it hard to say no, even when Didier's non-drinking wife joined us for dinner. The meal was delicious and well prepared, and the bottles were all drunk by my colleagues in the course of dinner. Conversations started to take place, from local politics to holidays. Then the next topic was decided, red wines from South America, and I was invited to join them for a wine tasting organized by the chemist, Jean-Paul, at his sister's vineyards in Vosne-Romanée. It was clear that the wine club provided them with an opportunity to meet and enjoy their friendship, and was not a space for social performance and competition. Even if sometimes they did not agree on the individual appreciation of the wine, nevertheless a consensual decision was always made by the dominant figure of the group, be it the oenologist or, in his absence, the wine grower's brother.

What these episodes illustrate is the multifaceted nature of wine drinking culture and consumption and the sites devoted to its expression as a growing passion of the affluent middle classes. If it is true that wine consumption has become an elitist and distinctive social practice, it is nevertheless the case that it also enables social relations and facilitates connections between individuals in a society in transition. Moreover, wine culture with its growing importance in French society plays an important role in creating a moderate and knowledgeable wine consumption transmitted by several groups of experts and mediated by a codified system of rules. Yet at the same time this culture has been used as a cultural resource to promote regional and social interests to the detriment of a more unified and simplified body of knowledge.

Notes

1. I should like to thank Berg Publishers for allowing me to reproduce parts of this chapter, which had previously appeared as Marion Demossier, 'Consuming wine in France: the "wandering drinker" and the "Vin-anomie"', in Thomas N. Wilson (ed.), *Drinking Cultures* (Oxford and New York: Berg, 2005), pp. 129–54.
2. M. Bernard uses a database of 300 local experts who will be asked each year to taste wines.
3. The INAO (Institut National des Appellations d'Origine Contrôlées) has created a glass, the internationally recognized Wine-Tasting Glass, which is now marketed as the "compulsory" tool for sensory evaluation of wine in any contentious tasting. The egg-shaped bowl is designed to enhance fully the concentration of aroma and allow the wine to be swirled without spilling. According to Robert Parker, it is 'the finest inexpensive tasting glass in the world'.
4. Jean-Pierre Albert, 'La nouvelle culture du vin', *Terrain*, 13 (1989), 117–24.
5. Especially under the Mitterrand presidency of 1981, a new era of cultural democratization was starting. However, this was later criticized by various intellectuals such as Marc Fumaroli.
6. See for a telling exemple, *http://www.chablis-garnier.com/page5.htm*.
7. Gil Morrot, 'Peut-on améliorer les performances des dégustateurs?', *Vigne et Vin* (1999), 31–7 and François Casabianca and Christine de Sainte Marie, 'L'évaluation sensorielle des produits typiques. Concevoir et instrumenter l'épreuve de typicité', in *The Socio-economics of Origin Labelled Products in Agro-food Supply Chains: Spatial, Institutional and Co-ordination aspects*, 67th EAAE Seminar, le Mans, 28–30 October 1999.
8. See for example the following website: *http://www.domaine-buisson.com/fr/presse.htm* consulted on 30 September 2008.
9. Sarah Blowen, Marion Demossier and Jeanine Picard, *Recollections of France. Memories, Identities and Heritage in Contemporary France* (Oxford and New York: Berghahn, 2000).
10. Robert C. Ulin, 'Work as cultural production: labor and self-identity among southwest French wine growers', *Journal of the Royal Anthropological Institute*, 8, 4 (2001), 696.
11. The head office is situated in Orange, southern France
12. Philippe Chaudat, 'In imago veritas. Images souhaitées, images produites', *Ethnologie Française*, 37 (2001–2), 717–23.
13. Chaudat, 'In imago veritas', 722. My own translation.
14. Ipsos-Insight Marketing, *Les Français et le vin*, survey conducted for ONIVINS; personal communication.
15. For more details about the Confrérie des Chevaliers du Tastevin, see Laferté, 'Un «folklore» pour journalistes. La Confréra des Chevaliers du Tastevin', *Ethnologies Comparées* 8 (Spring 2005), 1–32.
16. I was asked years later to talk about the festival to a village near Dijon which had been selected for hosting the *Saint-Vincent Tournante*, and

during one of the preparatory meetings I brought the film we made about it. Watching cases of drunkenness, most of the wine growers in the room were completely shocked by these scenes.

17 Jean-Pierre Plichon, 'Les mutations du tourisme viti-vinicole en Bordelais', in *Des vignobles et des vins à travers le monde*, p. 131.

18 Wine lovers very often refer to the *Guide des Vins de France* to select their wines, and this could be explained by their use of the internet and the influence of the *Revue des Vins de France* (see chapter 5).

19 The JCE (Jeune Chambre Économique) is a local association of young professionals (they have to be less than forty years old) who want to be involved in local matters and share the same interests. They organize various activities, projects, charities and travels, and are structured by the local Chambre de Commerce. They are an important port of social integration for any professionals coming to a specific area.

20 They have put the emphasis on this when talking about their passion for wine.

Chapter Six
Passion for Wine and Life-Stories

The study of wine consumption necessitates taking into account the spaces where it occurs, the various contexts in which individuals define and enact their wine consumption, as well as the narratives they use to construct their relationship to wine and alcohol drinking. Compared with other types of alcohol, wine is seen by many French consumers as part of their national heritage and as a symbol of a lifestyle which now has little to do with the realities of actual wine consumption. The passion for wine is very often described by consumers as a lifetime interest which takes several forms, from the average wine drinker to the intense wine lover.[1] It could also be argued that sometimes this passion transforms itself into a professional occupation, as many of the wine lovers encountered as part of this study have become involved in wine activities in parallel to their wine hobby, organizing tastings in their companies or writing articles for the press. What wine consumers have in common is their use of wine to fulfil social and personal needs, and wine is often presented as a medium enabling them to connect to or to engage with social networks.

By following five individuals selected during the course of my fieldwork on the basis of their proclaimed interest for wines and their particular stance relative to wine culture and wine consumption, this chapter argues that consumption enables individuals to create a sense of solidarity and sociability and to express or construct their identity through wine consumption. In return, this intensifies the nature of their relationships through alcohol consumption and creates a sense of belonging which enables them to identify with other groups or to subscribe to a number of shared values produced collectively. It also contributes to their social construction as individuals belonging to the French nation, facilitating connections with others, family and friends, rooting them in a territory which provides them with some emblematic values that they endorse. In their quest for landmarks, wine and gastronomic tourism, the discovery of regional heritage and direct contacts with the producer help to create a sense of stability or timelessness in reaction to the fluidity of modern life, the salience of contemporary identities and the ephemeral nature of our societies.[2] To some extent, it could be argued that wine consumption enables them to shape modernity, to make it theirs in their own terms.

There are almost as many wines in France as there are ways of drinking. Yet wine drinking in France refers to a set of values which are connected to ideal representations of the nation, most obviously that of the rural idyll.[3] Furthermore, France is usually treated by commentators and journalists in stereotypical terms as if it were culturally homogeneous, which is far from true.[4] What we could argue from the following examples is that wine consumption takes different forms, and even if there is a common framework, individuals engage in very different ways in relation to their consumption. This combination of values, such as friendship, egalitarianism, artisanship, collectivism, relationship to nature and collective heritage underlining wine consumption, challenges traditional understandings of consumption as utilitarian or mass-driven, and demonstrates the complex and varied patterns of responses to economic change by both producers and consumers, neither of whom are content to accept it passively, showing how they contribute to the redefinition of individual and collective identities.[5] The series of case studies presented in this chapter illustrate the dynamic, reflexive and collective processes behind wine consumption by connecting individual stories to wider developments occurring at regional, national and global levels. Each of them was selected because of their particular relationship to wine and because these five examples encompass some of the general characteristics encountered in relation to wine consumption in France. The interviews were focused on each individual and their relationship to the product, enabling them to tell their story and demonstrating that self-reflexivity and passion are constructed around wine.

1. Louis Dubreuil, retired self-proclaimed wine consumer, South of France, 2001

I first met Louis through an old friend of mine who is a talented photographer and invited my husband and me to spend a weekend in his parents' house in the South of France near Saint-Raphaël. Louis, retired after a successful career at the EDF (Électricité de France) in Paris, had built his dream home near the Mediterranean coast to enjoy, at fifty-two, an early retirement. His wife devoted her life to the education of their only child and to the housekeeping of their flat in Paris and, later, their house-to-be. She also took up different hobbies and wrote a book for her own pleasure. During our first meeting in his Paris flat, he expressed his passion for wines when he learned that I had completed a Ph.D. on the subject of Burgundian viticulture. I remember that our first visit was also marked by the tasting of 'very precious bottles' from Burgundy that he kept only for 'special occasions'. Years later when I started working on wine consumption, I decided to reflect on my stay in their house in 2001 to analyse Louis's passion for wine. This represented a unique occasion to witness how this passion was performed and displayed in the context of the private sphere, and how I remembered it as a social experience. Contrary to most of the wine consumers interviewed, Louis was not well known for his volubility as far as wines were concerned. He could be defined as a typical affluent middle-class male, and it is why I chose to include him in this chapter. His love for wine was confined to drinking it, every day, in moderate proportions, and enjoying it on specific festive and social occasions. In terms of his social profile, Louis belongs to the declining group of traditional wine drinkers. His wife did not drink wine but consumed water during our stay.

For Louis, our meeting was part of a festive weekend which needed to be organized in advance. He made the point that he expected us to follow a calendar of activities, from dawn till dusk, punctuated by gargantuan meals and incredible wine tastings. Most of his preparation, he insisted, was devoted to the choice of what we would consume at lunch and dinner time. Every item had been carefully selected, bought from the local market or the butcher, prepared and complemented by what he thought was an 'appropriate' bottle. The Saturday lunch was, for example, typical of a summer Provençal menu, with fish *terrine* as a starter and steak on a barbecue, followed by salad and cheeses, completed by a Norwegian ice *bombe*. Most of our other eating experiences worked on the same principle. Red wines were selected to go with cheeses and the steak on the barbecue, while white wines were served for the fish starter and the dessert. The meticulous organization was orchestrated with almost military precision, and the whole experience was clearly directed towards our pleasure, a collective hedonism, exchange and friendship.

When we arrived at their house on the Friday evening, it was clear that his meticulous organization was not only confined to the context of the weekend. The house was as spotless as if it were ready to be photographed by *Homes and Gardens*, a beautiful modern Provençal house shaped in an L around a magnificent swimming pool set in an exuberant and flourishing garden. A big table, which would be the centre of our activities for the next three days, stood on the patio with an aperitif already prepared. The whole experience would have stood comparison with a five-star hotel, and their hospitality went beyond mere form. We were allocated a beautiful bedroom, on the first floor, with an ensuite and a large balcony over the pool. Every detail had been thought about, and the same carefulness applied to every aspect of our stay.

On our arrival, the first thing Louis wanted us to visit was his cellar, which he had especially built into the rock in 1992. The cellar that he described as a 'sanctuary' was located next to the garage and was a room of nine square metres with a 2-metre-high ceiling. Air conditioning had been installed to keep the temperature around 16 degrees with a hygrometry of 70–90. It was an exact replica of the traditional wine cellar, with gravel on the floor, a barrel in the middle of the room and wine racks along two of the walls. Hundreds of bottles were displayed, classified by region and vintage. Each of the bottles was labelled and marked precisely, and Louis kept a record of his possessions in a notebook located on a small table in the corner of the room. Corkscrews and several types of glasses were exhibited on a shelf next to framed wine labels and advertising posters. Louis explained to us that his cellar contained over 250 bottles, of which eighty were from the Bordeaux region (ten white), sixty-five from Burgundy (fifteen white), twenty-five from Loire (fifteen white), ten white from Alsace, thirty red Côtes du Rh'ne, twenty-five from Provence (ten white, ten red and five rosé), ten Champagne, and five ciders. He did not go into the details of each denomination of origin, but he was proud of the fact that his oldest bottle dated back to 1957 and that the average age of a bottle was at least ten years. His precious collection was protected by an alarm. He then explained that most of his wines were bought from wine fairs organized by supermarkets or following the advice given to him by family and friends. He had also inherited some bottles which had previously been kept in the family cellar, but which were divided up following the death of his parents. This inheritance had previously been stored in the cellar of the family farmhouse in Burgundy. He reckoned that his annual spending on wines could be estimated at around £200–£250, which is not very much, and that he never bought any wines which were more than four years old, as the main objective of his cellar was to enable wines to age.

Apart from his cellar, no other signs indicated the exercise of a passion, there were no books on wines, no guides and no visible expression of this interest. His whole energy was focused upon an almost obsessive attention to detail during the preparation of the meal to demonstrate what he saw as a 'special and festive' occasion. The ceremonial surrounding each meal emphasized the need for Louis to display his culinary talents from breakfast to dinner, and his attention to detail regarding the choice of alcohol and wines consumed throughout the festivities. The aperitif started with a choice of drinks, ranging from *kir* to *aligoté*, *pastis* and *dorédor* accompanied by nibbles and elaborate canapés of melon and Parma ham. These were followed by a succession of bottles from the cellar, especially selected to match each dish, from the starter to the dessert. Bordeaux and Burgundy dominated our wine consumption, but some less well known local wines were also drunk such as Côteaux de Provence for the desserts. Louis could be classified as a French *bon vivant* who just enjoys eating and drinking, but he is also conscious of being a representative of a certain bourgeois tradition, as he emphasized that 'this is a family tradition that we need to keep alive'. His consumption during these festive occasions focused on pleasure, hedonism and good company. It was not about a display of his own knowledge and 'distinction' in relation to wines, and during most of the drinking he did not comment on the wines tasted, but it was more about a model of social presentation, as he was clearly anxious to project the image of a successful and affluent middle-class man with his own cellar and a passion for conviviality. When questioned about it, he said that, for him, it forms part of what it means to be French and that there is nothing exceptional in demonstrating what he termed a 'family heritage'. It is clear that wine consumption represents a link with his past and his attachment to a region, a proof of his social positioning in relation to his family and, more precisely, his brothers, as he made clear several times, and wider society. Moreover what dominated this social exchange was the demonstration of his culinary and cultural capital through the sharing of his bottles with friends. He was, as he made clear, very proud to be able to share these special wines with 'friends who can appreciate'.

2. Matthieu Nathan, Paris, wealthy wine collector, 2004

As we have seen above, drinking wine is in part a social experience for the French, providing a context for socializing with friends, reminiscence about times past or speculation about the future.[6] Yet the example of Matthieu Nathan, a son of the Gournoff family who had inherited one of the most famous modern and contemporary art galleries in Paris, offers an illustration of another type of young moderate consumer combining his love for landscape, cycling and Burgundy with aestheticism and a contemporary lifestyle. When his Russian aunt, Katia Gournoff, came to France in 1926 she opened a gallery which exhibited, amongst other artists, Marc Chagall, Pierre Bonnard, Édouard Vuillard, Georges Bouche, Amédée de la Patellière, and Foujita. In 1955 she was the first to show one of Monet's *Water Lilies* in a Paris gallery, and since she retired, a succession of new artists have been presented including Bellegarde, Messagier, Rebeyrolle, Arnaud d'Aunay and Isabel Michel. Matthieu's profession as an art dealer clearly relates to his passion for wines, and parallels could be established between both worlds, with their status at auctions for instance. However, when we met in the gallery in June 2004 he never drew the link between wine and art, preferring to discuss his passion for landscapes and *terroir*.[7] The visual however occupies an important place in his story.

I met Matthieu Nathan through an old acquaintance of my mother, Mme Pion, a retired wine merchant in Paris who had specialized in Burgundy wines. When I contacted her about my work on wine consumers and then interviewed her, she mentioned Matthieu, whom she described as a 'discreet connoisseur'. I rang him the following day, and he gave me an appointment at the gallery located on the Rive Gauche for the next morning. I had known his gallery by reputation and because some of the works exhibited were amongst those by my favourite artists. I arrived at ten o'clock and I was welcomed by his secretary, who said that he had not yet arrived. This coincided with a delivery made to the gallery of four cases of wine coming from Tollot-Beaut in Chorey-les-Beaune (Burgundy), which is one of a very select band of Côte d'Or vineyards. The 24 hectares of Tollot-Beaut sit modestly in the centre of Chorey-lès-Beaune. Today the 'front of house' face of the *domaine* is Nathalie Tollot, yet there are many other Tollots to be seen in the *cuverie* and the vineyards; uncle Jack, father Alain and Nathalie's cousins Jean-Paul and Olivier. Initially the family owned vines only in Chorey, but successive generations made small acquisitions in Savigny, Aloxe and Beaune, and much more recently their new 'monopole' Chorey-lès-Beaune 'Pièce du Chapitre'.

This delivery provided me with a great opportunity to start the interview and as soon as Matthieu arrived, I congratulated him on his choice of wines, explaining that I had tasted Nathalie's production several years before when I was working with her at the GJPV (Groupe des Jeunes Professionnels de la Vigne, Group of Young Professional Wine Growers) on rural women in Europe. Matthieu responded that these were 'his favourite wines from Burgundy, his favourite region'. Then I was asked to follow him, and the interview took place in the next room called the salon *Boiserie*, which was full of famous paintings by Chagall, Friesz, Rouault and Zadkine. A modern white desk and two chairs were in the middle of the room, and we took our places around the table in order to start the interview.

During the course of our discussion, Matthieu demonstrated a keen interest in everything related to landscape, travelling and the discovery of the various regions he had visited. In his thirties, fit and very handsome, he dressed in an effortlessly chic style and was not typical of the wine consumers I had met before, and he did not represent the traditional *bon vivant* or the classical 'wine spotter'. He presented himself as somebody who likes to discover France through his cycling excursions and to order wines from the producers directly rather than buying from supermarkets. His passion revealed itself during the interview when he mentioned that his interest in Burgundy was fostered by our common acquaintance Mme Pion. Through his various peregrinations over the years, he has got to know some of the 'best' producers who were either selected by the

Parker guide or were recommended by specialist magazines such as *Bourgogne Aujourd'hui*. He introduced his parents to Burgundian wines, taking them on a number of occasions on voyages of discovery around famous vineyards.[8] When asked about his trips to French wine regions, he insisted that the landscape is at the heart of the *terroir*, giving the example of Burgundy, with its tapestry of wines and soils: 'When you are on your bike, it is obvious, you look at the plots and the soil and you see differences.' Then he discussed the role of wine growers in making these differences more visible through wine-making, and how he liked to discover some of the wine growers already cited and reviewed in the specialist press. Despite his personal wealth, he claimed that most of the wines he bought had to offer a good relationship between quality and price, as he likes to drink some famous bottles but also enjoys exploring lesser-known products, new tastes and regions like Corsica or the Loire. What is striking in his narrative is the sense of time and historicity, and the fact that he is able to comment on wines from the 1970s, the 1980s and more recent vintages. The family cellar contains, according to him, some 7,000 to 8,000 bottles, with different vintages and denominations of origin, and he keeps a regular record of what he drinks. His tastes could be seen as quite eclectic, even if he emphasizes that he drinks only French wines: 'In France you have so much diversity' and as many *grands crus* than *petits vins de pays*.'

When discussing wine consumption, Matthieu evokes a division between ordinary consumption of wines, which is basically what he described as one bottle of wine per day consumed with his partner when dining, followed sometimes by a period of abstinence, and what he calls consumption of 'good wines' which refers to a special occasion described as 'the right time', 'the right meal' or the 'right occasion'. This consumption could involve both famous and expensive wines such as La Tâche as well as cheap and unknown ones like the Côteaux du Ventoux. For him, what matters when discussing wine consumption is again the idea of sharing a good bottle and having friends around to compare tastes ('There is always one wine which provides unanimity') and discuss matters related to the region from which the wine is produced. The main interest lies in the discovery of something unusual or surprising which will enable the subsequent organization of a trip to the region and the producer. Gastronomy and tourism thus become part of the ingredients of this new quest and the main aim is to meet another producer who will join the list of possible contacts which will then circulate amongst friends and colleagues in Paris.

For the reasons outlined above, Matthieu offers an example of the urban touristic consumer looking for his roots and some certainties. Wine consumption offers him the opportunity for an intimate relationship with a culture and a territory that is now separate from his own experience. By drinking, he is able to travel and incorporate the other. The wide range of wines and thus tastes and culinary sensations on offer provides him with an opportunity to travel in time and in space. These culinary and oenological journeys define his identity in a society where fragmentation is combined with modernity. Drinking wines for him provides a way of discovering new areas, their cultural and oenological heritage and traditions, but also a means of bringing back some of these memories to Paris by tasting these wines in a different context amongst friends and in the family setting. The yearning for a return to the countryside is part of the process of reinvention of a rural and peasant identity by urban consumers, but it is also an expression of a desire for landscape appropriation and a life in communities where togetherness, personal recognition and collective participation are easily combined, all these values being perceived as less salient in modern urban societies.

3. Marie-Laure Garcia, my *terroir* and my family, Burgundy, 2004

The idea of finding roots and meaning through gastronomical and oenological experiences is quite common in French society and the example of Marie-Laure Garcia is revealing because, when she was interviewed about her passion for wine, the discussion turned out to be more about her life story than a simple narrative of consumption. Marie-Laure is a well-known figure in the Burgundian tourist industry as she has been a guide and a lecturer at the tourist office in Beaune since the 1970s. She was one of the first women to organize visits and wine tastings in a region where the wine industry was traditionally dominated by men. I met her several times between 1999 and 2004, and I have always been impressed by her wide knowledge of the region and its wines, and also by her constant energy and enthusiasm for learning and exchanging her knowledge with others.

Marie-Laure Garcia was born in Burgundy, in the department of Sône-et-Loire where the river meets the plains and a new landscape offers a contrast to tourists accustomed to the hills of the nearby vineyards. As an orphan raised in local government care, she was brought up in a rural environment, but felt 'on her own'. She discovered Beaune when she started her education in a religious school. At the time, her options in terms of career were 'restricted to joining the army or working in tourism'. In October 1970, an opportunity arose with a one-month placement at the Beaune tourist board under the supervision of M. Delagrange, who took her under his wing and advised her to learn other languages before coming back. Marie-Laure, who found her vocation in tourism, left Burgundy to go to Germany to learn the language before being recalled once there was a vacancy and she joined the tourist board on a permanent basis.

Her recollections of this period are marked by the fact that she was on a learning curve, having to familiarize herself with various disciplines, from history of art, German, English and local history. She subsequently took all the necessary examinations to become a lecturer-guide, which was the highest professional qualification in the tourist industry at the time. In 1974, when wine tourism began to be developed and structured at local level with the influence of the CIVB, she decided to join some of their classes and workshops to be initiated into the arts of wine tasting by experts such as Max Léglise. She confirmed that her initial professional interest transformed quickly into a real passion and a lifestyle, and since 1974 she has acted as a wine expert for regional panels and has organized wine seminars for French companies. This passion also found an echo when she married a local chef, who shared her enthusiasm for food and wine. During the various interviews, she often underlined that her job is 'more than a simple passion, it is the family I never had'. Rightly, she is known beyond the confines of Beaune, and she contributes to the construction of the region as a rich historical heritage site, a complex landscape constituted by a mosaic of vines and a mapping of the vineyard constituted by domains and wine merchants which needs to be read with the help of an expert eye.

Among the skills that Marie-Laure had acquired, learning how to taste was the most challenging.[9] During all of our interviews, references to specific wines and their corresponding aromas were made such as 'Chambolle-Musigny is my favourite wine – coffee, cocoa and sometimes something animal and earthy.' Her education in wine, and especially the vocabulary of wine tasting, could be summarized by the attention she devotes to smell and the olfactory memory attached to the wines tasted. As a starting-point, she cited the example of the French perfume shop Sephora where you can smell 500 types of aromas. She also used the essences compiled by Jean Lenoir in his book of scents, *Le Nez du vin* (Aromas of Wine), which is very useful for beginners. Moreover, for Marie-Laure, the constitution of her olfactory memory was mediated by her own writings as she took notes on everything she tasted over the years, where and with whom. What is for her the most important element to transmit is the simplicity of the language, not too scientifically defined, not too poetic either.

Her experiences of other wine tastings helped her to constitute her own vocabulary and a sort of 'library of aromas' typical of the region and its most famous wines. Because of the vast diversity of consumers she meets, from Japanese tourists to groups of chefs, she wanted to make sure that her description remains close to the experiences of consumers. For her, wine tasting is first and foremost about objectivity, and there is a common basis to aromas and tastes that she wanted to acquire, but there is a lot of personal judgement that she also wanted consumers to understand. She always made the point that when she describes wines, her own individual judgement is at stake: 'It is what I feel; it does not mean I am right.'[10] Most of her experiences have moreover been mediated by her knowledge of gastronomy. During the interview, she emphasized that her love of food and cooking, which is shared by her husband, has enabled her to construct her knowledge about Burgundy and its wines. On one occasion, she had to convince a tourist that Burgundian wines were as good as those of the Bordelais. This visitor, during a stop at the Clos de Vougeot, disrupted her description of the wines of the Côtes de Nuits by saying, 'Anyway, I prefer Bordeaux wines.' It took three consecutive years before this 'collector of labels' as she termed him was convinced that the region was full of treasures.

Marie-Laure contributes to the construction of Burgundy as a tourist region by organizing visits to some of the most famous local sites including the Hôtel Dieu and the Château of La Rochepôt, and she also organizes trips to selected domains to taste their products, and gives lectures on wines. Most of her clientele is recruited from the world of business, mainly educated men over forty-five years of age, or she takes groups of young female and male professionals in their twenties who want to learn about wines. She helps companies to prepare organized tours, and with her knowledge of local services she plans meals in specific historical sites such as the Clos de Vougeot and takes the group through a commented wine tasting during dinner. Her humour, her personality and her cordial welcome are all the ingredients of this discovery of local wines, and once, as the ambiance relaxed, she found herself joined by the members of one of the local folkloric choirs to sing 'Joyeux enfants de la Bourgogne'. It was in this atmosphere of conviviality and excessive consumption that visitors found themselves in an exhilarating social situation, and this became the occasion for them to establish friendships. Her passion thus goes beyond professional duty, and her professional and private lives are constructed around a passion for food and drink. She likes 'talking about wine', and even if she is not a member of a website or a devoted reader of guides, transmits her knowledge and passion for Burgundian viticulture and gastronomy to visitors passing through Burgundy.

4. Théodore Magnien, wine lover and bank manager, Luxembourg, 2004

Compared with Marie-Laure, Théodore Magnien not only talks about wine, but loves writing about it. During the analysis of three wine websites (see chapter 7), I noticed that the name of Théodore Magnien came back repeatedly on the messages posted with *DC* (*Degustateurs.com*), and when I circulated my request to interview wine lovers, he contacted me immediately. Of all the wine consumers I encountered, he was the most critical and inquisitive about his passion, sending me, at regular intervals, fragments of analysis relating to some of the areas of my investigation or reactions to some of my questions such as how this passion has developed or what a 'good' wine is. He was also the most voluble wine consumer, and I have archived hours of interviews and email discussions with him. To some extent, he had all the qualities needed to become a sociologist and he confessed early on in our relationship that it was a new passion of his: 'I have become interested in sociology these last four years basically. It is a change of direction, but I am more sensitive to that than I was, and now, with wine, this offers a fabulous means to understand what is going on.'[11]

Without his contribution and his incisive comments on the nature of his passion for sociology, this book would not be what it is, as some of our discussions helped me greatly. Because of his own critical distance and, at the same time, his involvement in different aspects of his passion, he has a crucial place in this chapter. It is also the case that his story offers a different stance on wine consumption as he incarnates the traditional wine lover, but combines eclectic tastes with a global lifestyle. I welcomed him to my Burgundian village house near Beaune and cooked him a meal to which he contributed by bringing different French wines. I remembered the care I took to prepare some of the traditional dishes transmitted to me by my mother, as I wanted to make sure I could take up the gastronomic challenge. On that occasion, he brought me a bottle of wine, which he explained was the worst in his cellar. I discovered with amusement that in fact, it was a Beaune 1971 from the Couvent des Cordeliers, a company founded by my grandfather in the 1930s and subsequently sold to Patriarche, another famous Burgundian wine merchant. I could not quibble, as the bottle was indeed pretty awful.

Alsatian by birth, Théodore studied in Strasbourg and then went on to Nancy to the School of Engineering from which he subsequently graduated. Then after working in the mining industry for a while and completing his military service, he went on to work for the French embassy in Washington and decided to stay in America for two years. There he worked in a computing business based in Chicago until its bankruptcy obliged him to return to Europe. He was appointed to a post in Luxemburg by Accenture and was sent for two years to Finland to look after one of their clients. Finally he ended up in 1996 working for Fortes back in Luxemburg as a human resources manager where he says his passion for wines started to evolve. In 1997 he decided for the first time to take notes on all the wines he tasted and he started to buy books, read the specialized journals and attend his first wine seminars. He justified his new interest in wines during this period by his social status as a young, single and wealthy male professional. This new hobby developed in the context of a group of five or six colleagues in a similar position who were anxious to learn more about wines. According to him, it also corresponded with a major period of speculation in wine (in 1997 and 1998) that gave him the opportunity to buy at auction bottles of famous wines with the help of the *Guide Hachette*.

The group organized wine tastings of twelve bottles, deciding on a particular theme, region or variety of grapes, and learning their particular characteristics in terms of tastes. Then they went on to compare French with foreign wines, and later to have blind tastings, making it more professional and challenging. After this period, which he described as 'having wine tastings to taste forty famous wines without learning anything, it has no purpose, it is useless except to show your trophies; for my part, I try to make sure that people can remember something about it,' Théodore wanted to take up a new challenge. After his initiation in famous and expensive wines, he went on to organize more structured and educative sessions, and for this purpose, in 1999, he spent no less than 30,000 euros on wines from three or four local *cavistes*. As his current job obliges him to travel on a regular basis between Paris, Strasbourg, Brussels and Lyon, he found it difficult to devote as much as time as before to wine tasting. During his peregrinations, food and gastronomic breaks were always cited, and he made the point that his wine consumption took place in the context of either a wine tasting or a convivial meal taken in a restaurant or at home with friends. Yet his consumption had taken a new turn and was no longer devoted to expensive bottles. 'I like to please myself with a good Beaujolais or a good Morgon when I go climbing, I take it out of my bag and when you are a bit hungry, this has a great taste!'

For Théodore, another of the most important features of wine consumption is sociability, and on several occasions, he cited the social benefits that wine consumption has brought to him. The convivial nature of wine drinking plays a major role in the experience of consumption as the product acts as a social fluid, but it also reveals the nature of the other. This is an element that was emphasized by most of the wine consumers that I encountered, and the figure of the producer is very often presented in parallel with that of the product. Sociability is also cited by wine lovers when they visit wine producers, and according to Théodore,

> when wine growers give them some sort of recognition by saying 'You are a good wine taster', then they say he is a good wine grower; but when the wine grower is shy or reticent, they say he is a dead loss and his wines are bad. It is true that drinking the wine of a friendly wine grower is something special; this is one of the best experiences.

For Théodore, there is an important distinction between a blind wine tasting and meeting the producer, wine being appreciated in relation to the context in which it is consumed. The wine experience with the producer is an integral part of drinking, and this direct contact with the producer is always seen by consumers as the most important feature of their experience of wine consumption.

For Théodore, sharing his knowledge and love of wine involves not only wine tasting, but also the act of writing. As we have seen, he takes notes on everything he drinks, and most of our discussions following the interviews took place in the context of the polished texts he has written and put on the DC website to be read and reacted to. For him, writing about wine necessitates the adoption of a common vocabulary, which is not easy to establish, and what he aims for is to find the 'correct' word for each sensation, making sure that it can be shared whenever possible. He evoked on different occasions the balance between emotions and technical language with the aim of sharing and not just showing off his knowledge. Many of the conversations between wine lovers oscillate between a pseudo-intellectualization of the product and an exercise in self-esteem, which Théodore perceived as devoid of any real meaning:

> *Lots of discussions turn around this idea that you've bought these, you've drunk these. I know best, and what is cheaper. This is not helpful because we do not want to hear that, putting others down to make yourself better, it does not work ... DC is not like that, we put our notes on the web and we do not discuss them, we just talk.*

After all, for him, wine consumption is about having pleasure and exchanging with others.

5. Marie-Hélène Tardieu, labels and memories

Marie-Hélène Tardieu would not qualify herself as a wine lover even if she was introduced to me by a friend of mine as somebody 'who knows a lot about wine'. However, when we met, Marie-Hélène insisted that her passion was less for wine than for wine culture, collecting labels and discovering French geography through names and images. She also emphasized that she was not a discerning buyer as far as wine was concerned ('I buy anything really'), reducing her consumption to a simple act of just choosing wine in supermarkets where most of her shopping was done and then consuming them with friends and relatives. Working in Burgundy for an association specializing in women's issues and gender equality, she is divorced and a mother of two adolescents, combining a full-time job with various commitments to local associations where she lives. In her fifties, she also has many hobbies including walking, running and wine drinking. She characterized her active life as one devoted to voluntary groups and the organization of local events. She was for several years one of the main organizers of the MJC Maison des Jeunes et de la Culture, a community arts centre and youth club, where she contributed to the creation of a wine club. The MJC invited different speakers to talk about wines and taste some samples from different regions. Once she was no longer eligible for membership of the MJC, the age limit of membership being forty, she and some friends formed a small group of wine lovers who meet on a regular basis to discuss politics and wine.

According to Marie-Hélène, her interest in drinking wine is limited to this wine club and some social occasions, as she is very busy professionally. When describing the activities of the wine club, she emphasized that their aim is to know more about the region and to link their holidays and weekends in France to the discovery of the local wines encountered. However, when they organize the tasting, their selection of products is based on the local supermarket, and the price guides them in their selections. Then they prepare a file in relation to the region to look at a map and the names of the relevant villages and their producers. The wines selected were commented on by the group, but no consensus was reached between members. For Marie-Hélène, the aim of their meeting was mainly to learn about France and to discuss politics, and she stated: 'Most of the time, we finished by arguing, as Jean is National Front and I am left-wing. Last time, we had such an argument that since then he has not spoken to me and he refused to contribute to the last tasting.'

Marie-Hélène's interest in wine is closely connected to her own life story, and she has, for example, long collected labels. Her childhood was mentioned several times when she started to elaborate on her family passion for wine and her attachment to the region. As she expressed matters, 'They lived in the Bordelais, so you see that they appreciated wine, and we always drank wine at home. My father, who was a GP, was also a collector of wine labels.' Much of her childhood was passed in the family house in the Lot where all the various relatives gathered to share the summer vacations. Her family initiated her into wine culture by discussing what they drank and by encouraging her to taste local wines. Later, when her grandparents died, her parents bought a house in Buzet, another wine region, and all her memories of her adolescence are related to discovering this part of France and other wines from the Lot. This exploration of France is reflected in her hobby of collecting labels, something which was transmitted to her by her father when he retired. Marie-Hélène started to become passionate about wine through this collection of labels that she has constituted over the years, and it is also through this collection that she met her husband. After their marriage, they moved to Paris as he worked in the nuclear industry, and it is only later that they moved to Nuits-Saint-Georges. She kept all her collection in shoe boxes, showing me the oldest one, a 1903 Château Fronsac.

For Marie-Hélène, the collection is less about wine drinking or the status of the bottle and more about the images and memories constructed around them. Her memory of each wine is associated with a reminiscence associated with some well-known names that she describes to me. For her, the collection provides a tenuous link to members of the family, and each occasion was another opportunity to enrich the series. 'I have even kept the Côtes de Castillon that I drank over the years and I have a long chronological series of labels.' Most of our interview was devoted to going through the collection, and it is remarkable that she associated an interview on wine consumption with a discussion of wine labels. Her knowledge of French vineyards was confined to the list of *crus* and plots on display, and she never mentioned any other aspects of wine culture or consumption. Her appreciation of taste in wines was absent from our discussion, and at one point she declared that most of the time she does not consume wine, and it is only in the context of the wine club and family events that she will drink it.

Atypical in her story of wine consumption, Marie-Hélène illustrates another dimension of wine drinking, that of the consumption of images and representations of regions and wines detached from the act of drinking and from a self-reflexive approach to wine. Her story is that of a passive wine consumer absorbing the imaginary representations of the wine industry and creating by herself a memory of France which will privilege images rather than experiences. Because her case represents another aspect of wine consumption pushed to the extreme (she hardly mentioned drinking itself), it is revealing of some of the processes taking place at national level. The ideal of consumption is also part of this process, and the gap between these ideals and the reality of a declining, fragmented and occasional drinking culture is growing.

Through this ethnographic presentation of five case studies, wine consumption as a social object covers very different individual narratives and social situations. All of our consumers see wine drinking in a positive light and do not raise the issue of health or the dangers associated with drinking alcohol. Indeed most are proud of their consumption. They associate wine drinking with social exchanges, festive occasions and the discovery of French geography. They also put great emphasis on the social inclusion attached to the act of consuming and the necessity of conforming for most drinkers. According to these individuals, drinking wine is above all done in a collective context, but it is also associated with the opportunity to establish new networks of individuals and friends, on a smaller interpersonal scale, who have different tastes and interests. The common framework for thinking about their consumption is that as individuals they all belong to the middle class and they have the economic means and the time needed to enjoy wines. They construct their social identification and belonging through a shared set of values which define them as French against the forces of modernization that they actively engage with.

Drinking wine has become a major social activity in France, as is demonstrated by the growing number of wine clubs and other social activities that surround it in every city or small town. However, in this new environment, eating and drinking have become the sites of resistance to the decline of traditional alimentary patterns and to the 'McDonaldization' of French society. The growth of these activities around wine has facilitated new forms of social relations, linking producers to consumers. French wine producers have opened their cellars and have started to talk about their wines and, in doing so, have contributed to the political construction of France as a natural, traditional and authentic nation. The male middle class has become the major but not the only consumer of this new France, rediscovering the regions and their products during their leisure time and their vacations. By exploring the new representations at the core of this consumption, it could be argued that wine is a key part of the process by which France has become an object of consumption, a new commodity for its citizens. Wine drinking has in the process been transformed into both a self-reflexive and interactive activity enabling individuals to make sense of the world around them and to define their own identity through consumption. In an increasingly urbanized society, wine has become a powerful vehicle for the politics and economics of *ruralité* and regionalism. This is associated with a mythical golden age as well as supposed common values promoted by French producers and wine organizations.

Notes

1 Marion Demossier. 'Les passionnés du vin ou le mariage du cœur et de la raison', in Bromberger, *Passions ordinaires*, pp. 163–88. For an introduction to the definition of passion see Bromberger's introduction to the volume.
2 Sarah Blowen, Marion Demossier and Jeanine Picard, *Recollections of France, Memories, Identities and Heritage in Contemporary France* (Oxford and New York: Berghahn, 2000).
3 For a discussion of the concept of rural idyll, see the excellent thesis of Peter Howland, Pinot Pilgrims: Metro-rurality, social distinction and ideal reflexive individuality in Martinborough, PhD thesis, University of Canterbury, Anthropology, (2007).
4 Dwight B. Heath, *Drinking Occasions. Comparative Perspectives on Alcohol and Culture* (Philadelphia: Brunner-Routledge, 2000), p. 107.
5 In our work, consumption is defined as a means to construct your identity and in this sense consuming wine does encapsulate more than a simple need for sociability or distinction. The context in which wine consumption takes place confers specific meanings on consumption. In addition, the ways in which individuals engage, consciously or not, in consumption contribute to our analysis of alcohol consumption.
6 Heath, *Drinking Occasions*, p. 110.
7 For a discussion on wine and art, see the excellent chapter on Corbières: Christiane Amiel, 'Le vin à l'épreuve de l'art', in V. Nahoum-Grappe and O. Vincent (eds), *Le Goût des belles choses* (Paris: Éditions de la Maison des Sciences de l'Homme, 2004).
8 For a general discussion on wine routes and their impact at local level, see the example of Italy in Gianluca Brunori and Adanella Rossi, 'Synergy and coherence through collective action: some insights from wine routes in Tuscany', *Sociologia Ruralis*, 40, 4 (October 2000), 409–23.
9 Her position as a woman was very often challenged by men when she described the wines tasted However, Marie-Laure always emphasized that at the end of the day, to be a woman was also a trump card.

10　Experts have shown that judging a wine is a matter of subjectivity. For more discussion of wine tasting and the subjective character of wine evaluation, see François Casabianca and Christine de Sainte Marie, 'L'évaluation sensorielle des produits typiques. Concevoir et instrumenter l'épreuve de typicité', in *The Socio-economics of Origin-Labelled Products in the Agro-food Supply Chain: Spatial, Institutional and Coordination Aspects*, 67th EAAE seminar, le Mans, 28–30 October 1999, and Gil Morrot, 'Peut-on améliorer les performances des dégustateurs?', *Vigne et Vin* (1999), 31–7. Finally, Geneviève Teil, 'La production du jugement esthétique sur les vins par la critique vinicole', *Sociologie du Travail*, 43 (2001), 67–89, and her very interesting book *De la coupe aux lèvres. Pratiques de la perception et mise en marché des vins de qualité* (Toulouse : Editions Octarès, 2004).

11　As an informer, Théodore was a very useful social commentator as he had read all the literature of Bourdieu and was able to comment on some of my analysis of wine lovers. I should like to thank him for inspiring some of my comments.

Chapter Seven
Between Self-Reflexivity, 'Distinction' and Social Connectedness[1]

According to Ulrich Beck[2] and Anthony Giddens[3], reflexive individuality is an element of our late modern societies. Following the break-up of traditional social classes in the second half of the twentieth century, western Europeans are now confronted by a bewildering array of separate social identities, lifestyles, opinions and groups or subcultures. Attachments to social classes have weakened, people have separated from the traditional support networks provided by family or neighbourhood, and work has lost its importance as the primary focus of identity formation. France has not escaped these broader social changes, but the country remains unique in terms of its social landscapes, combining gradual modernization with more traditional social patterns of change. France today is an increasingly fragmented society, with multiple fault lines and new social divisions. In one sense, society has opened up, generating new opportunities for self-expression. But this also means that those unable to take advantage of new opportunities are left behind, creating new categories of 'excluded'. The middle class has been one of the principal beneficiaries of these changes and, as such, it occupies a central position in terms of economic power and leisure time.

Wine consumption offers a window on to these societal transformations. The growing middle class in France has been drawn towards fields of action where they perceive the greatest capacity for reflexive autonomy or choice, and wine consumption offers one such arena. If for centuries, wine culture was confined to the upper class and a handful of experts and connoisseurs, today it has become a more democratized form of consumption, a place for the maintenance or negotiation of identities. Despite this progressive democratization, it is still the case that a sizeable proportion of the population remains excluded from this wine culture. The majority of French wine lovers are white middle-class males of affluent economic means. They have time and money. Women, ethnic minorities and the less economically well-off have all, to a greater or lesser extent, been excluded from this new wine drinking culture and are notable by their absence in any statistical analysis of wine consumption.

Over recent years, wine, its production and culture have become an object of debate and exchange through a range of media including the internet, television and the press. Wine has become a global object of communication, enabling individuals to acquire knowledge and to experiment and explore taste on a scale that would have been unimaginable only a generation ago. What remains distinctive about wine consumption is that it offers a platform for combining the modern characteristics of the middle class, such as self reflexivity and distinction, with more traditional agrarian values like social communication through connectedness with other wine lovers sharing the same core of representations and values around the product. Some of these values such as the iconic status of the wine grower or the notion of *terroir*, could be seen as nationally embedded, but they could also, arguably, refer to globalization as a process of homogenization or reflect individualism as a reflexive activity. It is undeniable that wine culture and consumption are characterized by a more complex process of identity-building than just a national construction reinvented at different periods of time.

This chapter focuses on wine lovers and their personal narratives about wine. Through both a self-reflexive and an interactive process, individuals are engaged in an identity-building process. Wine websites offer a place where, through conspicuous consumption, intentional social connectedness and articulation of public narratives, individuals aspire to construct images of the self and of the other. By communicating, competing and arguing with others about the meaning of taste, the importance of regions and producers and, in some instances, French politics, they seek to establish territories, landmarks and networks of relationships, provoking debates and discussions about the world they live in. An essentialist vision of France, emphasizing the traditional work of the wine grower as the paragon of quality, and the uniqueness of *terroir* as a French characteristic, dominates the content of their debates, but it is increasingly confronted by a more liberal and critical perspective. Amongst the core values discussed are: work, artisanship, quality, sociability, friendship, belonging and commensality, all of which can be seen as providing reassurance and a sense of stability in a period of economic transition. Yet these values are not only limited to fictional narratives or self-proclaimed identities; they are activated and transformed into fields of action converting the virtual network into a real community or *gemeinschaft*. Ultimately, their primary function is to create groups and to establish social ties at national level through wine consumption.

The following analysis is based upon an ethnographic observation of three of the most popular French websites devoted to wine consumption in 2004.[4] The results of my research suggest that wine lovers constitute a particular group of consumers defined by their higher level of commitment and their intense relationship to the product, illustrated by the fact that they have joined a website or a forum. As a result, they form a separate and distinct group compared with the 'wandering drinker', who is absent from these fora. Once I had joined the websites as a member, one of the principal challenges, from an anthropological perspective, was to observe the salient characteristics of the communications they established between themselves and then to use some of these linguistic peculiarities to facilitate my integration into the virtual group. After several days of continuous observation, I noticed that humour was an integral part of their exchanges; it was a means of not taking their passion too seriously. Another characteristic was that most of the discussions rarely mentioned wines from abroad but focused on French wines. So I decided to send a message to the list under the provoking title 'Seeking wine lover desperately', making an allusion to a popular American film of the 1980s and their passion for wines. Discussions started immediately, and I was able to arrange interviews with members of the list throughout France. Most of these interviews involved sharing a bottle and a meal, and in one or two cases, I cooked a traditional Burgundian meal for them when they came to visit me. As argued by Geneviève Teil, what differentiates the wine lover, *amateur* or passionate consumer, from the average wine drinker is the intensity of his or her relationship to the product: As she describes matters: 'If experts and neophytes differ [from average consumers], this is perhaps more because of the difference of attention to wine and the reflexive nature of their tasting skills than the possession of a true or trustworthy knowledge.'[5]

It is clear that the internet is used as much for self-reflexivity as for the articulation of individual identity through connection and dialogue with others. According to Thomas Wilson, 'Drinking is a communicative act, a performance of identity.'[6] The performance of wine culture, through tastes, conscious enjoyment, knowledge and the evaluation of the quality of wine, defines the drinker in relation to the internet community to which he or she wishes to belong. Here again, as in most of the contexts observed where wine drinking culture was displayed, women are largely absent. Moreover, it is through exchanges with others that individuals establish a network of friendships based on common values and shared interests, but also negotiate the establishment of reputations in specific territories of the French nation, especially Bordeaux and Burgundy, through 'distinction' and thus intense competition. Self reflexivity, 'distinction' and connectedness characterize in a paradoxical fashion the consumption of these postmodern drinkers.[7]

The arrival of the internet as a means of communication has radically transformed the world of wine lovers, providing them with the opportunity to go beyond the confined circle of families and friends to talk about wine, talk about their experiences and knowledge, and establish networks around the sharing of the product.[8] This development has found an echo in the growing *culturalization* of wine consumption in both France and Europe, whereby multiple and differentiated sites have mushroomed, from wine bars to wine libraries. Thus wine lovers and the internet sites where they meet offer an interesting window on to wine consumption as they play a major role in the circulation of knowledge. Many of these wine lovers run wine-tasting classes at a local level, and through their mediating position between experts and consumers, contribute to the dissemination of knowledge and expertise.

The first internet site devoted to wine, *Magnum Vinum*, was created at the end of the 1990s as the result of a growing interest expressed by one of the leading specialist journals, the *Revue des Vins de France*. Its initial objective was to provide a new platform for wine lovers who needed help and direction when buying wines. As a respected source, the *RVF* saw the launch of *Magnum Vinum* as a means of consolidating its position in the market as the leading determinant of taste in high quality wines and as an adviser for other initiatives in this area. As P.E., one of the original contributors to the website noted, 'This was linked to *Magnum Vinum* and its initiative with a commercial partner, a *caviste*. Their idea was to create a community of wine lovers sufficiently malleable to be given some paternalistic advice by experienced journalists ... thus to have a dialogue going only in one direction.' However, after two or three years, most of the wine lovers left *Magnum Vinum* to establish parallel internet sites dedicated to their passion in order to escape from the *RVF* that many found 'patronising'.[9]

Since then, the number of internet sites has proliferated and the majority of them have seen their membership expand, with examples such as *La Passion du vin* (Passion for Wine) ranked in 257th place amongst the most popular French websites or *Liaisons oenophiles* (Oenophile Affairs) positioned in 4,657 place, with a 17 per cent membership increase demonstrating the success and popularity of such activity.[10] The wide range of sites devoted to wine consumption illustrates the growing interest of the affluent middle class, which has sought to use wine forums as a means of engaging with an 'imagined community' of consumers and to establish through competition and oenological connectedness a self-reflexive social activity. From *oenophiles* to *amateurs*, *passionnés* and *amis du vin* (friends of wine), what these internet sites have in common is the relationship between wine and individuals. While the majority of them put great emphasis on the sociable and friendly nature of the relationship, as can be seen from the names of their internet sites, others deliberately emphasize the competitive character of their meetings, as illustrated by *Dégustateurs DC* (wine taster) or *Iacchos* (the site of *amateurs* of great wines), or are defining what is at the core of their consumption like the French website *ABoire* (to drink).

The website of *La Passion du vin* provides a useful insight into the motivations of some of the more active websites.[11] They describe themselves as follows:

> *We are seven individuals living in the four corners of Europe and even the world, whom passion and specific events have brought together with the aim of establishing this site. Our horizons, geographic, cultural and social, are different and these differences are the richness of our meetings, necessary complements expressed by tastes and a variety of interests.*

Each of the wine lovers, in his individual narrative, emphasized drinking as 'an act of identification, of differentiation and integration and of the projection of homogeneity and heterogeneity'. The editor of the website *La Passion du vin* emphasizes that 'Drinking practices are active elements in individual and group identifications, and the sites where drinking takes place, the locales of regular and celebrated drinking, are places where meanings are made, shared, disputed, reproduced, where identities take shape, flourish and change.'[12]

The websites also emphasize that wine drinking is a means of communicating and connecting. As one internet wine club member noted, 'My biggest satisfaction today is to recognize that *LPV* (*La Passion du vin*) has enabled me to meet several other wine amateurs some of whom some have become my friends.'

1. Declining passions

Message 08/03/04 Les forums de degustateurs.com.chronique. Au fil du vin: Eclectism posted by T.M a wine lover in his thirties, single, working in human resources in Luxemburg

What is a good wine lover? Someone who has the best cellar, someone who has been able to buy some famous Bordeaux in 1961 and has kept them until now, despite their high prices at auctions? Someone who has in his cellar some Yquem, Latour, Romanée Conti and Moulin? On paper, it is impressive. However, this description lacks passion. Does passion express itself through the sharing of famous labels, a bit like a keen reader who proclaims he owns La Pléiade in his library? Surely not ... The passion focuses on sharing wines, independently of brands and labels. This is the best way to escape the stressful spiral of finding wine notes and paying the high price for constituting his wine cellar ... Very often the less famous wines are surprisingly the best, not so far from the well-renowned wines. We need to capitalize on the previous generations that have identified good wines and have educated their palates to recognize the finest and greatest wines. Otherwise, how to recognize these qualities in a Grange des Pères? Tasting famous wines enables us to be more adventurous with the others ... My cellar will be the greatest if I am able to surprise my fellow wine lovers by the eclecticism of my choices ... You have understood that we all know amongst our friends somebody able to come up with a great bottle that will surprise us and make us forget stars, guides and the political correctness of the passion for wine. The main thing is to have him amongst your friends!

The analysis of three internet sites, *Iacchos*, *LPV* (Passion for Wine) and *DC* (Wine Taster), provides a window on to wine drinking culture as self-reflexive and conspicuous consumption defying generalizations about wine consumption in France. The oldest of them, *Iacchos*, created in 1999, is presented as a very active list; on average a dozen messages are sent per day with strong variations between the evening and the weekend, which are both very intense periods of communication. The surfers on this list are named *Iaks* and their website combines a passion for wines and a passion for cigars, even if most of the discussions concerned wine. The list promotes specific wine growers and illustrates the incarnation of the wine grower as the paragon of quality. Specific articles and reviews are written about French wine growers with their pictures and list of wines accompanying the wine-tasting notes. Their passion for wine growers goes so far as naming them *Iacchosiens* when they fulfil all the criteria expected by the group of wine lovers: 'Who are the *Iacchosien* wine growers present? I have read that J. C. Le Brun will be there and I have been told that in previous years Hervé Bizeul attended' (D.B., 20 January 2004). Indeed to be seen as an *Iacchosien* wine grower refers to a whole philosophy shared by the members of the list: they are, above all, wine growers who are happy to open their doors to wine lovers and to spend some quality time discussing with them their job and their philosophy of wine drinking.

This is a form of blessing conferred by the members of the website endorsing community and agrarian values. For most wine lovers who know about *Iacchos*, the list is seen as elitist and exclusive:

> *They are not open because they have a history between them ... in fact they have a language, they have a list of wine growers who are their friends, they drink only their wines and they are the best wines, and therefore they get reinforced in their convictions.*

The *Iacchos* forum, which is the active platform for the website, has received more than 19,330 emails sent since its creation in 2003. It counts eighty different participants, but only two women and six proclaimed 'foreigners' were registered at the time of the observation. During the period studied, between 23 and 30 January 2004, most of the exchanges concerned the circulation of information about the world of wines in France (47.65 per cent divided by order of importance between information on the network, general information on wine culture and, finally, friends and special occasions), notes on wine tasting (22.61 per cent) and politics (18.45 per cent). These discussions were chaired by a group of wine growers previously employed by the specialized journal *RVF*, but who subsequently became the owners of a wine estate in the South of France. It could be argued that *Iacchos* is the most politicized of the three websites observed, as most of the conversations contained a political comment. Out of 168 messages exchanged during the period of observation, thirty-one were related to politics and were moderated by Jean Clavel, one of the leading wine growers from the South of France. The discussions cover issues related to the definition of wine as an alcohol product and the economic state of the wine industry or the institutional context.

Newcomers to *Iacchos* have to follow a number of steps in order to be accepted, and their initiation is always guided by other members of the list. Firstly, there is an application to fill in to become a member of the list, which one recent member described as 'a community apart that I see as not very open'. Then the initiation takes place progressively as described by another member: 'This is quite hard; you cannot speak just like that or you will be hammered; you have to stay humble.' The list has established some rules to follow, emphasizing that the debates have to remain under control. The list provides its members with the opportunity to test their knowledge, and every year, a *Iacchos* Masters competition is held in Bordeaux, which is presented as 'the international wine amateurs' wine tasting competition' by one of the members, a sports teacher. Held over the course of a day, teams of four wine lovers, with a maximum of two wine professionals per team, are constituted to taste fifteen different French and world wines, while being quizzed about their knowledge of wine. Throughout the competition, the ability to make a precise identification of wines by country, region, label, producer and vintage plays a crucial role in determining the quality of the team. The emphasis placed on encyclopaedic knowledge and competence in wine tasting is at the heart of this competition, and it is also reflected in the organization of the site, which prides itself on its closeness and elitism. This explains why the site is perceived as quite 'separate' from the others, a closed community and why the organizer of the competition is named the 'encyclopaedist'.[13]

The second website, *LPV* (passion for wine) where members use the informal *tu*, unlike *Iacchos,* is at the extreme other end of the continuum, as it is more open, less elitist, described as 'left-wing' by its competitors and quite focused on transmitting wine culture through enthusiasms. According to a leading figure in the rival website *DC*: '*LPV* is condemned to attract a growing number of consumers because effectively it is a site where individuals speak freely without any inhibition and in the trajectory of a wine lover, he needs to do this work before discussing contradictions and counter-examples.' The emphasis is on the pedagogic transmission of a wine culture. The site was launched by a group of seven, middle-class Frenchmen in 2003 following a rupture with *Magnum Vinum*, the old *RVF* website. The forum, presented itself as a place to exchange and meet, where the visitor could discuss freely, give his own impressions and talk about wines, in a spirit of tolerance and openness. Photos of the main participants, stories and narratives animate the website, and human warmth characterizes the nature of the possible encounter with the product. Access to the forum is straightforward, and the discussions are facilitated by the wholehearted and humorous atmosphere.

Among the list of forums proposed to the members, the most popular are Bordeaux (8,173 messages during the period observed (23–30 January 2004)), the section 'By the way' (5,549), Languedoc–Roussillon (2,948), Rhône (2,229), *cavistes* and restaurants (1,601), and finally wine tasting (1,491), which occupies only a minority of the exchanges. Presenting wine as a less elitist and more approachable product, *LPV* recognizes that its members 'are conscious of the gaps in their knowledge and that they are working on improving it'. As of 17 February 2004, more than 38,849 messages had been received since the launch of the website in February 2003, attesting its success in terms of strategy, and also its appeal as a less competitive site. Like *Iacchos*, *LPV* is organized around a bunch of key personalities, each of them associated with a specific territory or wine-producing region of France. The list, by its structure and management, gives concrete expression to the specialization of each key member of the website, leading in some cases to the establishment of territorial chapels: 'P. knows Burgundy very well; on the other hand for Bordeaux it is J.-P.' This is organized so that anyone can get his little empire. J.-P. is Gaillac, and nobody dares to say to him 'You know nothing about it ... We agree with you, but when you drink Burgundy wines, you do the same, you say P. is really good ...'. The organization of a wine tasting in the Côtes de Nuits, a reputed area of Burgundy, and the subsequent editing online of wine-tasting notes created a major clash between the two leading figures on the list, one described and recognized as the expert on the Burgundy region and the other, a Bordeaux specialist, who attended the tasting but disputed the evaluation of the wines. The debate led to their respective departures and the establishment of two separate websites, *LPV* and *DC*. *LPV* at the time of writing remains the most popular French site devoted to the passion for wines.

Indeed, contrasting with the two successful examples of *LPV* and *Iacchos*, the last website *DC* (*Degustateurs.com*) saw the light after the splitting up of the first recognized site for wine lovers *Magnum Vinum*. Presenting itself as an independent and demanding site for wine lovers, its creator, a sports teacher married to the daughter of a wine grower in Burgundy, had been one of the leading wine amateurs for *Magnum Vinum* before its disappearance. He remains the representative of the *RVF* in Burgundy and, as such, he is invited to all the official wine tastings organized in the region. It is also interesting to point out that his site has witnessed a decline in membership since its creation in 2003. In 2004, only one woman was an active member of the list, and it was because she combined the status of oenologist with being married to a wine lover, who was also a sports teacher and a devoted member of the site, that she became responsible for the section on oenology. The website is again mainly structured by region, and Burgundy comes to the fore in terms of the territorial coverage, with 2,356 messages during the period under observation, while Bordeaux had 1,967, Alsace 935, Loire 724 (during February 2004). The notes for wine tastings occupy most of the website, and they are defined as horizontal wine tastings (in a horizontal tasting, the wines are all from the same vintage but are from different wineries), as opposed to vertical wine tasting (where different years of the same wine are sampled) and thematic wine tasting (organized by themes such as regions, colour or countries and so on), emphasizing the highly competitive and professional approach to wine. Most of the discussions take place around wines and their evaluation. Unlike the *LPV*, the pedagogy of transmitting a wine culture is far from their principal preoccupation. The forum is freely accessible, and the use of the more formal term of address of *vous* is compulsory. Its specificity is that it is organized around a handful of *Décéiens* who share a distinctive passion for wine.

From an ethnographical perspective, *DC* has been the most interesting site for the observer because it has enabled me to meet several wine lovers and to interview them subsequently about their passion. It certainly seems that they have adopted a more critical and objective stance towards wine drinking culture than other websites. The interviews conducted with its members have also proved to be valuable when examining other examples of websites devoted to the passion for wines. Defining such a passion is extremely difficult, but belonging to a club or communicating through the internet contributes to defining one's self reflexive individuality. Through the communication and writing of one's passion, it is possible to grasp some of the collective national mythical representations or tensions in the making of wine drinking culture. By focusing on wine lovers as cultural mediators at the core of a dynamic, differentiated and fragmented wine drinking culture, it remains possible to analyse wine consumption as a unique, conspicuous, self reflexive process by which individuals engage with the world they live in and with a nation which has constantly reminded them that space, territory, hierarchy and rural values play a major role in the maintenance and negotiation of collective identities.

2. Drinking or tasting?

Message 17/05/04 Les forums de dégustateurs.com.chronique.Au fil du vin: pour boire pour déguster?

Christmas holidays have given me the opportunity to discover that I became a wine drinker, as well as a wine taster. The distinction is more subtle than it looks. Tasting is very often associated with the gourmet: he tastes little sips, symbol of a great pleasure. In contrast, drinking wine represents for the wine lover a crude pleasure, associated often with alcoholics drinking red plonk, and I do not mention the stars of Parker's guide or of the RVF! Synthesis of both, the gourmet who stuffs himself with wine is from the past ... Where is the paradox between drinking and tasting? Very often we start by drinking and then we taste, or drink on special occasions. I remember time I worked in a metallurgic firm in the Nièvre (Burgundy), where all the workers met at five thirty in the morning before starting at six o'clock to drink a glass of red wine. There were snacks as well as the wines, these dry white wines, drunk sometimes from the same bottle at the top of a high mountain, or the red accompanying sandwiches from the lunch box ... A simple wine, well done, at the right time is very good. The pleasure is here and your friends are happy to be convinced.

The difference between drinking and tasting is a major cleavage in the representations surrounding wine drinking culture, and its presentation through internet sites or wine clubs, illustrated by the following comment from a wine connoisseur. As one wine connoisseur argued, 'A wine club that is well thought of is a club that provides pleasure, where one has to like wine, not only to taste it ... there are too many clubs which are established on this pseudo-intellectualism of wine.' This tension between wine drinking seen as a pleasurable and sociable activity in which individuals consume wine and enjoy being *bon vivants* and wine tasting by which individuals negotiate their social status and position through the display and performance of their cultural knowledge and tasting ability relates to the division between what wine enthusiasts conceptualize as 'sociability' versus 'intellect'. As one of the wine lovers puts it,

> *For me, wine tasting, becomes nearly an intellectual exercise; it is what I do too often, that is to say tasting, giving a mark, passing a judgement, an appreciation, evaluation. The pleasure is gone. For me, as a wine lover, there is pleasure, one has to like drinking, there are no sub-categories in the wine lovers' group. For me, as soon as somebody comes to visit me and is happy to drink one of the wines I serve, he is potentially a wine lover ... For me, a good wine is above all something shared. This is an emotion felt, good or bad, this is visceral. I think of the good times I had recently tasting wine, and I drank some very famous wines, but the best time I had, was last night with a simple red Burgundy that I shared with a friend who came by surprise.*

Jean-Luc Fernandez describes the pleasure of drinking as inherent in wine drinking culture, wine tasting being a fundamental wine passion.[14] However, his analysis neglects the intoxicating nature of the product and the need to differentiate the product perceived as a social fluid from that of the elitist and status-seeking activity surrounding it.

Many examples can be found to illustrate this opposition between drinking and tasting, from sites named *Goûte ce vin* (Taste this Wine) or *Liaisons oenophiles* (Oenophile Affairs) to *Parlons du vin* (Let's Speak about Wine), *Tout savoir sur le vin* (To Know Everything about Wines) or *Très Grand Jury parisien'* (Famous Parisian Wine Jury) and the types of wine clubs encountered in our ethnographic travels. A message posted by a young wine lover, Robert, on 18 February 2004 on *Iacchos* confirms this contradiction between drinking and tasting, the love of the product or the intellectual exercise which seems to establish separate territories in the world of wine consumers. As an anonymous internet surfer described matters,

> *You have here a good sample of the tribe of wine lovers of the divine bottle; they revisit the bacchanals and they meet often for low mass, or I could say for tasting as an excuse for orgies. They are very dangerous individuals and above all in Alsace, where one of these specimens ravages the region. This persuasion is divided into several sects, the Carignan lovers from whom some gurus come to preach the good word on this forum. You also have the pro Burgundy, well known as the intellectual wine tasters, and the various ramifications which are fine wines or wines from the terroir, and the anti-Burgundy, known as the hedonists. These two groups are always in conflict to take power. At the moment, the only truth is in the glass.*

The passion for wine relates to language, memory, hierarchy and power, and thus individuals, whatever their position in relation to wine drinking culture – along the continuum of drinking or tasting – belong to the same universe where territories and legitimacies are established and negotiated. By communicating around wines, they define where they position themselves. Yet by joining these forums, they are fully aware that their knowledge about wine will be tested and collectively evaluated. However, the social character of wine tasting always emphasized by wine lovers paradoxically counterbalances the competitive and sometimes intense relationship established between drinkers. What they endorse in common is the festive and gregarious nature of their passion which, through the establishment of a strict codification of drinking through tasting, confines them to a model of drinking culture where moderation, slow ingestion and description using normative language control the whole process of consumption. A common wine culture and language are used to communicate and evaluate the product. Yet as wine tasting remains largely subjective, tensions emerge in the definition of what are called 'good' wines, or between wine as a sociable product or wine as an object of intellectualism. At the heart of this activity, language plays a determining role, and through language, people construct their accounts of what they do, what they taste and what they believe.

In a thought-provoking article, Nigel Bruce argues that the wine community operates as a 'knowledge territory' developing discourses of classification, hierarchy and authority.[15] Taking as an example the work of the oenologist and famous wine writer, Émile Peynaud, Bruce demonstrates that what Peynaud called the informed amateurs or wine enthusiasts 'do not always express themselves precisely'. For Peynaud, oenology as a science needs to be able to establish a common vocabulary linking sensation to expression, word and quality, principles which distinguish the wine lover from the oenologist. Thus language is the key essence of the establishment of hierarchy and access to power, even among wine lovers. Yet there is no consensus about what a good wine is. However what is striking is that throughout the fieldwork upon which this book is based, French wines have never been described as 'bad'.

3. 'Good' wines

Les forums de degustateurs.com.chronique. A votre avis: Emotions vin, Un diner en famille août 2001

Before leaving for Idaho, we had a family dinner [lunch in France]. The wines on the menu were: Meursault Blagny 96 Lopuis Latour, le Meursault de Bourrée and as a back-up Corton Charlemagne Clos Frantin 1995 Bichot. We start by opening the Blagny ... hmm ... It is drunk mechanically while we talk. Then follows the tasting of Perrières. Once the cork is extracted, I sniff ... Nothing to say. I say to one of my brothers who was there, 'What do you think?' He responds 'Floral.' 'Are you sure?' We put the bottle on the table and we talk again while starting with the crabs. Suddenly, a smell of perfume comes to my attention. My mother was sitting next to me and I said to her, 'Are you wearing perfume?' 'No,' she says slightly offended. That is when the excitement started. Note that we did not yet have any wine in our glasses. We pour the wine. Progressively, the table is inundated by the smell of violet. Fantastic! We stuck our nose into the glass and remained like that. The taste was too complex for my inexperienced palate. It was not as long in the mouth as the Corton Charlemagne 94 of Bouchard, but it gave me as much pleasure. Simply, another level. More extrovert, more floating. We were happy. The back-up, we drank it. Good as well.

The average wine consumer traditionally assumes that there is somewhere a true and objective description of wine available to the discerning and experienced drinker. The reality is far more complex, not to say subjective, and the relationship between language and sensory impressions is described by theorists such as Terry Eagleton as an ideology which aims to bridge the gap between nature and society.[16] The literature on tastes opposes two broad schools of thoughts. For sociologists, people have a tendency to define 'good taste' as a universal standard to which they can aspire,[17] while for social scientists, the notion of 'cultural capital' as conceptualised by Pierre Bourdieu is the result of their acculturation.[18] For the latter, tastes define your social position. However, wine seems to offer a more complex and less unified field for action than fashion, art, music or the choice of a name for your child. This is mainly because wine, like food, is absorbed and therefore it is at the interface between the biological and the social. Individuals are not equal when drinking wine. They have different abilities and competences. Moreover, wine is an alcoholic product which means that its consumption can lead to intoxication and thus a distortion of the senses which vary from one individual to another. According to Tim Hanni, many wine flavours are not naturally appealing to the human taste buds, but are the result of a long process of acculturation.[19] Some individuals do not like the taste of wine. So there are biological and social factors explaining the differences in the appreciation of wines. Moreover, as argued previously, wine tasting remains a subjective activity and each taster has his own profile of preferences, and these are very disparate.[20] It could be argued that they are also constructed through their drinking experience and formatted by the context in which they take place.

What is striking when observing the exchanges on the websites is the socially mediated character of the experience of wine tasting, and how individuals are shaping the experience of wine drinking to make it a normative and objective activity. Most of the wine lovers encountered on internet sites devote a substantial amount of their time and energy to the writing and circulation of notes on the wines they have consumed. This activity was at the core of the three websites analysed. As one of the wine connoisseurs interviewed noted, 'I started to be passionate about wines on the day in April 1997 when I began to keep a notebook about the wines I had drunk.' Writing about wines can take many forms, from brief and professional descriptions to more humorous and caustic accounts. The forms taken by the notes enable us to map the websites in relation to culture and knowledge, sociability or intellectualism. For example, TGJP, a Parisian website famous for its humour and derision, presents one of the dinners organized by their eight members emphasizing gastronomy, pleasure, hedonistic values and social atmosphere:

> **Starter:** *Canapés à la tapenade and au caviar d'aubergine + VdP Michel Issaly 2005 Les Cavaillès Bas + VdP des C'tes de Gascogne Pellehaut 2005 Ampelomeryx*
>
> *The white wine of Issaly is welcomed. A guest wine lover found it to have a peculiar nose, but his opinion does not reach a consensus. We find fruits and a nice balance. The second white wine seems a bit more ambitious, reveals itself to be quite bitter in the mouth, a sign of the grapes according to some.*

This example demonstrates that the display of their gastronomic associations with wine are disseminated through the internet to other gastronomes or to wine lovers seeking conviviality and pleasure.

DC, on the other hand, speaks in a different language, separating the notes from the convivial experience and adopting a professional and descriptive position:

> *Thierry starts by explaining to us the geology of the Alsace wine region using Google Earth. But let's taste the wines. They are served by year and are essentially Schlossberg and Fürstentum.*
>
> *Then is it granite or limestone ?*
>
> **Schlossberg 2004**: *the nose is toasted bread, smoky with jam citrus fruit. The taste is slightly round but becomes full-bodied and heavy with a touch of acidity. This is light. The taste is long and promising. A classic of terroir and a great success for the wine grower15/20.*

The variety of these descriptions reflects different hierarchical, fragmented and differentiated universes where subjectivity remains at the core of any evaluation of the product. Some wine lovers conduct their tastings during social occasions, while others argue that they taste at home in specific conditions, enabling them to remain 'objective'. While they recognize the subjective value of their taste, they nevertheless look for some sort of objectivity when evaluating the wines. Some take notes, while others just enjoy the social experience. The context of consumption is always mentioned and the nature of the tasting – individual or collective, professional or friendly – is systematically underlined. In communicating about what he has tasted, the drinker seeks to legitimize his perception of the product by establishing networks of individuals sharing the same values and tastes or the same passions for specific wine growers or regions. By the same token, individuals construct territories of tastes and friendship and transform an individual drinking performance into a collective and identity-building experience. A common culture and language are shared by all the participants, and are aimed at differentiating 'good' wines from the ordinary. During these exchanges, sociability and specific social affinities contribute to the evaluation of wines and, sometimes are seen as detrimental to the establishment of objective and discerning judgements. This point is often raised by some of the wine clubs, which deliberately refuse to meet the producers before tasting their wines, as they argue that 'it will influence our perception of the product; so we asked a local oenologist we know to send us some samples.'[21]

It is clear from all the wine tastings observed as part of this research that they are occasions not only for meeting other people, but also for sharing ideas, learning about others' perceptions, and finally controlling, through the exercise of evaluation and writing, the act of drinking. Wine consumption is thus mediated by culture. Language plays a crucial role in this process as bottles are named *flacons* and wines 'noble beverages', categories clearly imported from the commercial sphere and from an imagined past. The language used emphasizes the highly emblematic image of wine, and it is very rare that a wine is described as 'bad', especially when it is a French wine. Most of the notes are positive and poetic, ranging from scientific descriptions to bucolic and evocative phrases. The acquisition of this specialist language is largely controlled by the group, and the key personalities of each website, who are in the overwhelming majority of cases men, occupy a bridging position between the professional and the amateur worlds. Individuals such as P.E. for *DC* or J.L. for *Iacchos* dominate the sites and exemplify the dynamic and complex character of the field of wine tasting.

The acquisition of a specialist language and vocabulary plays a key role in disseminating wine drinking culture. Claude Fischler, in his book, *Du vin*, opposes broadly what he describes as cold drinking (*boire froid*), which is a technical term in oenological language, to the 'warm drinking', which is incarnated by *sommeliers* and is seen as hedonistic and humanistic language. Yet the observation of wine tastings demonstrates that it goes far beyond the issue of language and the simple dichotomy between technical and hedonistic vocabulary. Individuals are engaged in a dynamic process of evaluation, comparing notes and acquiring skills and competences. Some of them feel the need to refer back to the judgements of recognized experts, while others are trying to evaluate their own experience in relation to the public performance of the more confident drinkers. It is through these sensorial exchanges that individuals learn about themselves and others. Wine and its taste become pretexts to express identity and measure one's abilities, but also to create a sense of belonging to a community of shared interests and passions.

This progressive integration and socialization of individuals through the internet is illustrated by the arrival of newcomers on the websites. You cannot arrive and claim competence and knowledge without first following the implicit rules underlining internet communication. Some newcomers confess immediately that they do not know anything about wine and keep excusing themselves in case they make a *faux pas*, while others join the forum and face criticism or exclusion as soon as they proclaim their firm opinions. Fernandez describes the initiation followed by neophytes who are building up their expertise through interaction with recognized wine lovers.[22] Messages such as 'I have bought six bottles of X; what do you think?' are often formulated as 'What do you think of X?', which shows that individuals look for confirmation of their purchase. If somebody dares to say that the wine X is not good, and for the price it is possible to find something much better, the exchange often degenerates into a social struggle where the protagonists accuse each other of not knowing anything about wine. Modesty, humour and respect help newcomers to integrate in the list or forum and to have access to a mentor who may become a friend. For example, the forum *A votre avis* on the *DC* website enables newcomers to start discussions, like the young wine lover who first wanted to know how long he could keep some of his wines in the cellar and a month later felt sufficiently confident to put his wine notes on the website.

The trajectory is very often the same, beginning with a practical question related to the constitution of a cellar or a visit to one of the wine regions: 'I am going to Burgundy. Could you please recommend a wine grower?' Then the next step is for the inexperienced wine lover to buy wines without consulting members of the list, but just tasting the products and trusting his evaluation. The progression goes step by step with the support of some of his new internet partners – like this less confident individual asking, 'Which wines from my cellar are ready to be drunk?' and facing comments such as 'Taste them first and then decide which ones are ready.' Once his experience has been consolidated and positively encouraged by the members of the list, he progressively establishes himself and his tastes in the community. The final stage of his integration consists in the display of his wine notes, which then become visible to the members of the list.

However, this final step presents a challenge, as most wine connoisseurs are then evaluated by the other members of the list, and one of the wine lovers interviewed who loves writing commented:

> *That is a problem, individuals who speak well and taste less well, they are very influential because they speak well; others who do not speak well and do not taste well, we do not care. Those who taste well and talk well, we would like to see more of them, and sadly those who taste well, but do not speak, we do not know them.*

Through the process of writing notes, some individuals emerge as the determiners of taste, and what remains at the core of their recognition is their independent positioning in relation to taste, but above all their mastering of language as declared by the main protagonist of *DC*: 'They talk always of Bettane and Parker, and one day I told them: you are very nice, but either you talk about the wines you have tasted, or you go somewhere else ... I want to see only wine notes from the websurfers.' The expression of taste does not refer to a so-called objectivization of the product based upon sensorial competences or scientific method. The opinion on a specific wine acquired credibility and legitimacy through the exchanges and communication around the product and through the use of a common language. As several of my interviewees noted, 'If somebody wants you to discover his passions and you are ready to follow him, especially if it is done with simple words, without authority or without being peremptory, it will work.' In the end, it is through the establishment and negotiation of relationships that wine lovers acquire a wine culture that provides them not only with a certain competence and an ability to evaluate the product, but also a worldview in which *communitas*, friendship and sociability constitute them as individuals in relation to others. Wine enables this identification and common belonging despite the competitive and social nature of collective drinking.

Notes

1. The basis of this chapter, and especially the concept of self-reflexivity, have been inspired by Peter Howland's thesis on wines in Martinborough: 'Pinot pilgrims: metro-rurality, social distinction and ideal reflexive individuality in Martinborough', Ph.D. thesis, University of Canterbury, New Zealand, 2007. I should like to thank him for inviting me to be one of his external examiners.
2. Ulrich Beck and Elisabeth Beck-Gernsheim, *Individualization: Institutionalized Individualism and its Social and Political Consequences* (London: Sage, 2002).
3. Anthony Giddens, *Modernity and Self-Identity: Self and Society in the Late Modern Age* (Cambridge: Polity, 1991).
4. The three main websites studied have been selected according to their popularity with French consumers and their public visibility. There are as many websites as wine clubs, and therefore our principal aim was to locate the most popular and most visible to conduct our ethnographic work. Each website has been observed and analysed during several weeks at different monthly intervals, and the discussions taking place have been transcribed and analysed. From the methodological point of view, the selection of these three sites was based on some of the interviews I conducted over the years with professionals, consumers and wine lovers. These three sites came up in several discussions as examples of contrasted types of wine passions, and that is why I decided, after following some of their discussions, to become an official member of each of them. As a women representing only 1 per cent of the surfers, I was immediately spotted, and to make sure that my study remained as objective as possible, I presented myself as a French academic living in the UK who has already published a book on wine growers in Burgundy. Because of this social positioning as a female writer working on wine, I was admitted into the respective list. However, I then adopted different strategies to be able to meet some of the wine lovers and interview them for the purpose of this study. In each case, I had to draw attention to my social positioning and also to what they assume to be my expertise on wine. Throughout the fieldwork, I maintained an objective and quite detached position as a social actor and I emphasized my true identity as a female married academic who likes

drinking wine, but would define herself as far away as possible from being a sort of train spotter obsessed with wine.

5   Geneviève Teil, *De la coupe aux lèvres. Pratiques de la perception et mise en marché des vins de qualité* (Toulouse: Editions Octarès, 2004), p. 326.
6   Thomas M. Wilson (ed.), *Drinking Cultures: Alcohol and Identity* (Oxford and New York: Berg, 2005).
7   See Peter Howland's work on New Zealand. My argument is of a different nature as French consumption not only emphasizes, constructs and reaffirms ideals of wine, the rural/metro idyll, middle-class distinction and reflexive individualism, but French consumers use these ideals to generate a more egalitarian society, or at least to establish networks of friendship based on common values which are embedded in the national story about French wines.
8   For a discussion on the internet and the idea of community, see the remarkable work of Daniel Miller and Don Slater, *The Internet: An Ethnographic Approach* (Oxford: Berg, 2000).
9   This feeling was expressed by most of the wine connoisseurs interviewed during the fieldwork.
10 For more information about French websites and their success, see http://www.hit-parade.com/. These sites were all consulted in March 2004.
11 See http://www.lapassionduvin.com.
12 Wilson, *Drinking Cultures*, p. 10.
13 See chapter 5 for the ethnography of the club and the encounter with the encyclopaedist.
14 Jean-Luc Fernandez, *La Critique vinicole en France, Pouvoir de prescription et construction de la confiance*, Logiques sociales (Paris: L'Harmattan, 2004), p. 101.
15 See his webpage http://ec.hku.hk/njbruce/MainPage.htm and more precisely his two publications on language and wine: 'Classification and hierarchy in the discourse of wine: Émile Peynaud's "The Taste of Wine"' and 'A certain "je sais quoi": the voice of authority in Émile Peynaud's "The Taste of Wine"', both accessible online.
16 Terry Eagleton, *Ideology: An Introduction* (London: Verso, 1991), p. 200.
17 Deborah Lupton, *Food, the Body and the Self* (London: Sage, 1996).
18 Pierre Bourdieu, *La Distinction. Critique sociale du jugement* (Paris: Les Éditions de Minuit, 1979).
19 Cited by Bruce in 'A certain "je sais quoi"', in *Cause and Effect of Wine and Food*, Seminar given at the 1996 Wines of the Pacific Rim Fair, Hong Kong, May 1996.
20 Gil Morrot, 'Peut-on améliorer les performances des dégustateurs?', *Vigne et Vin* (1999), 31–7.
21 Noted by several wine drinkers, especially the members of the club in Chalon-sur-Sa'ne.
22 Fernandez, *La Critique vinicole*, p. 16.

Chapter Eight
Globalization, Nation and the Region: The New Wine Drinking Culture

As we have seen, wine drinking and its attendant culture play an important role in the historical and contemporary imagining of the French nation.[1] Yet wine culture cannot be discussed today without contextualizing it relative to the wider web of social and political meanings and the changing dimensions of national and global culture. In France the notion of a homogeneous wine drinking culture has been kept alive, in part, because of the high rates of alcohol consumption that were maintained for much of the twentieth century. Yet in reality, a national French wine drinking culture was always a myth, and somewhat paradoxically, as overall wine consumption has declined, a new mass wine drinking culture has emerged. In this process, wine elites, professional regional bodies, institutions such as the INAO, amateurs and professionals have constructed a specific relationship to the product and have sought to exercise a dominant influence over the dissemination of this new wine drinking culture. As part of this process, wine schools, wine tastings, regional tourism linking the leisure industry to the gastronomic experience, wine literature and the internet have all contributed significantly. While the cultural impact of wine and wine drinking has undoubtedly been growing in France in parallel with the decline of alcohol consumption, the types and uses of drinking behaviour remain the basis for a remarkably divergent social and cultural identification. Moreover the new French wine culture is something that needs to be seen as part of a broader international phenomenon as wine has entered the public sphere.

This chapter explores how French wine drinking culture has adapted to globalization, exploring some of the major elements of practices and discourses such as the hierarchy of *terroir*, the cult of the wine grower, the value of artisanship and authenticity, and finally science and modernity as sites of contestation and negotiation between local and global actors. These cultural representations, disseminated by the new wine drinking culture, create, invent and summon up theories of 'place'. Indeed the creation of a notion of 'place' connects both regionalism and an individual sense of consciousness and belonging.[2] In numerical terms, women are undoubtedly less likely to participate in this wine drinking culture, but as new wine consumers they increasingly enjoy drinking wine.

The regional dimension in particular has come to play a new role as the focus of this wine drinking culture by reshaping cultural artefacts in an imaginative fashion, as a continuity between past and present, combining traditional and modern elements. The region has also come to provide a complex site of identification for the nation as part of a wider narrative attached to the national 'rural idyll', by which wine consumers experience others, not only through the incorporation of glasses of wine, but also by the consumption of a landscape, closer contact to the producer as the paragon of quality, the authentic experience of collective drinking and the progressive acquisition of a complex and distinctive drinking culture rooted in a *terroir*. Yet this consumption simultaneously integrates global and political elements, which are then translated and integrated at national level, because to consume a *vin de terroir* also has resonances with a sense of Frenchness and national identification. This Frenchness based upon the region and articulated through wine drinking culture demonstrates how wine consumers have incorporated some of the values orchestrated relentlessly by the state, and the wine profession, and its attendant experts in their promotion of the product. The successful promotion of better-quality wines associated with the AOC, the promotion of wine as a symbol of French cultural distinctiveness and its association with supposedly timeless French values of *terroir* and artisanship have provided national viticulture with a powerful armoury with which to combat the effects of declining alcohol consumption and global competition. It also links together production and consumption as part of an attempt to engage consumers with wider global issues affecting the French vineyards.

For the French, globalization is often broadly perceived as a one-way process, a synonym for political, cultural and economic

Americanization. The examples of the notorious Mondavi affair and of the film *Mondovino* as they were commented on in the press reveal both the misconceptions and the mythic dimensions of globalization as it is conceived in the French imaginary. In a stimulating article, Diane Barthel-Bouchier and Lauretta Clough convincingly argue that the Mondavi affair was portrayed as a 'struggle between little guys and bad guys, people attached to the *terroir* versus people concerned with profit, small friendly family businesses versus global corporations', while the underlying economics and politics was far more complex.[3] In fact, the locals were far from simple peasants defending their *terroir*, and the opposition to the arrival of Mondavi in Languedoc involved a variety of groups whose different motivations ranged from populist hunters protecting their environment to politicians obsessed with maintaining legitimacy in their political fiefs as well as individuals in quest of economic legitimacy. According to Barthel-Bouchier and Clough, what is interesting in the development of this affair is how Languedoc offers an illustration of an emerging global professional culture of wine that can be observed both in France and elsewhere.[4] As they argued in their conclusion, 'Many of the locals are also global and eager to profit from sophisticated marketing and production techniques without losing respect for tradition and *terroir*.' Recent work by Aliziz Gouez and Boris Petric confirms the complex social configuration of Languedoc–Roussillon, with a diversity of actors contributing to the reshaping of the region as a centre of viticulture.[5] To some extent, the region illustrates the changes affecting the French vineyards as a whole, and especially those regions with less well established reputations: new marketing of the wine region as a global viticultural area defined by grapes or brands; new international and financial actors joining in wine production, and neo-ruralism becoming one of the ingredients of regionalism.

In a similar way, the film *Mondovino* chooses to downplay the complexities of local situations to emphasize broader conceptions or cleavages commonly present in the wine industry. It is undeniable that the French wine industry with its 467 denominations of origin is in decline, while the New World, presented as its opponent, is forecast to grow rapidly. Yet the trend for consumers to drink less but better wine should favour those French regions which have a global reputation for quality. Still there are a number of obstacles that force the French wine industry to ask the state for assistance because the current European Union regulations prevent innovation and radical technical changes, making French products less competitive. I met several producers all over France who denounced the traditional and conservative position of the INAO and the Ministry of Agriculture when innovation is possible. Arguably, the French wine industry despite its national dimension remains a global activity, and its future depends on the ability of the profession to adapt to global changes while enhancing quality and preserving uniqueness based on diversity, regional identification and rural values. In terms of its export markets, it has now to face international competition while remaining attached to quality and established reputation.

French wine regions

The concept of *Appellations d'origine contrôlées*, which is at the heart of the French wine industry, is used to embody regional uniqueness acting as a kind of trademark and guarantee of quality for wines. In Burgundy, for example, the name of the region refers to a wide range of famous wines which have established their reputation over several centuries. In an age of global consumerism, the wine region is thus commodified as a 'local space' defined by its uniqueness and essentialism offering a direct tie to the producer and to the *terroir*. It is also a powerful way of conceptualizing place and identity in the context of globalization. In terms of economic and productive space, the region has traditionally provided the administrative foundations upon which the industry established itself through a complex web of interconnections with the nation state. However, administrative decentralization since the 1970s means that more and more responsibilities have been transferred to the regions, which have gained a new voice as a consequence. The wine industry has adapted to these changes, with some regions being proactive while others have been content to rest upon their reputation. Regional professional bodies and institutions have reflected the variety of socio-economic situations and social configurations of the actors involved, be they politicians, wine professionals or *entrepreneurs*.

When examining the region as a place of identification and as a cultural entity, any definition needs to encompass a whole range of territorial practices promoted consciously to the rank of emblematic items emphasizing distinctiveness in a positive way as a source of pride for its inhabitants. For instance, as Philippe Chaudat has demonstrated, supermarkets in the Jura region use the notions of *terroir*, tradition and authenticity to promote local wines by presenting their products with a number of emblematic regional items such as the local *charcuterie*, the *comté* cheese, objects from the powerful local timber industry and elements of local architecture or heritage.[6] All of these ingredients contribute to the construction of regional identity, and the population takes pride in identifying with them at the local level. In the majority of cases, a cultural item, the pipe in the case of the Jura, is chosen by local actors and professionals to be exhibited, presented and promoted to the outside world. Some of these cultural items play an important role in consolidating the image and representation of a territory in the context of the region, being not only a tool for spatial categorization, but also a means of establishing a hierarchy between competitive and increasingly interconnected entities at a higher level.[7]

There are other examples of more proactive regions which strong leadership has enabled to adopt a modern stance in the promotion of their wines relative to the international markets. Aliziz Gouez and Boris Petric have argued that the role of Georges Frêche in Languedoc–Roussillon was central to the shaping of the wine region as a new competitor in global markets. As they note,

> On the very day of his installation, in 2004 and following the furrow so often ploughed by those Midi elected representatives speaking against Parisian power, the new president attacked the name of Languedoc–Roussillon as the fruit of an artificial identity determined by the French state ('a corpse I do not wish to continue dragging'), whereas his proposal of 'Septimanie' would better suit the true regional identity.[8]

Georges Frêche argued that, at international level, nobody knows the Languedoc–Roussillon region or where it is, and that the most successful territories in the great game of world competition are those that have played the card of the brand like 'Roquefort' or 'Champagne'. Aliziz Gouez and Boris Petric emphasized that what was needed was a brand with an evocative name to back the promotion of the territory and local production.[9] The idea of bolstering the regional image attracted a broad consensus behind it, as many recognized the need to unite in order to survive at global level. In the end Georges Frêche had to give up his 'Septimanie' idea in 2005 for another name 'Languedoc–Roussillon/Sud de France' adopted in 2006. Thus the emergence of the brand 'Sud de France' spells out a redefinition of the relationship to the regional territory and has now become one of the marketing branding names to advertise wine from the region.

Wine-producing regions constantly mobilize regional distinctiveness to promote their products, and it could be argued that specific historical elements such as social characteristics or a particular feature of the vineyard are picked up and emblematized through a complex process of what Robert Ulin calls 'power differentials' between regional actors.[10] This involves negotiations and bargaining at different levels of the region, not only in relation to the social configuration of the regional wine industry, but also increasingly with outsiders from the tourist industry, cultural mediators and professional partners from other areas of expertise such as public relations or journalism, all of whom contribute to the articulation of the region as a cultural representation. Politicians, as observed before, can also choose to play a proactive role in the rebranding of the region. The 'power differentials' defined by Ulin in his case study of the south-west placed those with limited resources in a position subordinate to elites and thus marginalized their voices in the construction and production of wine-growing discourse and knowledge. Yet this social configuration has become even more complex as the region is today integrated into a global system and the relationship between both – local and global – is now based on a more complex web of interconnections than before. The making of the image of the wine region which prevailed between the wars has today become a more complex and dynamic process in the hands of a chain of multiple actors.

However, in terms of models of regional wine cultures, there has always been a clear distinction between Bordeaux and Burgundy wines. If this is not as clear-cut today, it remains nevertheless true that each region still uses more or less the same traditional repertoire of cultural icons in order to promote its distinctiveness. Bordeaux wines still play on the image of the château as a sign of continuity between their wines and an aristocratic past, while Burgundy remains the *terroir béni des dieux* (soil blessed by the gods), emphasizing its religious and peasant roots. As part of this campaign, the emphasis is placed on a range of themes, including colours, aromas to inform the drinker of the regional subtleties of the soil, women as new consumers or new professionals in the wine industry.

In a recent book published on the rivalry between Bordeaux and Burgundy, the human geographer Jean-Robert Pitte presented them as competing civilizations, arguing that their respective economic and cultural histories placed them in very different positions in the international market. According to his analysis, wine producers in the two regions are very distinct:

> *Caricaturing only a little, the Bordelais have diplomas, they speak English and sometimes another language, they read the economic press, they travel a lot to Paris and abroad, they dress like English gentlemen farmers, play tennis or polo and are stylish. The Burgundians, on the other hand, most of them, have not studied, like to wear casual or sports clothes, do not bother about their appearance so much, and look like proud peasants.*[11]

Yet his publication is itself part of the myth constructed around Burgundy and Bordeaux, and it was published in the Hachette Littératures series. Both regional models seem to go back to the opposition between urban and rural: Bordeaux is the name of both a city and a wine region while Burgundy is the name of a rural region and a wine region. While most of Burgundy is defined by the *crus* which name exceptional wines of a distinctive typicity within a *terroir*, Bordeaux wines relie less on *terroir* but more on château and a blending process to constitute their originality.

Labels and promotional materials collected over the years in both regions display various cultural references which we could argue are almost always presented in opposition. The Bordeaux aristocratic *propriétaire* (wine owner) is often contrasted with the Burgundian *vigneron* (wine grower), dynasties of aristocrats with families and lineages, the château with the soil and vines, industrialization and science with artisanship and tradition. This broad differentiation has been documented by Gilles Laferté for the interwar period in Burgundy, where he examines how the *vigneron* tradition was used as a repertoire by local elites and academics to foster a new regional image. If many of these traits are still apparent, the actual cultural repertoire converges towards a more modern version emphasizing nature, technical knowledge, tastes and the role of the oenologist.

Each wine region has its own cultural repertoire with its references to local history, monuments, famous personalities and emblematic scenery. Yet some regions have chosen to rebrand themselves playing the global card by displaying the variety of their grapes or the wider denomination attached to the image of their *terroir* such as 'Vins du Sud'. The various political and socio-economic contexts, in which the region situates itself determine the items or elements it will present or exhibit. Competition and globalization have also meant that some of these symbols have been borrowed and appropriated by other wine regions. A good example is provided by the famous Confrérie des Chevaliers du Tastevin created in Burgundy in 1934 by the local elite, whose success in publicizing their wines inspired the many other confraternities organized subsequently in the Loire, Bordeaux and other less well-known wine regions such as Champlitte in the Haute-Marne. Today the emphasis is increasingly placed upon the technical side of wine-making or the role of oenologists, and even the most traditional regions have adopted these images as part of their narrative.

Festivals, museums, wine tourism and wine routes all contribute to the construction of the image of the region and are often combined with those of global culture to make their products accessible to local, national and international consumers. The same cultural material is offered to the visitor, but depending on his status as an international or national tourist, regional visitor or local, the reading and the identification with that material will differ. It is also striking that a global wine culture enables a common identification with the product through the framework of a single and codified culture, whatever the region or the country. The 'rural idyll' is orchestrated in a similar fashion in Martinborough in New Zealand to that in Burgundy; only the process and the outcomes of identification change depending on the audience, whether New Zealander, Parisian or English and so on.[12] At a time of intense circulation of goods, ideas and people, these regional cultural models have been adopted on a global scale, as the example of India demonstrates, where new wines produced at Château Indage make the news and seek to attract the expanding Indian middle class which is also being drawn into a global wine drinking culture.

Terroir

Among the various cards played by French producers in response to globalization, the concept of *terroir* has proved to be the most successful one. Linking places, tastes, type of agriculture and quality, it has now been adopted throughout the world. Historically speaking, the concept of *terroir* is rooted in the development of the French vineyards and their legal protection as a particular parcel of land with specific characteristics of soil, landscape and location that are revealed through the work of the producer, who is defined as an artisan. In her innovative work, the anthropologist Amy Trubek, who offers an American take on *terroir*, argues that it has been used to explain agriculture for centuries, but its association with taste, place and quality is more recent, a reaction to changing markets and the mechanization of the farming industry.[13] *Terroir* as explained by Trubek is a category that frames perceptions and practices, a worldview or, as she puts it, a foodview. If it is undeniable that *terroir* is a consensual and collective reality for the majority of French people, who use the expression in everyday life, its definition nevertheless becomes more confused and ambiguous once experts start to debate what it means in practice. For French consumers, there is no doubt that *terroir* was invented by the French (this time it is the true) and is associated with quality, as even French supermarkets use it as a marketing trope to identify local products in relation to the mass of standardized products they sell. For most producers, especially wine producers, there is a significant advantage in believing in the natural virtues of the soil, especially if you own a plot in the Clos Vougeot, which places you in a tremendously advantageous economic position.

The AOC system is built primarily on the notion of *terroir*, and it has increasingly come to associate it with the idea of typicity. According to the geologists, a wine has a specific aromatic profile, which is partly defined by its *terroir*, and it is possible to guess where it comes from by reading this profile. Yet the profession is divided about this idea of typicity, and the INAO, the institution which initially founded the AOC, is still debating it.[14] Despite the absence of a legal definition of the concept of *terroir*, the AOC system is informed by the concept as it provided historically the building block for discussions between the *syndicats* representing the wine producers and the INAO. Interestingly enough, several producers in Burgundy and elsewhere expressed reservations in relation to the notion of *terroir*, as their wines were not recognized by the system of classification at the time of their creation and they felt that some of their wines were comparable to the ones that were given the AOC.[15] To sum up, the concept of *terroir* is in part an ideological tool which has enabled the construction of a more regulated, normalized and

organized wine sector, creating hierarchies and sha[...]
also linking a product to a place and to specific know-h[...]

From a historical perspective, it is clear that the concep[t...] has continuously evolved, reflecting a reinterpretation of the p[...] well as a sense of place by wine producers, the elites and the sta[te.] Far from encapsulating a fixed and monolithic view of French vineyards, it has evolved into a broader category defining the distinctive character of French rural production with an atomized landownership, a system promoting agrarian values and artisanship at a time of major agricultural change and rapid industrialization. The use of ideas about place to make arguments about quality became increasingly important in the late nineteenth century, and it was part of a serious socio-political movement to protect French agricultural products from internal and external forces in the early twentieth century. The studies of Kolleen Guyon on Champagne and Gilles Laferté and Philip Whalen on Burgundy have demonstrated that France and its *terroir*, commodified by regions, were sold as an international commodity to elites travelling around the globe.[16] Today, when many consumers have lost confidence in, and connections to, the rural world, *terroir* encapsulates notions of tie to a place, local products and quality in an era of mass production and concern about adulterated foods. This could be seen as a successful story of globalization providing consumers with a different way of drinking and eating, preserving at the same time the local social fabric and protecting notions of quality.

For most French consumers, *terroir* means quality and guarantees the origin of the products consumed. Yet if they have come to recognize and consume it as a commodity for which they are ready to pay more, they still remain puzzled and largely ignorant about the realities of the system of AOC for wines. With thousands of AOCs, consumers face a complex edifice which is extremely difficult to decipher when making decisions about the choice of what wines to drink. In 2001, the French minister of agriculture commissioned the audit controller, General Jacques Berthomeau, to examine the future position of the wine industry.[17] Among the five major problems identified, four were related to the AOC system, which was seen as 'confusing', 'misleading', 'unknown' to the consumer, 'too regulated'. Recent consumer surveys demonstrate that the majority of French people cannot make sense of the complex system of categorization of wines are concerned. For the producers, it is also

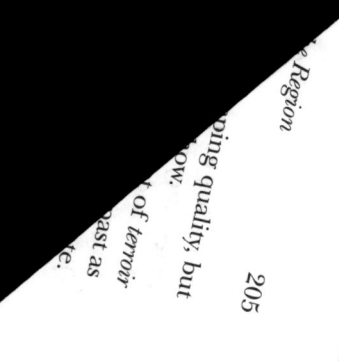

sked about the *terroir* of their AOC
imous when it comes to offering a
se about what, in reality, it means.[18]
as part of a recent research project
AOC Fleurie (Beaujolais) show clearly
no idea at all of the characteristics of
cognition is presented as collective, but
ers, INAO experts and key players, who
to impose their vision of the *terroir* on the
rest of ... ter and Pettigrew have demonstrated, all
of these processes ... an attempt to fix the quality of wine, an
aesthetic product in which the concept of quality and the criteria
for defining it are notoriously opaque.[19]

The cult of the wine grower

The dominant figure of the wine grower in France as a cultural icon of the *terroir* is another important feature of the process of reinventing and reconstructing the French nation through the region. As we have seen, the French wine grower has recently been reborn as an icon of modernity, a national hero of our time, a symbol of a civilization threatened by globalization, but also as the figure synthesizing the ambiguous paradoxes of global and regional identity. Television programmes, newspapers, books and exhibitions have since the 1980s devoted considerable attention to the *vigneron*, a character exemplified by Aimée Guibert in *Mondovino* or by the publication in 2002 of *Les Nouveaux Vignerons* by Rigaux and Bon. This cult of the wine grower is distinguished by the voice given to them by writers or film-makers in relation to specific issues identifying them as unique characters. They have also become the stars of soap operas and crime fiction on French television. The emphasis is put on the authenticity of the producer, his story, his family history, tradition and artisanship. Very few if any women are chosen to illustrate the modern wine grower. He is very often filmed or photographed in his rural setting, wearing his working clothes or in front of his estate with his family, his wife and children next to him. His accent is always edged with regional intonations and his strong personality transpires through the interview. He is presented as an 'honest' and 'true' human being.

The figure of the wine grower as an artist or artisan provides the foundation for the expression of a wine imaginary and has become commonplace in several professional discourses.[20] He remains associated for consumers with the guarantee of quality, while the figure of the wine merchant is almost totally absent from discourses on wine and on the promotion of the region or *terroir*. As far as wine lovers are concerned, the wine grower incarnates a valued form of social capital, and counting one of them amongst your friends is a clear sign of your status as an expert. During my fieldwork with wine professionals and wine lovers, it was clear that a competitive field was established around the acquisition of a network of wine growers. Several times I was asked to prove myself in reference to that field. Interestingly enough, having worked for many years with producers, this point was never mentioned to me by either producers or the profession during our interviews, implying that it is far less significant for them.

Susan Carol Rogers, a pioneering American anthropologist working in France, noted twenty years ago that certain features of French society were strikingly different from those of the United States, especially 'the French preoccupation with history and traditions, and the importance of rural life in French thought'.[21] The cult of the wine grower does indeed refer to agrarian values, and this could be seen as the continuity of the image of the peasant which has been disappearing following the modernization of French society. Rogers explored the role of the peasant in French culture, arguing that the peasant, or *le paysan*, functioned as an important symbolic category. The peasant, like food, was 'good to think'. The idea of the peasant – the small farmer embedded in rural areas and upholding the French agrarian legacy – often served as a lightning rod in contemporary debates about what made France unique and the French people remarkable. As Rogers points out, France has

> *two often conflicting views of itself. On the one hand, France is a highly centralized, modern civilization with a strong sense of national identity ... On the other hand, its identity is tied to a long history of deeply rooted traditions, many anchored in French soil.*

The imagined peasant thus has been replaced by the figure of the wine grower as spokesman for the benefits of national progress or the pain and loss of cultural change.

As a discursive and essentialist element of what Peter Howland names the 'rural idyll', the wine grower is not a recent invention.[22]

Gilles Laferté, in his book on Burgundy and its wines, has shown that during the inter-war period, a commercial and regionalist folklore focusing on the wine grower as the paragon of quality, the artisan of an authentic product, was promoted by local elites as part of a strategy designed to integrate them into the national economy. Philip Whalen, in a similar vein, has demonstrated how the 1937 Universal Exhibition marketed artisan workmanship, gastronomical traditions, vernacular architecture and folkloric traditions to create a commercial paradigm of French national identity which was rooted in Burgundian provincial productivity.[23] Yet for Laferté the construction between folklore and economy was more subtle, as the image of the producers of quality wines was imposed alongside that of the region, this fusion being illustrated by the cellar which was the main room of the pavilion and the incarnation of various conflicting values, between folklore and elite culture.[24]

It is therefore clear that the image of the wine grower has deep roots, and the historian Herman Lebovics has argued that the idea of a 'true France' during the inter-war period was politically loaded with the 'blood and soil' ideology of fascist and ultra-conservative thought. As Whalen hints in a recent article, a new perspective on the issue of regionalism is needed, and we have to go beyond an oversimplification of the concept. According to the historian Julian Wright,

> Regionalism has for long been seen either as a feature of right-wing fascisant discourse, full of danger for the unitarist, Jacobin values on which French republicanism is based (according to the dominant, but not necessarily correct, school of thought); or regionalism can be seen as a less politically dangerous but nevertheless deleterious ideology, based on a loose and vague sentimentalism that, through its very looseness, undermines the more developed republican philosophical values in that same republican construct.[25]

However, it could be said that there are important connections between left-wing regionalism in the 1930s and indeed the 1990s. What we learn from the contemporary perspective is that individuals interpret the meaning of regionalism either as the hub of a nostalgia for a 'rural idyll', as a symbol of French resistance against globalization, as a symbol of left-wing ideology against the forces of capitalism, or as an essentialist and right-wing element of a political ideology. Several interpretations coexist, and the wine grower is presented here as a bastion against modernity, linking the past with the present. Yet this construction is quite telling as the image of the wine grower as the paragon of quality is undeniably the result of the growing contribution of the wine profession, and wine growers in particular, to the construction of their own image, despite mediation by other cultural actors in this process of reinvention.

The French example can be compared with the figure of the winemaker examined by Peter Howland as part of the New Zealand rural idyll.[26] It is possible to argue that the figure of the French wine grower was reinvented as part of the response to the growing internationalization of the wine economy. For Howland, Martinborough's tourists replicate the pervasive New World and New Zealand ethos of the 'cult of the winemaker', which fundamentally opposes the classic French notion of *terroir* and thus, casts the winemakers and their palate, production philosophies and personality as crucial in determining the taste and quality of wine. For them, the cult of the winemaker results from the New Zealand wine industry's comparatively short history and consequent lack of appreciation of the role of *terroir* in winemaking. In the French case, the national model has been built on regional diversity, with some regions downplaying the role of wine growers while others, like Burgundy, the Jura and the Loire, have emphasized their value as icons of modernity. However, the regional model of the wine grower again became a national affair only recently, and it is today characterized by several tensions as other icons of wine modernity have also emerged, for example the oenologist and the *sommelier*. The 'flying winemaker' who was once a symbol of New World wines, is now often cited on the label as another element of French wine modernity, illustrating the impact of globalization on wine culture. Over the years, we have met an increasing number of wine producers who travel to New Zealand or Australia for the grape harvest as they gain experience in their winemaking techniques and learn from their colleagues. Literature, television and tourism emphasize the social position of the wine grower, while in reality most consumers still face closed doors and suspicious faces when trying to taste wines directly from producers.

Authenticity and artisanship or technicity and modernity

Another important image associated with wine drinking culture is the emphasis upon wine as an 'authentic, natural and artisanal product', reflecting the *terroir* as a myth widely rooted in the conception of Frenchness. Most wine growers play the local, traditional and natural cards even when they are almost entirely detached from their social environment, do not cultivate their lands or do not even make their wines themselves. As I have argued elsewhere, the ethos of the wine grower as a professional is constructed around the idea of authenticity even when his/her winemaking and wine-growing techniques are very modern or leave, in some cases, little space for his/her intervention. For a wine grower, working your plot defines you as a member of the community, as a peasant who still has a link with the *terroir* and ties to the local community. However this conception has been increasingly challenged by the consequences of economic and commercial success or by the integration of key players into a global network going beyond the village, which in turn led to a questioning of the organization of the community. The traditional image of the *vigneron* has prevailed for decades despite periods of intense modernization of French agriculture, which threatened the concept of *terroir* based around the idea of working the land and respecting nature. Even if modernity has become the key element of the wine industry, the emphasis is nevertheless on the link with nature. The image of authenticity is widely shared by the various actors of the wine sector and marketing practice refers to it as one of the main elements marking the specificity of French wines.

Whatever the reality of the relationship between wine grower and *terroir*, modern consumers are seeking out authentic brands and experiences, which are core components of commercial success because they form part of a unique identity. Luxury wine producers in particular simultaneously embraced basic marketing techniques, while also distancing themselves from images of industrial production and commerce. Authenticity as connection to time and place is therefore an important element of wine production. Ulin notes that by defining wine as a natural product, as opposed to an industrial mass-produced one, social, cultural and historical claims of authenticity were presented as 'natural'.[27] Champagne, on the other hand, became synonymous with the interests of France, and identified with the development of symbolic links to nature to distance producers from the reality of what is a very industrialized process of production.[28] This strategy was a crucial means of differentiation during an age of mass production and helped position 'true champagne' in foreign markets. Images of authenticity still play an important role, especially for the traditional and well-established vineyards. Many of these changes affecting wine markets reflect wider movements at a global level. For instance authenticity is associated with time. Wine is often presented as a temporal marker, its origin is given by date, it is a product improved by time, and as a product it can be seen to integrate history. Yet if time was long regarded as an important criterion in wine consumption, especially with vintages being recognized as 'art objects', this is an increasingly isolated phenomenon, as most consumers will disregard the vintage when buying wine unless they are experts, collectors or wine lovers. The concept of vintage in our modern society has lost its appeal as most consumers do not have cellars to keep their wine until they are at the optimum point to be drunk.

In his study of twenty-six luxury wine firms located in different corners of the world, Beverland has argued that authenticity was expressed in the commitment to *terroir*, with wines expressing differences by seasonal variations being seen as 'real'.[29] Strategic actions that were designed to bolster brand authenticity include commitment to high quality, maintenance of stylistic consistency, and instrumental use of history and place as positive referents. The use of *terroir* as a positioning statement and guiding philosophy was expressed in a number of ways, with some identifying themselves as merely stewards of nature and taking a great deal of care to emphasize that they are non-interventionist in their approach, even though the actions needed to ensure consistency of quality in poor seasons require a degree of intervention. Other approaches take a broader view of expression of place, identifying the important role of the individual, the efforts of previous owners and workers as an expression of uniqueness and distinction. Beverland argues that there is an element of hypocrisy and manipulation in discussing impressions of brand authenticity, such as when producers appear to put themselves above commercial considerations while actively marketing their brands, and in decrying modern production methods while using them all the same.[30] This study demonstrates that claims about authenticity are part of a deliberate strategy to create a sense of differentiation in a field of cultural production.

Like other fields of cultural production, it could be argued that 'authenticity' in wines reinforces the privilege of wine elites and wine growers by eclipsing the cultural mediation of time and work, and hence the social constitution of the natural. Yet differentiation plays a major role, as from one producer to another or from one region to the next there will be major differences in the way wines are marketed or branded. In the Loire, for example, Gamble and Taddei have shown that individual producers develop their own understanding of the market and either do not want or will not share this model with anyone else.[31] Their ideas are often informed by direct sales, popular with producers in the Loire. Some vineyards such as Château Langlois (owned by the champagne house Bollinger) do this well, while many small producers invest considerable effort in direct personal sales that may result in the purchase of few bottles. The same could apply to other vineyards, and even in the rich Burgundy region some small producers still rely on very traditional and old-fashioned images that serve no commercial purposes in today's wine market.

This new wine drinking culture is first and foremost more dynamic than previously assumed, as it integrates progressively and at various paces some elements of our global modernity, linking the region as the locus of culture to global forces shaking the wine industry. Some elements discussed in this chapter reveal that there are continuities between the peasant and rural society and the wine grower and the *terroir*, illustrating the appeal of the national rural idyll to modern consumers. The historian James Lehning, taking up Rogers's exegesis of the French peasant, sees the domination of what he terms a 'metanarrative' in histories of the nineteenth and twentieth centuries.[32] This metanarrative tells a story of the absorption of the French peasant and regional rural practices and lifestyles into the more powerful homogenizing impulses of the French state. Narrative plots rely on a sense of comedy (the savage peasant tamed) or tragedy (rural culture destroyed). He describes the French interest in rural landscape as what he calls a metaphor for the culture of the countryside, a space on which individuals make meaning as they live their lives. This is certainly true for the period prior to the 1970s. The emergence of wine drinking culture in the 1980s demonstrates that the wine grower has taken the place of the French peasant in this rural idyll, and that a new metanarrative is emerging linking the region as a unit of cultural production to the wine grower and a combination of traditional and modern elements which make wine drinking culture a new locus of culture between local and global realities.

As we have seen, wine amateurs and to some extent some general consumers have appropriated specific representations attached to the new wine drinking culture. Yet this process has not affected all consumers in the same way. If we speak about French to foreign consumers, they are more likely to share different representations of French wines. Moreover, the New World wines have also adopted some elements of this wine modernity, using for example family lineages, as with Mondavi's promotional material presenting the owner's daughter as the wine grower or with the AVA (Viticultural Area), the American equivalent of the French *terroir*. In the context of a postmodern society, individuals have also become more actively involved and critically engaged in the process of consumption. The image of a rural idyll portrayed alongside that of the wine grower as the paragon of quality, and of a traditional rural regional culture anchored in the *terroir* and its specific tastes articulated through the gastronomic experience, has come to be attacked in the face of growing preoccupations about health, identity and lifestyles, and globalization simplifying the rules of production. Some of the traditional elements associated with the rural idyll have been displayed for two centuries, and the old recipes of the past need now to be reconceptualized in the context of new emerging vineyards in different parts of the world and increasing competition for good-quality wines. The *terroir* was a useful trump card to play, but as wine drinking culture and expertise have democratized, images and representations may become superfluous and international consumers may turn their attention to a more objective definition of quality and to products seen to offer better value for money.

Notes

1 For a useful discussion of regional culture and the making of identity, see Martina Avanza and Gilles Laferté, 'Dépasser la "construction des identités"? Identification, image sociale, appartenance', *Genèses*, 61 (2005), 154–67. For a more recent contribution to the debate on wine in France, see the excellent work of Marie-France Garcia-Parpet, *Le Marché de l'excellence. Les Grands Crus à l'épreuve de la mondialisation*, Collection Liber (Paris: Seuil, 2009).
2 The link between regionalism and culture has been remarkably discussed by Wendy Griswold in her book *Regionalism and the Reading Class* (Chicago: University of Chicago Press, 2008).
3 Diane Barthel-Bouchier and Lauretta Clough, 'From Mondavi to Depardieu: the global/local politics of wine', *French Politics, Culture*

and *Society*, 23, 2 (summer 2005), 71–90. For more discussion of this case, read Alun Jones, '"Power in place": viticultural spatialities of globalisation and community empowerment in the Languedoc', *Transactions of the Institute of British Geographers*, 28, (2003), 367–82.

4 Barthel-Bouchier and Clough, 'From Mondavi to Depardieu', 71–90.
5 Aziliz Gouez and Boris Petric, *Wine and Europe: The Metamorphoses of a Land of Choice*, Notre Europe, case study 1, http://www.notre-europe.eu/uploads/tx_publication/Etude56-Gouez-Petric-VinetEurope-en.pdf.
6 Philippe Chaudat, 'In imago veritas. Images souhaitées, images produites', *Ethnologie Française*, 37 (2001–2), 717–23.
7 Gilles Laferté, *La Bourgogne et ses vins. Image d'origine contrôlée* (Paris: Belin, 2006).
8 Gouez and Petric, *Wine and Europe*.
9 Gouez and Petric, *Wine and Europe*.
10 Robert C. Ulin, *Vintages and Traditions: An Ethnohistory of Southwest French Wine Cooperatives* (Washington: Smithsonian Institution Press, 1996).
11 Jean-Robert Pitte, *Bordeaux-Bourgogne. Les Passions rivales* (Paris: Hachette Littératures, 2005), p. 169.
12 Peter Howland, 'Pinot pilgrims: metro-rurality, social distinction and ideal reflexive individuality in Martinborough', Ph.D. thesis, University of Canterbury, New Zealand (2007).
13 Amy Trubek, *The Taste of Place: A Cultural Journey into Terroir* (Berkeley: University of California Press, 2008).
14 For a discussion on typicity, see the publications produced by the INAO and the INRA.
15 For an example of the discussions on the AOC, see for example Laferté, *La Bourgogne et ses vins*, pp. 41–65.
16 Kolleen M. Guy. *When Champagne Became French: Wine and the Making of a National Identity*, Johns Hopkins University Studies in Historical and Political Science, 121st Series (Baltimore: Johns Hopkins University Press, 2003), Gilles Laferté, *La Bourgogne et ses vins* and Philip Whalen, 'Burgundian regionalism and French republican commercial culture at the 1937 Paris International Exposition', *Cultural Analysis*, 6 (2007), 31–69.
17 Jacques Berthomeau, *Comment mieux positionner les vins français sur les marchés d'exportation*, Rapport remis à Jean Glavany, ministre de l'agriculture et de la pêche, 31 July 2001.
18 Personal communication with a member of the INAO commission of the Fleurie AOC, June 2008.
19 Steve Charters and Simone Pettigrew, 'Is wine consumption an aesthetic experience?', *Journal of Wine Research*, 16, 2 (August 2005), 121–36.
20 Christiane Amiel, 'Le vin à l'épreuve de l'art', in V. Nahoum-Grappe and O. Vincent *Le Goût des belles choses* (Paris: Éditions de la Maison des Sciences de l'Homme, 2004), pp. 83–108.
21 Susan Carol Rogers, 'Good to think: The "peasant" in contemporary France', *Anthropological Quarterly*, 60, 2 (1987), 56–63; more recently

'Which heritage? Nature, culture and identity in French rural tourism', *French Historical Studies*, 25, 3 (Summer 2002), 475–503.
22 Howland, 'Pinot pilgrims', especially chapters 3, 4 and 5.
23 Whalen, 'Burgundian regionalism'.
24 Laferté, *La Bourgogne et ses vins*, p. 208.
25 Julian Wright, 'Tradition, modernity and the regionalist Republic: a response to Philip Whalen', *Cultural Analysis*, 6 (2008), 63–6.
26 See Howland, 'Pinot pilgrims', pp. 283–315.
27 Ulin, *Vintages and Traditions*.
28 Guy, *When Champagne Became French*.
29 Michael B. Beverland, 'Crafting brand authenticity: the case of luxury wines', *Journal of Management Studies*, 42, 5 (July 2005), 1003–29.
30 Ibid.
31 Paul R. Gamble and Jean-Claude Taddei, 'Restructuring the French wine industry: the case of the Loire', *Journal of Wine Research*, 18, 3 (November 2007), 125–45.
32 James Lehning, *Peasants and French: Cultural Contact in Rural France during the Nineteenth Century* (Cambridge: Cambridge University Press, 1995).

Conclusion

The myth of a national wine drinking culture has inspired politicians, historians, the media and the wider French public for generations, and it has even become an accepted part of debate about alcohol consumption internationally, where the concept of a unique French drinking culture based on restraint and moderation is contrasted with the binge drinking of northern Europeans. But in reality the French were not only amongst the highest per capita consumers of alcohol; they were also, in general, largely ignorant of wine culture, which was essentially an elite phenomenon. For the peasants and workers who constituted the overwhelming majority of the French population, wine was something that was consumed daily as part of a staple diet, and this changed little before the final quarter of the twentieth century. Quality was not a consideration, people drank the local plonk. This is still true for part of the French population, which has not acquired a wine culture in the sense of understanding the subtleties of the *appellation* system or even being confident about distinguishing good wines from bad. Such knowledge was largely confined to the educated middle and upper classes, who through their connections and cultural capital constituted a group of wine *amateurs*. But this group had hardly any impact in cultural terms upon the habits of their fellow citizens. The elites consumed the gastronomy and wines of their region in the private sphere – that is to say, in the privacy of their dining rooms, clubs and confraternities. This was a closed and exclusive world where knowledge was shared but in no sense communicated to the outside world.

The economic crisis following the First World War led to a profound transformation of French viticulture, with increasing emphasis placed upon the production of quality wines as elites, professionals and the wine industry started to fight internal frauds and to respond to the internationalization of their market. The creation of the INAO with the system of AOC was a perfect example of the willingness of the professional elites to produce better-quality wines based on the idea of *terroir* or place of origin. Major innovations such as the *Code du vin* of 1936 provided the legal foundations of modern wine production introducing a distinction between AOC and ordinary wines. These regulations were intended to guarantee quality and outlaw the unregulated economic production that was responsible for frauds.

Terroir and its corollary the AOC provided the basis for the organization of wine production at local and regional levels, establishing hierarchies and strong social divisions in wine communities based on ownership of the most prestigious vineyards. Its appeal as a model of agricultural development has gone far beyond the boundaries of France, and similar systems have been adopted both by other European states, and even by the United States, which has also defined specific Agricultural and Viticultural Areas. Very often accused of inertia and resistance to change, the AOC has been transformed into an efficient tool for French economic development and territorial reorganization. Over the last fifty years, the AOC label has been applied to other foodstuffs, notably cheeses, as well as agricultural products including fruit and vegetables, and the INAO was recently renamed the *Institut National de l'Origine et de la Qualité*, and claims to be the guardian of quality. In the wine sector, in particular, the proliferation of AOCs, IGP (*Indication Géographique de Provenance*, label of origin) and other labels such as *vins de pays* has led to major territorial remapping, even in emblematic regions such as the south-west, where intense debates divide the Bordeaux vineyards from other peripheral or less prestigious regions. The first decade of the twenty-first century has been a period of crisis for French viticulture, which has led to serious questioning of the AOC system and an impetus towards the territorial remapping of regions and vineyards, leaving worries and uncertainties for many producers.

The emergence of the concept of *terroir* as part of the AOC legislation coincided with the campaign led by elites at regional level to create a gastronomic and oenological culture which reached its apogee during the interwar period in Champagne and Burgundy. They built upon a folkloric, traditional and nostalgic vision of France, which still holds sway in some of the more prosperous regions. It took different forms in each producing region, but wine became, part of the regional discourse, stressing local uniqueness, pride and territorial identification. It was also absorbed into a more general discourse about the French nation, which was aimed both at the internal group of French wine consumers and at international markets for an affluent and discerning clientele. What is striking about this construction is its broad and successful popular appeal, especially for the regions already boasting established reputations for producing high-quality wines. Bordeaux and Burgundy have progressively become synonymous with good-quality wines sustained by a wine culture promoting their noble virtues and elitist tastes. Diversity, complexity and authenticity were and still are the main ingredients of this edifice.

During the 1980s, the government of François Mitterrand launched a policy of decentralization, transferring power and authority to revived regional assemblies. More recently, this tendency has been reinforced by the European Union, which has sponsored regional development, encouraging issues of territoriality and local identities to come to the fore. The growing number of European initiatives requiring the active collaboration of the local authorities has dramatically increased the role of the regions in the field of economic development. In Burgundy and Champagne there is an almost symbiotic relationship between wine production, and regional development, with the two sides mutually reinforcing each other. The less economically privileged wine regions are at a marked disadvantage and have had to rebrand and restructure their wine production and by the same token have often been quick to take advantage of modern advertising techniques. The recent creation of the Sud de France label is a good example of how a name evocative of one of the most famous regions of France has been harnessed to promote both the wine industry and regional development.

The changes affecting the political and economic organization of French viticulture provide the background to the emergence of a new and much more socially democratic wine drinking culture. Although it is possible to trace its roots back to the nineteenth century, this new culture has proliferated over the last thirty years in line with the expansion of the middle-class. As the quantity of wine drunk has decreased, interest in its quality has grown. The urge of the French public to know more about wine has been reflected in the burgeoning of media interest, with television, radio, newspapers and magazines all devoting attention to the subject. There has also

Conclusion

been a rapid expansion of more specialized books and periodicals catering for a market of passionately dedicated wine lovers, who have themselves become a factor in the dissemination of wine drinking culture.

Wine consumption can also be interpreted as a cultural artefact as well as a commodity, through which French people engage with their past and construct their image of the present. Wine drinking has in the process been transformed into both a self-reflexive and an interactive activity, enabling individuals to make sense of the world around them and to define their own identity through consumption. It also provides a means of expressing differentiation or distinction in the context of a democratization of wine drinking culture and the emergence of a mass consumption headed by the middle class. Individuals now possess an immense choice in what they want to drink, and it is in this context that these complex processes of differentiation take place. There is a real tension between the 'wandering drinker', who reflects the fragmented type of wine consumption, and the 'wine lover', who is seen as a dominant and perennial figure in wine culture, preaching the virtues of *terroir* and direct contact with the idealized figure of the wine grower. Through wine drinking, individuals compete and construct their identities and lifestyle images through a process of appropriation and the shared normative orientations underlying their consumption. In an increasingly urbanized society, wine has become a powerful vehicle for the politics and economics of *ruralité* and regionalism. This is associated with a mythical golden age as well as supposed common values promoted by French producers and wine organizations. Wine thus provides a window on to the changing nature of what it means to be French, offering an insight into the relationship between consumption and cultural identity in an age of globalization and rapid political and economic change. It also offers an excellent example of how a national drinking culture is created, or recreated, and of how it relates to broader patterns of social and economic change.

In recent years, France has also seen the emergence of a specific group of wine lovers who are both an expression of a new wine drinking culture and its principal consumers. Their role as mediators in the construction of a wine drinking culture sheds light on the many paradoxes surrounding taste as a competitive and ideological concept. Wine lovers are not only negotiating their social status through wine tasting, but are also communicating and creating social networks around specific producers and wines. Moreover educating others in the art of wine consumption is an important aspect of the exercise of their passion. This passion has taken on new forms with the development of the internet, which plays an important role by permitting the rapid circulation and dissemination of information and ideas about the world of wine. By competing with others around the meanings of taste and the importance of regions, wine lovers seek to establish territories and networks of relationships, provoking positive, but also some negative, responses and reactions. In this global era of communication, an essentialist vision of France, emphasizing the traditional work of the wine grower as the paragon of quality, dominates the content of their debates, but it is increasingly confronted by a more liberal perspective. Amongst the core values that define their consumption are: work, artisanship, quality, sociability and commensality, all of which can be seen as providing reassurance and a sense of stability. Other values at stake have more to do with issues of class, 'distinction' and social empowerment, and drinking wine remains the prism by which ideas and values of Frenchness can be read.

For many French people, despite the modernization of their society, wine remains a 'cultural exception' and in this context, it is part of the French specificity. Wine as a culture and as an object of consumption has always been used in different ways, but its emblematic position as a landmark of cultural specificity helps to explain why, for many, it is still seen as a symbol of Frenchness. Today, consumption in France could be seen as a way of reshaping old ideologies, and it is certain that contradictory values are embedded in French wine drinking culture. The national dimension of wine culture no longer relies upon consumption, but has more to do with specific emblematic values which are today in danger of disappearing. The changing political, social and economic context has given rise to new expressions of local, regional and national identities based on differentiation and competition in the social sphere, which are negotiated between individuals, groups and society as a whole.

Changes in French wine consumption help us to illustrate these processes and the new relationships between national identity, regionalism and the individual. At first glance, this can appear as a conservative, defensive response, and it is easy to imagine how wine culture could be presented as a culture of exclusion. Such a conclusion would be misleading, and wine production is part of a far more dynamic movement of political, cultural and economic revival in the regions. Wine culture is also potentially more adaptive and inclusive than it might at first appear. While still predominantly a male, middle-class phenomenon, these pages have shown that it is also heterogeneous, with individuals helping to impose their own interpretation of what is in some ways a collective passion. It is also clear that a growing number of women are actively involved as both actors and consumers of the culture of wine. With its emphasis on place, timelessness and tradition, French wine culture can appear as backward-looking, nostalgic and out of touch with a modern urban and increasingly multiracial society. In this respect, it was interesting to listen to a recent national radio broadcast of a Muslim Algerian in the Montmartre district of Paris, who some years ago opened a wine shop, despite the unease of his own community, and who explained that wine had helped him to discover France, its regions, its diversity and its people, and that it was a knowledge that he hoped to transmit. In years to come, it will be interesting to see if his example proves typical and if wine culture succeeds in transcending social, religious and ethnic divides. If so, the French population will continue to believe that in drinking a glass of wine it is consuming France.

Glossary

AFIVIN	Agence Française d'Information sur le Vin
ANIVIT	Association Nationale Interprofessionnelle des Vins de Table et des Vins de Pays
ANPAA	Association Nationale pour la Prévention en Alcoologie et en Addictologie
AOC	*Appellation d'origine contrôlée* (label or denomination of origin)
BIVB	Bureau Interprofessionnel des Vins de Bourgogne
CCVF	Confédération des Coopératives Vinicoles de France
CIVB	Comité Interprofessionnel des Vins de Bordeaux
CIVC	Comité Interprofessionnel des Vins de Champagne
HCEIA	Haut Comité d'Etude et d'Information sur l'Alcoolisme
IGP	*Indication Géographique de Provenance*
INA	Institut National Audiovisuel
INAO	Institut National des Appellations d'Origine Contrôlées
JCE	Jeune Chambre Économique
ONIVINS	Office National Interprofessionnel des Vins.
RVF	*Revue des Vins de France*
SECODIP	Member of the Taylor Nelson Sofres Group
SIRC	Social Issues Research Centre, Oxford.
SOFRES	Institut d'Études Marketing et d'Opinion International
VDQS	*Vins délimités de qualité supérieure*
VINIFLHOR	Office National Interprofessionel des Fruits, des Légumes, des Vins et de l'Horticulture
WHO	World Health Organization

Bibliography

Aigrain, Patrick, Boulet, Daniel, Lalanne, Jean Bernard, Laporte, Jean-Pierre and Mélani, Christian, *Les Comportements individuels de consommation du vin en France. Évolution 1980–1995*, Rapport INRA ESR Montpellier (Paris: ONIVINS, 1996).

Aigrain, Patrick, Boulet, Daniel, Laporte, Jean-Pierre and Lambert, Jean Louis, 'La consommation du vin en France. Évolutions tendancielles et diversité des comportements', *Revue de l'Économie Méridionale*, 39 (1991), 155–6.

Albert, Jean-Pierre, 'La nouvelle culture du vin', *Terrain*, 13 (1989), 117–124.

Albert, Jean-Pierre, 'Le vin au présent', *Les Papiers*, 9 (1992), 192–7.

Amiel, Christiane, 'Le vin à l'épreuve de l'art', in Nahoum-Grappe and Vincent, *Le Goût des belles choses*.

Anderson, Benedict, *Imagined Communities: Reflections on the Origin and Spread of Nationalism* (London and New York: Verso, 1983).

Appadurai, Arjun, *The Social Life of Things* (Cambridge: Cambridge University Press, 1988).

Appadurai, Arjun, *Modernity at Large: Cultural Dimensions of Globalization* (Minneapolis: Minnesota University Press, 1996).

Assouly, Olivier, *Les Nourritures nostalgiques. Essai sur le mythe du terroir* (n.p., Actes Sud, 2004).

Avanza, Martina and Laferté, Gilles, 'Dépasser la "construction des identités"? Identification, image sociale, appartenance', *Genèses*, 61 (2005), 154–67.

Badouin, Robert, 'L'évolution de la consommation de vin en France', *Comptes-Rendus de l'Académie d'Agriculture de France*, 76, 7 (1990), 33–42.

Barham, Elizabeth, 'Translating terroir: the global challenge of French AOC labeling', *Journal of Rural Studies*, 19, 1 (January 2003), 127–38.

Barthel-Bouchier, Diane and Clough, Lauretta, 'From Mondavi to Depardieu: the global/local Politics of Wine', *French Politics, Culture and Society*, 23, 2 (Summer 2005), 71–90.

Barthes, Roland, *Mythologies* (Paris: Seuil, 1957).

Beck, Ulrich, *What is Globalization?* (Cambridge: Polity Press, 2000).

Beck, Ulrich and Beck-Gernsheim, Elisabeth, *Individualization: Institutionalized Individualism and its Social and Political Consequences* (London: Sage, 2002).

Bell, David and Valentine, Gill, *Consuming Geographies. We Are What We Eat* (London and New York: Routledge, 1997).

Berthomeau, Jacques, 'Comment mieux positionner les vins français sur les marchés d'exportation', Rapport remis à Jean Glavany, ministre de l'agriculture et de la pêche, 31 July 2001.

Besson, Danielle, 'Boissons alcoolisées: 40 ans de baisse de consommation', *INSEE Première*, 966 (May 2004).

Beverland, Michael B., 'Crafting brand authenticity: the case of luxury wines', *Journal of Management Studies*, 42, 5 (July 2005), 1003–29.

Billig, Michael, *Banal Nationalism* (London: Sage, 1995).

Bleton-Ruget, Annie and Poirrier, Philippe (eds), *Le Temps des Sciences Humaines. Gaston Roupnel et les années trente* (Paris: Éditions Le Manuscrit–MSH de Dijon, 2006).

Blowen, Sarah, Demossier, Marion and Picard, Jeanine (eds), *Recollections of France: Memories, Identities and Heritage in Contemporary France* (Oxford and New York: Berghahn, 2000).

Bocock, Robert, *Consumption* (London: Routledge, 1993).

Boisard, Pierre, *Camembert: A National Myth* (Berkeley: University of California Press, 2003).

Boizot, Christine, 'La demande de boissons des ménages. Une estimation de la consommation à domicile', *Économie et Statistique*, 324–5, 4, 5 (1999), 143–56.

Bologne, Jean-Claude, *Histoire morale et culturelle de nos boissons* (Paris: Robert Laffont, 1991).

Bourdieu, Pierre, *La Distinction. Critique sociale du jugement* (Paris: Les Éditions de Minuit, 1979).

Brennan, Thomas, *Public Drinking and Popular Culture in Eighteenth Century Paris* (Princeton: Princeton University Press, 1988).

Brewer, Johan and Trentmann, Frank, *Consuming Cultures, Global Perspectives: Historical Trajectories, Transational Exchanges* (Oxford and New York: Berg, 2006).

Brochot, Aline, 'Champagne. Objet de culture, objet de lutte', in Rautenberg,

Micoud, Bérard and Marchenay, *Campagnes de tous nos désirs*.

Bromberger, Christian (ed.), *Passions ordinaires* (Paris: Éditions Bayard, 1998).

Bromberger, Christian and Meyer, Mireille, 'Cultures régionales en débat', *Ethnologie Française*, 3 (July–September 2003), 357–61.

Brunori, Gianluca and Rossi, Adanella, 'Synergy and coherence through collective action: some insights from wine routes in Tuscany', *Sociologia Ruralis*, 40, 4 (October 2000), 409–23.

Casabianca, François and Sainte Marie, Christine de, 'L'évaluation sensorielle des produits typiques. Concevoir et instrumenter l'épreuve de typicité', in *The Socio-economics of Origin-labelled Products in the Agro-food Supply Chain: Spatial, Institutional and Coordination Aspects*, 67th EAAE seminar, le Mans, 28–30 October 1999.

Castelain, Jean-Pierre, *Manières de vivre, manières de boire. Alcool et sociabilité sur le port* (Paris: Imago, 1989).

Charters, Steve and Pettigrew, Simone, 'Is wine consumption an aesthetic experience?', *Journal of Wine Research*, 16, 2 (August 2005), 121–36.

Chaudat, Philippe, 'In imago veritas. Images souhaitées, images produites', *Ethnologie Française*, 37 (2001–2), 717–23.
Chiva, Matty, *Le Doux et l'amer* (Paris: PUF, 1985).
Clout, Hugh and Demossier, Marion (eds), *Politics, Tradition and Modernity in Rural France*, special issue of *Modern & Contemporary France*, 11, 3 (August 2003).
Cook, Malcolm and Davie, Grace (eds), *Modern France: Society in Transition* (London: Routledge, 1998).
Corbeau, Jean-Pierre, 'Une affaire de goûts et de couleurs', *GEO*, special issue, *La Folie des vins du monde* (2007), 82–3.
Corbeau, Jean-Pierre, 'De la présentation dramatisée des aliments à la représentation de leurs consommateurs', in Giachetti, *Identités des mangeurs*.
Counihan, Carole and Van Esterik, Penny (eds), *Food and Culture: A Reader* (London: Routledge, 1997).
Craplet, Michel, *A consommer avec modération* (Paris: Éditions Odile Jacob, 2005).
Demossier, Marion, 'Producing tradition and managing social changes in the French vineyards: the circle of time in Burgundy', *Ethnologia Europea*, 27, 1 (Spring 1997), 29–47.
Demossier, Marion, 'Les passionnés du vin ou le mariage du cœur et de la raison', in Bromberger, *Passions ordinaires*.
Demossier, Marion *Hommes et vins. Une Anthropologie du vignoble bourguignon* (Dijon: Éd. Universitaires de Dijon, 1999).
Demossier, Marion, 'Territoires, produits et identités en mutation. Les Hautes-Côtes en Bourgogne', *Ruralia*, 8 (2001), 141–58.
Demossier, Marion, 'Consuming wine in France: the "wandering" drinker and the "vin-anomie"', in Wilson, *Drinking Cultures*.
Demossier, Marion, 'Entre littérature et objet ethnologique, « Nono » ou la construction du vigneron comme archétype de la culture locale', in Bleton-Ruget and Poirrier, *Le temps des sciences humaines*.
Demossier, Marion, 'Le discours œnologique contemporain. Région contre nation au 21ème siècle', in Hache-Bissette and Saillard, *Gastronomie et Identité*.
Demossier, Marion and Milner, Susan, 'Differences: age and place related', in W. Kidd and S. Reynolds, *French Cultures, French Identities*.
Dine, Philip, 'Leisure and consumption', in Cook and Davie, *Modern France*.
Douglas, Mary, *Food in the Social Order: Studies of Food and Festivities in Three American Communities* (New York: Russell Sage Foundation, 1984).
Douglas, Mary, *Constructive Drinking: Perspectives on Drink from Anthropology* (Cambridge: Cambridge University Press, 1987).
Drout, H., *Notes d'un Dijonnais pendant l'occupation, 1940–1944* (Dijon: EUD, 1998).
Durand, Georges, 'La vigne et le vin', in Nora, *Les Lieux de mémoire*.
Eagleton, Terry, *Ideology: An Introduction* (London: Verso, 1991).
Faure, Christian, *Le Projet culturel de Vichy. Folklore et Révolution Nationale 1940–1944* (Lyon: Presses Universitaires de Lyon–Éditions du CNRS, 1989).

Fernandez, Jean-Luc, *La Critique vinicole en France. Pouvoir de prescription et construction de la confiance*, Logiques sociales (Paris: L'Harmattan, 2004).

Fillaut, Thierry, Garçon, Jack and Bernardin, Muriel, 'Les belles plantes ne s'arrosent pas à l'alcool. L'alcoolisme', *adsp*, 26 (March 1999), 20–2.

Fillaut, Thierry, Nahoum-Grappe, Véronique and Tsikounas, Myriam, *Histoire et alcool*, Logiques sociales (Paris: L'Harmattan, 1999).

Fischler, Claude, 'Food, self and identity', *Social Science Information*, 27 (1988), 275–92.

Fischler, Claude, *Du vin* (Paris: Odile Jacob, 1999).

Forbes, Jill and Hewlett, Nick, *Contemporary France: Essays and Texts on Politics, Economics and Society* (London: Longman, 1994).

Fouquet, Pierre and de Borde, Martine, *Histoire de l'alcool* (Paris: PUF,1990).

Fournier, Dominique and d'Onofrio, Salvatore, *Le Ferment divin* (Paris: Éditions de la Maison des Sciences de l'Homme, 1991).

Gamble, Paul R. and Taddei, Jean-Claude, 'Restructuring the French wine industry: the case of the Loire', *Journal of Wine Research*, 18, 3 (November 2007), 125–145.

Garcia-Parpet, Marie-France, 'Dispositions économiques et stratégies de reconversion. L'exemple de la nouvelle viticulture', *Ruralia*, 7 (2000), 129–57.

Garcia-Parpet, Marie-France, 'Le terroir, le cépage et la marque. Stratégies de valorisation des vins dans un contexte mondial', *Cahiers d'Économie et Sociologie Rurales*, 60–1 (2001), 150–80.

Garcia-Parpet, Marie-France, *Le Marché de l'excellence. Les Grands Crus à l'épreuve de la mondialisation*, Collection Liber (Paris: Seuil, 2009).

Garine, Igor de and Garine, Valérie de, *Drinking: Anthropological Approaches* (Oxford and New York: Berghahn, 2001).

Garrier, Gilbert, *Histoire sociale et culturelle du vin* (Paris: Bordas Cultures, 1995 ; new edition, 1998).

Gautier, Jean-François, *Histoire du vin*, Collection Que sais-je?, 2676 (Paris: PUF, 1992).

Gellner, Ernest, *Nations and Nationalism* (Ithaca: Cornell University Press, 1983).

Giachetti, Ismène (ed.), *Identités des mangeurs. Images des aliments* (Paris: Polytechnica, 1996).

Giddens, Anthony, *A Contemporary Critique of Historical Materialism*, vol. 1: *Power, Property and the State* (London: Macmillan, 1981).

Giddens, Anthony, *Modernity and Self-Identity: Self and Society in the Late Modern Age* (Cambridge: Polity, 1991).

Griswold, Wendy, *Regionalism and the Reading Class* (Chicago: University of Chicago Press, 2008).

Gual Antoni and Colomb, Joan, 'Why has alcohol consumption declined in countries of southern Europe?' *Addiction*, 92, 1 (1997).

Gusfield, Joseph, 'Passage to play: rituals of drinking time in American society', in Douglas, *Constructive Drinking*.

Guy, Kolleen M., *When Champagne Became French: Wine and the Making of a National Identity*, Johns Hopkins University Studies in Historical and Political Science, 121st Series (Baltimore: Johns Hopkins University Press. 2003).

Hache-Bissette, Françoise and Saillard, Denis (eds), *Gastronomie et identité culturelle française* (Paris: Nouveau Monde, 2007).
Heath, Dwight B, *Drinking Occasions: Comparative Perspectives on Alcohol and Culture* (Philadelphia: Brunner/Mazel, 2000).
Holmes, Douglas R., *Integral Europe: Fast-Capitalism, Multiculturalism, Neofascism* (Princeton: Princeton University Press, 2000).
Holtzman, Jon D., 'Food and Memory', *Annual Review of Anthropology*, 35 (2006), 361–78.
Howard, Sarah, 'Selling wine to the French: official attempts to increase wine consumption, 1931–1936', *Food and Foodways*, 12, 4 (2004), 197–224.
Howard, Sarah, *Les Images de l'alcool en France, 1915–42* (Paris: CNRS, 2006).
Howland, Peter, 'Pinot pilgrims: metro-rurality, social distinction and ideal reflexive individuality in Martinborough', Ph.D. thesis, University of Canterbury, New Zealand, 2007.
Jackson, Julian, *France: The Dark Years, 1940–1944* (Oxford: Oxford University Press, 2001)
Jacquet, Olivier, 'Les AOC à l'épreuve des fraudes en Bourgogne. Le négoce dans la tourmente', *Cahiers de l'Institut d'Histoire Contemporaine*, 6 (Dijon: EUD, 2001), 25–39.
Jacquet Olivier, *Un Siècle de construction du vignoble bourguignon. Les organisations vitivinicoles de 1884 aux AOC* (Dijon: EUD, 2009).
Jones, Alun, '"Power in place": viticultural spatialities of globalisation and community empowerment in the Languedoc', *Transactions of the Institute of British Geographers*, 28, 3 (2003), 367–82.
Kidd, William and Reynolds, Siân, *Contemporary French Cultural Studies* (London: Arnold, 2000).
Kladstrup, Don and Kladstrup, Petie, *Wine and War: The French, the Nazis, and the Battle for France's Greatest Treasure* (London: Hodder & Stoughton, 2002).
Lachiver, Marcel, *Vins, vignes et vignerons. Histoire du vignoble français* (Paris: Fayard, 1988).
Laferté, Gilles, 'Un "folklore" pour journalistes. La Confrérie des Chevaliers du Tastevin', *Ethnologies Comparées*, 8 (Spring 2005), 1–32.
Laferté, Gilles, *La Bourgogne et ses vins. Image d'origine contr'lée* (Paris: Belin, 2006).
Lalouette, Jacqueline, 'La consommation de vin et d'alcool au cours du dix-neuvième et au début du vingtième siècle', *Ethnologie Française*, 10, 3 (1980), 287–300.
Lalouette, Jacqueline, 'Alcoolisme et classe ouvrière en France aux alentours de 1900', *Cahiers d'Histoire*, 42, 1 (1997).
Laporte, Catherine, 'Système d'information sur la qualité et profit. Le cas des vins d'appellation d'origine contr'lée de Bourgogne', Thèse d'économie INRA-ENESAD, Dijon, 2000.
Lebovics, Herman, *True France: The Wars over Cultural Identity, 1900–1945* (Ithaca, NY and London: Cornell University Press, 1992).
Le Gars, Claudine and Roudié, Philippe (eds), *Des vignobles et des vins à travers le monde. Hommage à Alain Huetz de Lemps*, Collection Grappes et

Millésimes, Maison des Pays Ibériques (Bordeaux: Presses Universitaires de Bordeaux, 1996).

Léglise, Max, *Une Initiation à la dégustation des grands vins* (Marseille: Jean Laffitte, 1984).

Lehning, James, *Peasant and French: Cultural Contact in Rural France During the Nineteenth Century* (Cambridge: Cambridge University Press, 1995).

Loubère, Léo A., *The Wine Revolution in France: The Twentieth Century* (Princeton: Princeton University Press, 1990).

Lupton, Deborah, *Food, the Body and the Self* (London: Sage, 1996).

Mennell, Stephen, *All Manners of Food* (Oxford: Blackwell Science, 1985).

Miller, Daniel and Don Slater, *The Internet: An Ethnographic Approach* (Oxford: Berg, 2000).

Moentmann, Élise Marie, 'The search for French identity in the regions: national versus local visions of France in the 1930s', *French History*, 17/3 (2003), 307–27.

Montserrat Guibernau, M., 'Anthony Smith on nations and national identity: a critical assessment', *Nations and Nationalism*, 10, 1/2 (2004), 125–41.

Morrot, Gil, 'Peut-on améliorer les performances des dégustateurs?', *Vigne et Vin* (1999), 31–7.

Nahoum-Grappe, Véronique and Vincent, Odile (eds), *Le Goût des belles choses* (Paris: Éditions de la Maison des Sciences de l'Homme, 2004).

Neirinck, Jean and Poulain, Jean-Pierre, *Histoire de la cuisine et des cuisiniers* (Cachan: Éditions Jacques Lanore, 2000).

Nora, Pierre, *Les Lieux de mémoire*, vol. 2: *Traditions* (Paris: Gallimard, 1992).

Nourrisson, Didier, *Le Buveur du dix-neuvième siècle* (Paris: Albin Michel, 1990).

Ory, Pascal, *Le Discours gastronomique français des origines à nos jours* (Paris: Gallimard/Juillard, 1998).

Peer, Shanny, *France on Display: Peasants, Provincials, and Folklore in the 1937 Paris World's Fair*, SUNY Series in National Identities (Albany: State University of New York Press, 1998).

Peynaud, Émile, *Connaissance et travail du vin* (Paris: Dunod, 1971).

Peynaud, Émile, *The Taste of Wine* (London: Macdonald Orbis, 1987).

Peynaud, Émile, *Oenologue dans le siècle* (Paris: La Table Ronde, 1995).

Pitte, Jean-Robert, *Gastronomie française* (Paris: Fayard, 1991).

Pitte, Jean-Robert, 'La table', in Rioux and Sirinelli, *La France d'un siècle à l'autre: 1914–2000*.

Pitte, Jean-Robert, *Bordeaux-Bourgogne. Les Passions rivales* (Paris: Hachette Littératures, 2005).

Plichon, Jean-Pierre, 'Les mutations du tourisme viti-vinicole en Bordelais', in Legars, and Roudié, *Des vignobles et des vins à travers le monde*.

Puisais, Jacques, *Le Goût et l'enfant* (Paris: Flammarion, 1987).

Rainaut, J. and Balmes, J.-L., *Le Vigne et le vin. Les Enjeux pour demain* (Paris: Office International de la Vigne et du Vin, 1990).

Rautenberg, Michel, Micoud, André, Bérard, Laurence and Marchenay, Philippe (eds), *Campagnes de tous nos désirs* (Paris: Maison des Sciences de l'Homme, 2000).

Reckinger, Rachel, 'Les pratiques discursives oenophiles, entre normativité et appropriation. Contribution à une sociologie des cultures alimentaires', Thèse de doctorat, Marseille, 2 volumes, 2008.
Rioux, Jean-Pierre, 'Les Français et leur histoire', *L'Histoire*, 100 (May 1987).
Rioux, Jean-Pierre and Sirinelli, Jean-François, *La France d'un siècle à l'autre: 1914–2000. Dictionnaire critique* (Paris: Hachette Littératures, 1999).
Rogers, Susan Carol, 'Good to think: the "peasant" in contemporary France', *Anthropological Quarterly*, 60, 2 (1987), 56–63.
Rogers, Susan Carol, 'Which heritage? Nature, culture and identity in French rural tourism', *French Historical Studies*, 25, 3 (Summer 2002), 475–503.
Ross, Kristin, *Fast Cars, Clean Bodies: Decolonization and the Reordering of French Culture* (Cambridge, Mass.: MIT Press, 1995).
Sadoun, Roland, Lolli, Giorgio and Silverman, Milton, *Drinking in French Culture* (New Brunswick, NJ: Publications Division, Rutgers Center of Alcohol Studies, 1965).
Scholliers, Peter (ed.), *Food, drink and Identity: Cooking, Eating and Drinking in Europe since the Middle Ages* (Oxford: Berg, 2001).
Smith, Anthony D, *National Identity* (London: Penguin, 1991).
Sournia, Jean-Charles, *Histoire de l'alcoolisme* (Paris: Flammarion, 1986).
Stanziani, Alessandro, *La Qualité des produits en France, XVIIIe–XXe siècle* (Paris: Belin, 2003).
Strathern, Marylin, 'Grande-Bretagne: anthropology at home', *Ethnologie Française*, 2, 37 (2007), 197–212.
Sulkunen, Pekka, 'Drinking in France 1965–79: an analysis of household consumption data', *British Journal of Addiction*, 84 (1989), 61–72.
Sutton, David E., *Remembrances of Repast: An Anthropology of Food and Memory* (New York: Berg, 2001).
Teil, Geneviève, 'La production du jugement esthétique sur les vins par la critique vinicole', *Sociologie du Travail*, 43 (2001), 67–89.
Teil, Geneviève, *De la coupe aux lèvres. Pratiques de la perception et mise en marché des vins de qualité* (Toulouse: Éditions Octarès, 2004).
Terrio, Susan, *Crafting the Culture and History of French Chocolate* (Berkeley: University of California Press, 2000).
Thiesse, Anne-Marie, *La Création des identités nationales. Europe XVIIIe–XXe siècle* (Paris: Éditions du Seuil, 1999).
Trubek, Amy, *The Taste of Place: A Cultural Journey into Terroir* (Berkeley: University of California Press, 2008).
Ulin, Robert C, *Vintages and Traditions: An Ethnohistory of Southwest French Wine Cooperatives* (Washington: Smithsonian Institution Press, 1996).
Ulin, Robert C, 'Work as cultural production: labor and self-identity among southwest French wine growers', *Journal of the Royal Anthropological Institute*, 8, 4 (2001), 691–712.
Veblen, Thorstein, *The Theory of the Leisure Class* (Chicago: University of Chicago, 1899).
Veillon, Dominique, *Vivre et survivre en France, 1939–1947* (Paris: Histoire Payot, 1995).

Vigreux, Jean, *La Vigne du maréchal Pétain ou un faire-valoir bourguignon de la Révolution Nationale* (Dijon: EUD, 2005).

Warde, Alan, *Consumption, Food and Taste: Culinary Antinomies and Commodity Culture* (London: Sage, 1997).

Whalen, Philip, 'Burgundian regionalism and French republican commercial culture at the 1937 Paris International Exposition', *Cultural Analysis*, 6 (2007), 31–62.

Wright, Julian, 'Tradition, modernity and the regionalist Republic: a response to Philip Whalen', *Cultural Analysis*, 6 (2007), 63–6.

Wilson Thomas M. (ed.), *Drinking Cultures: Alcohol and Identity* (Oxford and New York: Berg, 2005).

Index

abstinence 83, 84, 92, 97, 104, 162
Académie du Vin 107, 122
AFIVIN 5, 16, 99
Agen 11
Albert, Jean-Pierre 69, 97, 153
Albi 11
alcohol 2, 4,5, 7, 8, 13–19, 22, 23, 27,28, 30, 38, 47–9, 54, 58–60, 66, 68, 69, 70, 74, 75, 82, 84, 87, 88, 91, 93–7, 99–100, 102–5, 123, 127, 131, 145, 155, 159, 172, 173, 182, 185, 189, 195, 196–7, 216
alcoholism 46, 93
Algeria 50, 221
Alsace 60, 87, 125, 131, 158, 184, 187, 190
amateurs 31, 80, 121, 128, 150, 175–95, 196, 213, 216, 221
Annales School 103
anti-alcohol rhetoric 92
AOC wines 2, 4, 12, 14, 16, 20, 25, 42, 43, 44, 50, 51, 53, 54, 57, 66–8, 76–7, 87, 95, 98, 109, 110, 113, 117, 125, 133–5, 139–42, 145, 151, 197, 204–6, 214–15, 217, 221
appellations 24, 43, 44, 57, 76, 77, 98, 153, 199
Argentina 6, 35, 122
aromas 164, 165, 201
Aron, Raymond 45
artisan 26, 34, 52, 67, 76, 113, 195, 204, 206–7
artisanship 13, 14, 32, 36, 44, 50, 54, 112, 113, 127, 156, 177, 197, 203, 205–6, 209–13, 220
artist 160–1, 206, 215
Athéneum 134

Aude 124, 131
Australia 97, 122, 209
authenticity 32, 34, 35, 37, 65, 76, 78, 92, 101, 112, 113, 115, 139, 141–2, 197, 200–6, 209–13, 215, 218
authority 44, 54, 188, 193, 195, 218

'bad' wines 3
ballon de rouge (glass of red wine) 103
Barthes, Roland 46, 66, 102–3
Bauman, Zygmunt 29
Bazin, Jean-François 105, 113, 129
Beaujolais 43, 63, 77, 78, 114, 119, 120, 125, 131, 168, 206
Beaune 4, 11, 25, 68, 90, 105–6, 110, 134, 135, 144, 163–4, 167
Beck, Ulrick 175, 194
beer 28, 60, 74, 87, 88, 91
belonging 22, 33, 36, 47, 142, 145, 155, 172, 177, 185, 192, 194, 197
Bettane, Michel 71, 109–10, 193, 195
BIVB (Bureau Interprofessionnel des Vins de Bourgogne) 4, 132–3
'Boire froid' 111, 192
'Boire chaud' 112
bon vivant 159, 161, 186
Bordeaux 4, 11, 21, 24, 47, 63, 70, 73, 77, 79–80, 88, 90, 96, 99, 106–8, 115, 125, 126, 131, 146–8, 158–9, 165, 178, 180, 182–4, 201–3, 214, 217–18
Bourdieu, Pierre 28, 60, 73, 89, 97, 99, 128, 174, 189, 195
Bové, José 114

brand 13, 24, 35–6, 91, 112, 127, 180, 198, 200–2, 210–12, 215, 218
Brest 93
Britain 15, 143
Brittany 22–3, 49, 60
broadcasts 101–31
Burgundy 4, 11, 21–6, 43, 45–7, 51–3, 63, 67, 73, 88, 96, 106–33, 136, 143, 155, 157–66, 178, 183–7, 193–5, 201–9, 212, 217–18

Caves Particulières 138–42
Caviste 42, 72, 79, 80, 102, 149, 168, 179, 183
Champagne 24–5, 38, 51–2, 55, 66–8, 125–31, 158, 200, 205, 210, 212, 214–15, 217–18
Château Margaux 115, 139
chefs 11, 61, 62, 114, 133, 165
CIVC (Comité Interprofessionnel des Vins de Champagne) 55
Clavel, Jean 182
colour 79, 124, 134, 184, 201
Comité National de Défense contre l'Alcoolisme 92
commensality 14, 33, 36–7, 91, 127, 177, 220
commodity 3, 18, 39, 42, 47, 52, 103, 111, 138, 141, 173, 205, 219
community 8, 13, 19–20, 24, 35, 50, 52, 54–5, 100–1, 116, 121, 123, 126–7, 170, 177–82, 188, 192–3, 210, 214, 221
Common Market 6, 57, 122
competition 3, 6, 7, 13, 16, 22, 26, 30, 35–7, 42, 43, 45, 53, 62, 75, 78–9, 82, 89, 101, 102, 110, 118, 122, 124–6, 135, 152, 178–9, 182, 197, 199, 200, 203, 213, 220
confraternities 21, 49, 104, 117, 202, 216
Confrérie des Chevaliers du Tastevin 143, 153, 203
connoisseurs 30, 46–7, 71, 86, 95–6, 110, 175, 189, 193, 195
co-operatives 5, 110
Corbeau, Jean-Pierre 78, 98, 131
Corbières 124, 131

coronary heart disease 74, 95, 104
Corsica 11, 162
Côtes du Rhône 77, 124, 131
coup de cœur 135, 147, 151
courtiers (brokers) 107, 133, 136
crisis 1, 3, 6, 13, 16, 25–6, 43, 55, 61, 64, 68, 75, 79, 101–2, 115, 129, 216–17
cultural capital 30, 68, 91, 109, 160, 189
cultural exception 12, 19, 37, 92, 116, 127, 220
cultural markers 61, 142
culturalisation 19, 178

De Garine and De Garine 7, 17
democratization 22, 63, 70, 73, 81, 91, 101, 135, 153, 175, 219
denomination of origin 2, 22, 34, 95, 110, 124, 140, 158
Desseauve, Thierry 108
dietary discourse 32, 86, 104
differentiation 3, 5, 9, 24, 30, 35, 37, 61, 71, 73, 75, 89, 90, 91, 138, 140, 143, 144, 179, 202, 210–13, 219–20
Dion, Roger 103
'distinction' 2, 12, 28–31, 60–1, 73, 77, 89–91, 99, 103, 124, 128, 138, 143, 146, 159, 169, 173, 175–95, 201, 211, 214, 217, 219, 220
doctors 94–5, 104
Douglas, Mary 7, 17, 30, 39, 65
drink-drive laws 3
Dublin agreements 123
Durand, Georges 46, 66

Eagleton, Terry 189, 195
Eastern Europe 122
elites 21, 25, 43, 49, 54, 128, 130, 196, 201–2, 205, 208, 211, 216–17
Elle 108
emotions 169, 188
empowerment 73, 214, 220
essentialism 8, 199
Europe 2, 5–8, 15–7, 23, 26, 35, 38, 52, 57, 74, 82, 91, 94, 97, 110,

116, 117, 122–3, 161, 167, 175, 178–9, 214, 216–18
European Commission 6
Europeanization 47
European Union 6, 123, 199
Évin law 3, 4, 93–5, 123–4
exports 3–5, 75, 117

festivals 11, 41, 64, 68, 71, 117–20, 145, 203
fieldwork 8, 10–11, 16, 25, 85, 88, 132, 148, 155, 207
Fischler, Claude 27, 111, 129, 191
folklore 24–6, 41, 52, 54, 68, 105, 113–14, 128, 136, 208
foreigners 181
fragmentation 14, 22, 29, 31, 32, 56, 60–2, 70, 80, 86, 88, 91, 93, 109, 163
frauds 43–4, 50, 117, 216–17
Frenchness 1, 44, 46–7, 103, 197, 210, 220
French paradox 74, 94–5, 104
friends 30, 65, 77, 80, 108, 120, 150, 152, 155–6, 158–63, 166, 168, 170, 172, 177–81, 186, 191, 194, 207

Garrier, Gilbert 2, 15, 57, 66, 80, 103
gastronomic associations 21, 94, 104, 114, 190, 196
gastronomic culture/norms 13, 42, 64, 106, 112, 137, 146, 208, 217
gastronomic literature 66, 103, 105
gastronomic writings 11, 108
gastronomy 49, 57, 71, 114, 156, 163, 168, 196, 213
GATT 15, 16, 123
Gayon, Ulysse 106, 109
gender 2, 10, 28, 32, 58, 60, 74, 81, 86–7, 121, 150, 170
generational rupture 28, 41
generations 27, 49, 61, 63, 66, 74, 78–81, 83–5, 107, 120, 145, 161, 176, 180, 216
geographic origin 79
Germany 44, 54, 122, 164

Giddens, Anthony 29, 111, 129, 175, 194
Ginestet, Bernard 115
globalization 2, 7, 14, 18, 27, 30, 31, 35–8, 42, 47, 78, 91, 101, 114, 128, 176, 196–215, 219
'good' wines 121, 162, 166, 187–94
grands crus (high premium) 10, 51, 53, 98, 129, 162, 213
grapes 22, 57, 76, 100, 104, 139, 168, 190, 198, 203
Groupe d'Études viticoles (Viticulture Study Group) 4, 123
Guide Hachette 109–10, 132–8, 151, 167
guru 71, 109–10, 113, 187

harvests 45, 118–20, 122
Haut Comité d'Étude et d'Information sur l'Alcoolisme 46, 58, 93, 94
Haut Brion 115
Hautes-Côtes 113, 129, 151–2
health 4–5, 13, 20, 26, 32, 59, 64, 74–5, 83, 86, 91–8, 102, 104–5, 123–4, 127, 145, 172, 213
Heath, Dwight B. 7, 8, 17
hedonism 54, 158–9
Hérault 124, 131
heritage 13, 14, 19, 22, 28, 43, 57, 64, 113–14, 130, 142, 155–6, 160, 163–4, 173
Hospices de Beaune 54, 55, 117, 118, 126

Iacchos 179–94
identification 19–21, 26–31, 47, 49, 102, 127–31, 172, 179–80, 182, 196–7, 199, 203, 213, 218
IGP (*Indication Géographique de Provenance*) 217
INAO (Institut National des Appellations d'Origine Contrôlées) 24, 44, 57, 77, 101, 122, 134, 139–40, 153, 196, 199, 204, 206, 217
internet forums 3, 12–13, 176, 178, 180, 185–9, 190, 192–4, 196, 220

interprofession 4, 55, 95, 132, 134
Italy 6, 87, 104, 115

Johnson, Hugh 109
Jura 131, 142, 200, 209

knowledge about wine 1, 3, 9, 28, 31, 36, 41, 49, 57, 62, 70, 73, 75, 77, 79, 89–92, 97, 106, 108, 109, 111, 114, 118, 135–6, 143, 149, 152, 159, 163, 165–6, 169, 171, 176–8, 182, 186–94, 201–2, 216, 221
Kolleen, M. Guy 24, 38, 66–7, 205

Laferté, Gilles 49, 52, 202, 205, 208
Languedoc-Roussillon 131, 183, 198, 200
Lebovics, Herman 36, 51, 115, 208
Léglise, Max 106–7, 164
leisure 13, 45, 55, 58, 60, 64, 101, 113, 121, 127, 141, 146, 150, 172, 175, 196
Lenoir, Jean 165
lifestyle theory 29, 61, 73, 83, 91, 105, 109, 175, 212, 219
lobby 32, 55, 59, 92, 95, 102, 111, 123
Loire 131, 158, 162, 184, 203, 209, 212

Maison du Beaujolais 78
media 3, 5, 9, 12–13, 33, 41, 62–4, 70, 90, 93, 95, 101–6, 108, 118, 122, 123, 125, 176, 218
mediatization 112
memory 18, 31–9, 41, 45, 47, 90, 120, 165, 171, 187
Mendès-France, Pierre 46, 66, 93
métiers de la vigne et du vin 112
middle-class 3, 79, 127, 157, 159, 176, 183, 218, 221
Ministry of Agriculture 32, 59, 102, 199
Ministry of Education 58
Ministry of Health 45, 32, 102
moderate consumption 21, 30, 70, 83, 95–6, 104, 144, 146

modernity 13–14, 26, 28, 30–2, 36–7, 45, 78, 84, 91, 128, 108–16, 126, 128, 156, 163, 197, 206, 209–10, 212–13
Mondavi affair 35, 198, 213–14
Monde (Le) 11, 98, 123
Mondovino 35, 198, 206
Morgon 168
Muscadet 119–20
Mythologies 102

national identity 6–9, 12–13, 15, 19–38, 89, 91, 92–3, 96, 98, 123, 126–7, 149, 155–72, 176–7, 185, 196–7, 132, 134, 138, 203, 206, 207, 216–21
nature, natural 3, 7–9, 14, 18–19, 27–9, 32, 46–7, 50–2, 59, 63–5, 74, 76, 86, 94, 96, 102, 105, 108, 111, 116, 118, 119, 141–3, 150–2
négociants 25, 42–3, 48, 50, 52, 71–2
Néo-ruralism 98
New World wines 3, 34, 209, 213
New Zealand 97, 194
Nogent (petit vin blanc) 119–20
Normandy 22–3, 60
North 60–1, 87–8
Nossiter, Jonathan 35
nostalgia 34, 37, 42, 112, 208
Nourrisson, Didier 2, 38, 41, 103, 128

occasional drinkers 2, 14, 70, 81, 84–8, 140, 145, 147, 172
oenologists 9, 11, 16, 42, 63, 71, 133, 136, 147, 152, 184, 188, 202, 209
oenological discourse 13, 42, 45, 57, 80, 89, 90, 102–31, 142, 163, 179, 192, 217
oenology 22, 45, 50, 58, 63, 184
oenophiles 39, 76, 179
Ory, Pascal 61–2, 69, 103, 128

PACA (Provence, Alpes, Côte d'Azur) 86
Paris 11–13, 25, 42, 51–4, 56, 58, 70, 88, 90, 93, 105, 107, 114, 119,

122, 138–9, 160, 163, 168, 171, 186, 195, 202, 203, 221
Paris Exhibition (1937) 26
Parker, Robert 71, 109, 117, 137, 153, 162
Peynaud, Emile 63, 106–7, 111, 188
phylloxéra crisis 25, 43
pinard (plonk) 20, 48–9, 105
Pitte, Jean-Robert 202
policies 14, 74, 92
politics of nostalgia *see* nostalgia
Portugal 122–3
power 7, 9, 24, 27, 30, 33, 36, 40, 44, 47–9, 60–3, 73–4, 77, 89, 92, 95, 102, 109, 111, 115–16, 123, 125–7, 138, 140, 150, 173, 175, 187, 197, 199, 200–1, 212
premium wines 57, 63
propriétaires-viticulteurs 25
Provence 49, 86, 131, 158–9

quality 1, 2, 14, 21, 26–7, 31, 33, 34, 36–7, 43–5, 50, 52–3, 57, 59, 62–5, 73, 76–9, 91, 93, 97, 101, 110, 112, 115, 133, 135, 137, 140, 145, 162, 170, 176–8, 181–2, 188, 197–8, 203–11, 216–20

reforms 48, 112, 123
regionalism 12, 15, 22, 32, 55, 104–5, 112–13, 124, 137, 173, 220
regional culture 11, 42, 51, 57, 60–2, 105, 114, 134–52
regional identity 7, 8–9, 11, 22–3, 23–31, 37–51, 72, 74, 77, 112, 134–52
regions 4, 12–15, 22, 41, 43, 48–9, 51, 70, 79, 80–2, 86–93, 96, 101, 107, 110, 113, 118, 120–7, 134–52, 156, 158, 160–5, 168, 170–3, 176, 182–5, 188, 190–3, 196–215, 216–21
regular drinkers 2, 54–5, 81, 84–8, 140, 180
retailers 36, 78–9
Ribereau-Gayon, Jean 57, 63
Rogers, Susan Carol 207, 212

Rothschild, Lafite 115, 126
ruralité 32, 65, 113, 173, 219
RVF (Revue des Vins de France) 11, 108, 185, 178–9, 182–5

Saint-Vincent tournante 143–7
Sarkozy, Nicolas 3, 104, 145, 148
self-reflexivity 156, 175–95
sensorial analysis 31, 95, 106–7, 111, 134, 192–3
Smith, Anthony 19, 38
sociability 14, 20, 23, 30, 37, 46, 91–2, 102, 127, 155, 168, 173, 175, 177, 186, 190–5, 220
social connectedness 175–95
social differentiation 3, 5, 9, 30, 61, 89, 138, 140
soil 54, 78, 142, 162, 201–2, 204, 207–8
solidarity 14, 20, 128, 155
sommeliers 11
Spain 6, 15, 57, 122–3, 151
Spurrier, Steven 107, 122
state 5, 22, 24, 30, 32, 43, 44, 50, 59, 91–100, 102, 111, 123, 198–200, 205, 212, 217
Suguenot, Alain 4, 96
Sulkunen, Petta 30, 74, 97
supermarket 36, 42, 56, 71, 72, 75, 79, 141, 142, 146, 151, 160–1, 169–70, 200, 204
syndicats 44, 113, 204

taste 11–14, 18, 33, 35–9, 49, 60, 62–3, 73, 76, 78–80, 89, 106–7, 109–10, 123, 133–43, 146–53, 159, 161–5, 167, 173, 176, 178–82, 185–95, 202–5, 209, 213, 218–20
tradition 10, 14, 19, 21, 22, 23–9, 34–8, 42, 50, 65, 78–9, 83, 86, 88, 92, 101, 104, 112, 115, 116, 135, 141, 159, 163, 198, 200, 202, 206, 207, 220
technical progress 5, 13, 127
television 101–31
temperance 49, 58, 93
territoriality 8, 218

terroir 4, 12–14, 20, 22, 25, 26–8, 32, 34, 36, 42–3, 49, 51, 54, 63, 76, 94, 95, 112–15, 118, 124, 127, 138, 141, 160, 162–3, 176, 187, 190, 197–8, 200, 217, 219
Thiesse, Anne-Marie 23, 38
tourism 11, 14, 51, 56–8, 64–5, 71, 101, 113, 124, 146, 156, 164, 196, 203, 209, 215
Trubek, Amy 204, 214
'true' France 50, 112, 116
typicité 33, 129

Ulin, Robert 201, 210
USA 6, 52, 76, 92, 143

VCC (*vins de consommation vourante*) 86
VDQS (*Vins délimité de qualité supérieure*) 43, 66
vente directe 34, 110, 112
Vinexpo 117
vinification 76
Vinothérapie 94, 104
vins ordinaires (everyday wines) 78
vins de pays 2, 66, 73, 77, 91, 98, 140, 162, 217
'Vins du Sud' 203
vins plaisirs (wine for pleasure) 140
viticulture 4–5, 25, 43–5, 48, 52–3, 57, 75–6, 101, 103, 105, 116–19, 123, 157–8, 197–8, 216–18

'wandering drinker' 29, 70, 72, 85, 89, 91, 147, 177, 219
Warde, Alan 27, 37
water 3–4, 28, 59
well-being 5, 95–6, 104
Whalen, Philip 208
WHO (World Health Organization) 15, 91, 96
Wilson, Thomas W. 20–1, 27, 143, 178
wine bars 3, 42, 72, 134, 144, 178
wine clubs 3, 11, 33, 70, 105, 172, 186, 191

wine crisis *see* crisis
wine critic 108
wine culture 3, 9, 12–14, 18–19, 28, 33, 37, 41–2, 47, 51, 57, 63, 65, 70–5, 85, 89–92, 102, 105, 107–8, 114, 117–18, 120–7, 132–4, 146, 151–2, 155, 169, 171, 175–6, 181–7, 194–6, 201, 203, 209, 216, 218–21
wine experts 32, 92, 94, 131, 134
wine festival *see* festivals
wine growers 3–4, 25, 42–4, 49, 51, 53, 55, 59, 63, 71–2, 75–6, 78–9, 91, 107, 110, 113–14, 116, 118, 127, 133, 135, 137, 140–54, 161–2, 168, 181–2, 194, 206–14
wine industry 4–6, 11, 14, 26, 34–6, 49, 52, 55, 57, 74, 92, 95, 101, 110–11, 118, 122, 136, 141, 151, 163, 171, 182, 198–9, 201, 205, 209–12
wine literature 111, 136, 196
wine lovers 3, 11, 12, 14, 19, 31–2, 34, 36–7, 59, 63, 70–2, 77, 92, 94, 107, 109, 112, 117, 121, 128, 133–5, 139, 141, 146, 155, 166, 168–70
winemakers 3, 76, 78, 98, 209
wine merchants 5, 13, 25, 42, 71, 75, 78–9, 107, 115, 127, 133, 164
wine production 1, 5, 11, 12, 57, 64, 75–8, 102, 107, 112, 115, 118, 126, 198, 210, 217–18, 221
wine regions 64, 99, 124–5, 162, 193, 199, 203, 218
wine routes 64, 78, 173, 203
wine tasting 3, 28, 33, 57–8, 63, 71, 73, 79, 89, 90, 108–14, 121–2, 129, 132–53, 155–74, 175–95, 196, 220
wine trade 11, 115
women 2, 28, 56, 60, 70, 79, 83, 86, 93, 108, 117, 121, 133, 140, 161, 163, 170, 176, 178, 181, 197, 201, 206, 221